Moral Indignation

Moral Indignation
Embryonic Stem Cells, DNA, and Christians

Sherman P Bastarache

Idein Publishing
Moncton N.B.
Canada

Moral Indignation

Copyright © 2010 by Sherman P. Bastarache:
Canada 1077137

Published in Canada by Idein Publishing ®TM 2018

ISBN 9780992159412

Sherman P Bastarache demonstrates a strong logic in his arrangement of ideas and asks the right questions at the right moment. References to experts in the field make the discussion even more interesting.

Reviewed by Christian Sia for Readers' Favorite

****

The debate was engaging and, while the book is clearly a case for embracing embryonic cell research, it also examined in detail a variety of other pertinent issues of the day which I found absolutely fascinating. Whether you agree with the arguments presented or not, there is no question that this book is all about doing what is right.

Reviewed by Amanda Rofe for Readers' Favorite

****

I believe it was in Chapter Seven: Impartment of a Soul, the moment I handed the book to my wife and told her she had to read it. The science cannot be ignored, but when it's paired with philosophy and good, old-fashioned common sense, it has to be shared.

Reviewed by Asher Syed for Readers' Favorite

In Memory of

Norm

Progress is impossible without change, and those who cannot change their minds cannot change anything.

George Bernard Shaw

Book Cover Design by
Tiffany A. Bastarache

Manuscript Edited by
Stoneburgh Editing Services

Contents

Preface

I was not going to include a preface in this book, but I felt it necessary to inform the reader of certain facts. The main one being that it is not possible to cover all the content of this subject in anything resembling complete detail.

I will cover God, as opposed to religion, wherein the latter, I am sure a complete book could be written with many facts that I must omit in this manuscript.

Likewise, I will cover science in its many subjects: physics, biology, chemistry, quantum mechanics, evolution, psychology, language, morals, abortion, euthanasia, and philosophy, which is not an extensive list, but would require books, or volumes of their own. For the purpose of this book, I must touch on these subjects in one chapter each. This requires leaving out many topics within topics. It also requires leaving out minute details of individual topics.

Perhaps, if we make a deal with the devil, we can accept less: the devil is in the details. I purpose this contra: We eschew the exactness of any factual measurements hitherto acquired by experts in their fields. In other words, we will not use the proper data or mathematical equations in any complicated, strict sense, but use them loosely for ease of understanding; in layman's terms as it were. I will use the following example for a better definition.

I was putting a car on the hoist the other day and my friend, who was working beside me, asked what I was doing. What he meant by this question was: am I doing an oil change, brake job, engine overhaul, etc. Being sarcastic like I am, I said that I was levitating the vehicle. No, he said, you are lifting it on the hoist; the hoist is lifting the car. I got really smart then!

No, I am using the force to levitate the car off the ground. I even did the Yoda hand jester! What force, he asked. The force that is distributed evenly throughout the fluid (the law of hydraulics). Yes, but you're not doing the lifting, he replied. Yes, I am doing the lifting, I said, and then I showed him that, I, it was—the Yoda thing again—who was pushing the button, ergo, I was, in fact, using the force in levitating the car.

Was I using the force to levitate the car? Yes! That would be the sweetened, condensed answer for the sweetened, condensed version. The "true" answer is still yes, but it needs more information. I was using an electromotive force (with a long explanation) to create a hydraulic force (with another long explanation) to move a mechanical device using mechanical force (with a third long explanation). In both cases, the answer is still yes: The agent was I—as Yoda would say—that caused the vehicle to become levitated!

Do, or do not! There is no try! Should we take a lesson from these two last paragraphs? Can we get a completed short version of a story that is still true, but lacks the long explanation to make any technical sense? How technical do we need to be for one to say I concede the point? Not everyone is interested in physics, after all. Or any other science, especially mathematics. I know, I know, I have a hard time believing that too!

For this book, I will require no mathematical thinking on your part, whatsoever, but I do require you to look at some formulas. My advice is that you do not have to understand the complex reasons, you only need to look at the overall picture to see if it makes theoretic sense. If it does, great, move on to the next topic. If not, continue reading, accepting that most of these concepts are widely accepted as true, either religiously, or scientifically.

Notice I said most of. I will, after all, add some of my own interpretations of scientific facts and religious inquires, most notably my interpretations of the soul.

The whole of this manuscript revolves around embryonic stem cell research and the moral issues that research entails. Before progress can be made, a lot of thinking must be overturned and new views held. I can only hope to perform admirably, the task at hand, in as little real estate as one chapter per topic.

Also of note: where I use biblical quotes, I mainly use the King James Version, however, I correct the older words like "thine" into the more common English word "your". Otherwise, any scriptures will be marked as NIV— New International Version when applicable. My notes are all written in my King James Version. Finally, the King James Version has been the most widely used version until recent time.

Chapter One

The Knowledge Tree

The man that wanders out of the way of understanding shall remain in the congregation of the dead.

— Proverbs. 21:16

In the words of Aristotle, "It is the mark of an enlightened mind to be able to entertain an idea without accepting it."

In dealing with faith and reason, some of you, reading this book, will be tempted to close your minds. I encourage you to keep your minds open and save the rejections for later. It is only in the review of every possible species of thought that one will become whole.

Already, we have two problems, which have surfaced in this first paragraphs. One: enlightenment, which this chapter will cover; two: having a closed mind. I will deal with the closed mind first.

There are certain personality types who cannot accept being wrong. These types will fight, even in light of being proven factually wrong. At that point, where they begin to see their error, they shut down and refuse to talk about the topic any longer—lest they have their eyes opened and cannot subscribe to their former belief. This applies to both the religious as well as the non-religious.

For that reason, I have my job cut out for me as I try to analyze every species of thought from every point in this spectrum. Perhaps, if you agree to entertain every idea while holding on to your beliefs, then you might be willing to accept a partial advancement over the complete loss that is ensured by the 'all or nothing' mode of thinking.

For example, while I was in a bible study group a few years ago, I happened to be reading a book called *God is Not Great,* Christopher Hitchens, which was listed as a number one international bestseller at the time. I was asked why I would read such a book. I gave two answers; it was a bible study after all. My response was to say: So that you don't have to read it! How are you going to recognize the enemy if you don't know what the enemy looks like? There was a point I wanted to share in his book at the bible study and it created a simple question for me, that is important in this book.

How are we going to recognize the real enemy, which is ignorance? Ignorance is relevant to both sides! Yes, both sides: faith and reason—science and religion! We must try to overcome our ignorance!

In both of these topics, some huge blunders need to be examined and I will attempt to tweak out some resolve. This brings up many important issues, which have become so blinding that neither science nor religion will ever see past them.

An indignant mind is a closed mind. I propose a compromise and argue for both faith and reason while you tag along, hopefully, in awe of my technique and creative abilities. Surely, that is promising more than I can deliver but I will try!

Why would I, a devout Christian, fight both sides of an exhausting battle, you might ask? In search of truth! The only truth I found is that neither side will go away because both faith and reason are needed at an integrated level. This is just my personal belief! It is not a statement of knowledge. I am sure of two things only: faith has a place in every life in some form or another and knowledge has its well-needed place among the faithful.

Therefore, in this chapter, I will examine knowledge in biblical terms to show that not only faith in God is required by the faithful, but also knowledge (enlightenment). If any embryonic stem cell issue is to be settled, there must be a level playing field. I must instill in you, the reader, that there is a "reason" we have faith, and "faith" in our reasoning. I will, therefore, expound the need for both faith and reason. Which is the topic of another chapter! Simply put, we need both! They are both real! This, I hope, will place a level playing field for us to battle the real enemy, which, in this case, are the moral issues involving the darkness of death.

There are two specific arguments I will deal with in this chapter: knowledge for the sake of knowledge, and playing God. These are just two of the arguments within the larger, embryonic stem cell battle. It only takes putting on an atheist hat, for one moment, to see where we stray. Let's examine wearing that atheist hat! We can wear a theological hat later, switch hats back and forth as needed, or wear both at the same time.

Any atheist worth his weight in salt should be able to read *your* bible, notice the God inference and ask this question, "Why, then, does *your* bible tell *you* that you are gods and yet, you furiously resist playing god?" The act of co-creation and co-problem solving probably comes from Gnosticism. Gnosticism originates from God's divine spark being trapped in humankind. Having knowledge— gnostic—of the divine spark would liberate humankind.

Every major religion believes we are co-creators with God, or the universe, and it is our duty to do whatever we possibly can to improve humanity, with the one general exception of Christianity. To be more concise, conservative Christians! Somehow, conservative Christians believe that Jesus is going to magically do everything for us.

"There is no God except Allah, and Muhammad is his messenger" is the adherence of Islamic culture. Strange, but the same applies to Christianity. "There is no God except Jove, and Jesus is His messenger demigod" Demigod because he was born from man, and God in perfect union.

Scripture states us as being gods. "There is no God except God, and god is his messenger" would fittingly apply. Likewise: "There is no Allah except Allah, and Allah is his messenger" are identical statements, being that the word Allah means God. Yes, Islamism believes that God created us in his image too. I could include the same statement in the tradition of Judaism, where Jesus is held as only a prophet.

Muslims believe we are co-creators in life, as do those of Jewish descent. As writers on the embryonic stem cell topic claim, why are so many conservative Christians groups or organisations, derived from the same Deity, the only groups against embryonic stem cell research? Is it because we believe ourselves as adopted "gods" and expect Him to take care of us, instead of us helping to take care of his works and our fellow human beings? Jesus did say, "My meat is to do the will of Him that sent me, and to finish His works." (John 4:33). Aren't we supposed to emulate that?

The same worthy atheist should be able to ask what we have against knowledge in general, and, more specifically, knowledge for the sake of knowledge. There are certainly several scriptures indicating that much. You don't even need to be a believer to gather this religious information. The atheist would demand fact, which he or she should, and a set standard for evidence.

Make this as real as possible, first, and hold that the bible is true and prove it to be true. I own several bibles and I can, at any point, go to them and quote any material therein. It is true that these things are written in every bible—sometimes altered in meaning from the original text—and we can, with absolute certainty, state them as *biblical* facts. There they are, in black and white, for anyone to read! Yes, the bible does exist! Yes, the many things written within the pages of the bible are truly written! This does not mean the bible is a true reflection of creation. Nor does it mean that it does not contain aspects of myths, or that every event pertains to God. Here, I am dealing with knowledge, but I will deal with fact and opinion in a separate chapter under a different guise.

I am a strong supporter of stem cell research on all levels as I believe it will yield the knowledge for most, if not all, cures for the sick. I am, by no means, a supporter of any method to get there, or any means necessary to attain this knowledge. In fact, as much as I strongly support the research, I am just as strongly against much of the horrors it could lead to. These will also be discussed in the following chapters. For now, I shall say that I think it is time to settle this matter on playing god and dissolving ignorance by taking the good while eschewing the evil. To eschew the evil, one must first look at evil and see why Christians, above any other religions, equate knowledge with evil. Then we can conclude where a proper stand should take place.

To have knowledge is not sin! What you do or do not do with the knowledge you have may or may not be sin. James 4:17 tells us, "Therefore to him that knows to do good, and does not do good, to him it is sin." To not do something good when you have the knowledge to do that good does count as sin. Biblical fact! Funny, but you don't hear this argument—not even once—when it comes to the embryonic stem cell research issues.

We should examine knowledge, what the bible says about knowledge, and whether it is good or bad. More, we should seek what knowledge a benevolent God requires of us and what to do with that knowledge. This one argument is very important and deserves to be looked at in detail. Barring all other moral points for the moment—our atheist hat—will allow an unbiased discussion of the theory that doing nothing is sin. This includes gaining knowledge just for the sake of knowledge and "playing God" as one of the arguments go.

Humans have discovered stem cells and the discovery could save millions of people great suffering, along with many lives. What is done with this knowledge may or may not be sin.

Now that stem cells and DNA are known, do you think we can just forget about them? Are we not responsible for finding ways to use this knowledge for the greater good? You might convince yourself that it is none of your business or moral obligation to support or contribute to the efforts being placed into stem cell research, but you would be wrong. True, there are some evils to be had along with the good, but we are certainly responsible to shine our light upon the darkness and resolve the issues.

This is the basis on which the concept of God is built. As I am writing a Christian case that is pro-stem cell research, I shall be dealing mainly with our Christian God. Omnipotent—all powerful, and omniscient—all-knowing, are two of the many attributes of God. Proclaiming, I didn't know as a means of self-justification will not make you innocent. We are talking about a God who does know your thoughts, your heart, and your crimes. Biblical fact!

It is important to note several facts surrounding the whole stem cell research topic. First, it is not only the religious who have moral issues with embryonic stem cell research. Humane societies do as well, not to mention some members of the scientific community. This should tell you something about the severity of the issue. Second, out of all the religions, Christians—as maintained by every author writing on the topic—are the only ones who have moral issues with anything about a fertilized egg, which just happens to be every issue possible. Some Conservative Christians protest not only embryonic stem cell research, but also much of stem cell research conditions and outcomes in general. Why?

> The official positions of conservative religions consider the embryo as a human being. The Southern Baptist Convention, noted for their long-standing position on abortion, strenuously opposes human embryo research and calls upon research centers to "cease and desist from research which destroys human embryos, the most vulnerable members of the human community." Both the Orthodox Christian and Methodist churches assert that embryo research is a fundamental violation of human life. The Anglican view, prepared as a brief for the House of Lords in 2002, elevates the moral status of the embryo as sacred, containing "the very beginning of each human being."
>
> The Catholic Church declares that God bestows personhood and a soul at the moment of conception. (Christopher Thomas Scott)

The moral issues of embryonic stem cell research are the most important issues to cover, but I will cover some of the medical promises of stem cell research and explain, somewhat, what these stem cells are in case you are not familiar with the scientific scope of this research. I only deal with the "promised miracles" so you understand what is at stake here. You can't understand what all the fuss is about if you don't understand the prize being sought.

Returning to the current topic, we find that one needs to know, or rather have knowledge, to apply or withhold it. This applying or withholding of knowledge falls under the direction of wisdom. It always works best when arguing positions or points of view that all the terms are defined up front. Wisdom then, for our purpose, will be defined as knowing the best way to apply one's knowledge to the situation at hand. The question of when and what sin is, under the topic of doing nothing, requires wisdom.

This leads us atheists, which is the hat we are currently wearing, back to Genesis for the moment while we inspect knowledge before continuing. Adam and Eve had communication with one another, which does necessitate the knowledge of language as the meanings of their words would have to be known. Adam reportedly named all the animals, which is no small feat and it does require knowledge; at least at the minimal to know the difference between plants, animals, and inanimate objects. They even knew they were not supposed to eat from the tree of knowledge of good and evil.

As the name indicates "of the tree", it was the tree of knowing the difference between good and evil—wisdom—and not a tree of knowledge. I briefly showed this to be the case in the last paragraph. As we just love to shorten phrases for faster communication purposes, one of the biggest mistakes theology has made was to shorten the phrase "the tree of knowledge of good and evil" into "the tree of knowledge."

Worse, everyone allowed this to happen! It now carries the connotation of knowledge being evil. It should have been shortened for faster communication by calling it the tree of good and evil or the tree of conscience, or wisdom. Later, we can examine it as "the tree of pro-conscious wisdom".

Knowledge is a must for many reasons. Adam could never have known or talked with God if man did not have the ability of knowledge in its many forms. First, speaking requires the knowledge of what the words mean or what concept is being communicated. Second, humans could not have eaten anything in the garden if they did not know about eating or food. Even from an evolutionary view, at its very heart, knowledge came from instinct.

Before you jump up and down screaming that God taught them as the need arose, consider your own confusion. Without a basic, instinctual knowledge to be able to learn being built into the human brain, teaching would be impossible. What you mean then is that God programmed mankind to be robots. With only a few modest examples, I think I can move on, unchallenged that true knowledge is a basic and fundamental need.

When the scriptures are brought under scrutiny, one can see that knowledge was never the issue; at least not during the "fall" in the garden. Genesis shows a clear and decisive conversation going on between a serpent and a woman, which would never have taken place without knowledge. I only need to look at two of the statements made:

> For God does know that in the day you eat thereof, then your eyes shall be opened, and you shall *be as gods*, knowing good from evil. (And) When the woman saw that the tree was good for food, and that it was pleasant to the eyes, and a tree to be desired to *make one wise*, she took of the fruit thereof, and did eat... (Genesis 3:5, and 6.)

Here we have a case where the woman thought knowing good from evil produced wisdom. This brings me to one of the opening sentences of this chapter, *To have knowledge is not sin! What you do or do not do with the knowledge you have may or may not be sin.*

This leaves some black and white areas as well as many gray areas. It puts into perspective the reason an all-powerful and all-knowing God does not intervene in the affairs of man, which the atheist argue proves the non-existence of a caring God, due to so much world suffering. You have wisdom, figure it out yourselves! Later, we shall see that God does, in fact, want us to act. Only, He wants us to figure it out for ourselves!

Besides redemption of the world, love and the likes, there are three major themes of the Bible. These are fear, knowledge, and faith. Possibly the most famous scripture on fear is:

> Have I not commanded you? Be strong and of good courage; be not afraid, neither be thou dismayed: for the Lord your God is with you whithersoever you go. (Joshua 1:9.)

Almost exclusively, the Old Testament uses "fear not" as a main theme. Faith has almost exclusively replaced fear in the New Testament and faith is the opposite of fear as I have heard several theologians argue on. Both the Old and New Testaments use knowledge throughout, and I might point out that the best way to relieve fear of darkness is to shine the light of knowledge upon it while believing you shall endure and overcome—faith.

That statement might offend many Christians as it is thought that, through faith used as belief, fear is destroyed, and when the bible talks of knowledge, it is referring to knowledge of faith in God. True, knowledge of how faith works is important, but it is not referring exclusively to faith, eschewing knowledge of everything else. It makes it sound as if one cannot have both faith and reason, which, personally, I find offensive. Really? I must choose one?

It is just my observation, but faith serves to empower you to overcome fear, acting despite your fear. Knowledge of the things that cause fear, dissolves fear or, at least, turns fear into reverence or respect for the thing feared. Action, despite fear, teaches you how to overcome that same fear. This is just one sense of the word faith and has nothing directly to do with the other senses of the word.

I will argue that not only can we have both faith and reason, but we need both. With a forced stance on either side of the faith-reason debate, it's no wonder science and religion feel indignant toward one another. What is the purpose to believe, if not to act on what we believe? Do we not act on what we believe from the knowledge that acting produces results? If results occur, then does it now become knowledge that your faith worked, because faith without work is dead? (James 2:26) Sounds to me as if the whole system is designed to produce knowledge, or reason, from faith!

I think I have advanced far enough now to qualify saying that when the Bible says knowledge, it is not prejudiced against knowledge of knowledge—reason, favoring knowledge of faith, but reconciles to both nicely.

Even if explicitly, it is referring to knowledge of God and God's way, then we must allow for God's way to be learned. I must ask if you, the reader, have any real or imagined reason that we should not come to know what God knows. The reason I asked if we should not come to know what God knows is to make you think about what God knows, what we should strive to know, and if our knowledge is a problem to God. The bible says no! Both implicitly and decidedly.

We can, for instance, derive the fact that God wants us to know everything he knows from the fact that Jesus taught us to call Him Father. I am a father and can only speak for myself, but I don't want my daughters to be as stupid as a wet paper towel. Not only do I want them to know what I know, thus teach them the best I can, I want them to know more than I know and do better for themselves than I did. The only real difference between us and God is that God is the highest form of everything, we are not. Thus, his sons and daughters need not fear to come to know more than God. I am sure, no convinced, that God wants us all to attain his status of love, knowledge, faith, forgiveness, power, and peace. If you have any doubts, read those very words, right in your own bible, for yourself. They are there!

I have made comments, which must now be defended. One can't liken themselves unto God without defending that position using God's very own words. Before I promote my striving to acquire knowledge in God's name as sons and daughters, thus gods ourselves, I must establish this as biblical fact. I will start with Genesis and follow as orderly as I can with the biblical proofs, but I leave two of them out of order for the last comment on the topic.

The first hint we have is that God created us in "his own image, in the image of God created he him," (Genesis 1:27). If God is a god and we are in his image, then what are we? Next, the devil tempts Eve:

> For God does know that in the day you eat thereof, then your eyes shall be opened, and you shall *be as gods*, knowing good from evil. (Genesis 3:5.)

You think God would call the devil a liar, wouldn't you? These are, after all, words spoken by the serpent of old. God acknowledges what the devil says as true:

Behold, the *man is become as one of us*, to know good from evil: and now, lest he put forth his hand and take also from the tree of life, and eat, and live forever. (Genesis 3:22.)

Does this not hint that, in some small way, we are gods? Think of it this way. We, humans, start out as babies, defenceless and ignorant, and we must grow and learn until we reach the full status of human—anima. As humans, in God's eyes, we are baby gods, which must grow and learn until we reach the full status of gods. I will spend plenty of time on the anima, also known as soul, later.

Another point to acknowledge is that in both of the above scriptures, there is nothing mentioned about knowledge itself, only good from evil.

We also see a predilection of Jesus making the Father-God connection in this psalm:

He shall cry unto me, you are my father, my God, and the rock of my salvation. Also I will make him my firstborn, higher than the kings of the earth. (Psalm 89:26, 27.)

I will take a few more of the many scriptures, both in the Old and New Testaments, which refer directly to God being our Father.

And call no man your father upon the earth: for one is your Father, which is in heaven. (Matthew 23:9)

Fear not, little flock; for it is your Father's good pleasure to give you the kingdom. (Luke 12:32)

- 13 -

Neither can they die any more: for they are equal unto the angels; and are the children of the resurrection. (Luke 20:36)

Then Jesus said, Father, forgive them; for they know not what they do. (Luke 23:34)

This next scripture I love to use as it fits together, in undeviating black and white biblical terms, all that I have written above, and no less a historical figure than Jesus himself made the statement.

Therefore, the Jews sought the more to kill him, because he not only had broken the Sabbath, but said also that God was his Father, making himself equal with God. Then answered Jesus and said unto them, Verily, verily, I say unto you, The Son can do nothing of himself, but what he sees the Father do; for whatsoever things he does, these also does the Son likewise. For the Father loves the Son, and shows him all things that [he] himself does; and he will show him greater works than these, that you may marvel. (John 5:18-20)

Continuing, we find it bluntly stated in the psalms. I will quote the whole psalm because it also deals with knowledge, then follow it directly with a comment Jesus makes referring to this very scripture.

A psalm of A-saph

God stands in the congregation of the mighty; he judges *among the gods*. How long will you judge unjustly, and except the persons of the wicked? Defend the poor and fatherless: do justice to the afflicted and needy. Deliver the poor and needy:

rid them out of the hand of the wicked. *They know not, neither will they understand; they walk on in darkness*: all the foundations of the earth are out of course. I have said, *you are gods; and all of you are the children of the most high.* But you shall die like men, and fall like one of the princes. Arise, O God, judge the earth: for you shall inherit all nations.

The Gospel of John

Jesus answered them, Many good works have I shown you from my Father: for which of those works do you stone me? The Jews answered him, saying, For a good work we stone you not; but for blasphemy; and because that you, being a man, makes yourself God. Jesus answered them, Is it not written in your law, *I said, you are gods*? If he called them gods, unto whom the word of God came, and the scripture cannot be broken; Say you of him, whom the Father has sanctified, and sent into the world, you blasphemy; because I said, I am the Son of God? If I do not [do] the works of my father, believe me not. But if I do, though you believe not me, believe the works: that you may *know, and believe*, that the father is in me, and I in him. (John 10:32-38; emphasis mine.)

This will end my comments on us being gods, and it is the perfect scripture to end with. Notice I have emphasized, both, know and believe. Reason orbits around knowledge! Faith orbits around belief! Would a reasonable, faithful Christian condemn me for desiring both faith and reason?

Strangely enough, one of the very arguments used against embryonic stem cell research is that we should not be "playing god". My stand on this comment is that we should not be playing gods, we should be working at perfecting being gods! Too strong of a statement? Not if the bible is true!

How much knowledge is too much knowledge? I don't think you could get any Christian, or, for that matter, any religion, to come right out publicly and say that having too much faith is not good. In fact, your bible says you should continually grow your faith and exercise it to become stronger. Can you ever have too much faith?

On the other hand, it is commonplace to hear people saying that you can have too much knowledge. We hear everything from, "Man is starting to know too much for his own good," to the term "Over-educated heathen," to the statement "Man is so smart now that we have forgotten how to think." Can you ever have too much knowledge? True, knowledge without the wisdom to use it is dangerous, but that is a different matter and should be dealt with separately.

Does the bible put a cap on what the maximum amount of faith you should acquire? Not one single scripture says such a thing. Don't confuse it with faith of a mustard seed! The analogy used was to take your mustard seed faith and grow it into a tree size faith that birds could take cover in.

Does the bible place a cap on what the maximum amount of knowledge you should acquire is? Again, not one single scripture says such a thing. In fact, the scriptures have completely thrown out the cap of acquired knowledge. I will show one scripture written in two different gospels, which, point blank, makes this very statement.

For there is nothing hid, which shall not be manifested; neither was anything kept secret, but that it should come abroad. (Mark 4:22)

For there is nothing covered, that shall not be revealed; neither hid, that shall not be known. (Luke 12:2)

Did God intend to hide anything from us? As I write this, I can envision hearing some reader saying this is not what the scripture refers to, based solely on not wanting it to be true. I might remind you that you agreed to be open-minded, whether you are religious or an atheist. Any opinions should be formed after a complete reading of this book. "There is a difference between keeping an open mind and believing something because you want it to be true." *Sub-Commander T'Pol: Star Trek: Enterprise.*

You have the same resources as I have, and are completely free to draw your own conclusions from the scriptures. Just remember, when you protest knowledge, you show the knowledgeable in faith the meaning of blind faith.

You are walking around with your eyes closed, believing you are never going to bump into things or trip. Christians are supposed to be an example unto the world and that example should not be stumbling around and tripping in the dark! He that does truth comes to the light... (John 3:21). If I may quote another scripture:

My people are destroyed for lack of knowledge: because you have rejected knowledge, I will also reject you, that you shall be no priest to me... (Hosea 4:6.NIV)

We should be looking at it this way: "My people are destroyed for lack of knowledge", so we believe ignorance to be the enemy of the world. Ignorance prevents peace, ignorance thrives on poverty, and ignorance keeps us in our infirmities; both, mentally and physically. Another thing to be noted here is the biblical fact that the word faith is not used in that scripture. It does not say, My people are destroyed from a lack of faith! It says we are destroyed from a lack of knowledge!

In case some Christian readers might think the Old Testament to be outdated upon Jesus's birth and death, maybe a scripture in Jesus's own words will make a difference to your thoughts.

> Woe to you experts in the law, because you have taken away the key to knowledge. You yourselves have not entered, and you have hindered those who were entering. (Luke 11:52 NIV)

Reopening the point of a child learning what a parent knows and God wanting us to know what he knows, imagine how your children feel when you do everything for them. My daughters used to get angry and fuss when they were babies and being fed. They wanted to feed themselves, but when they were given the spoon could not get the food into their mouths. Once they learned, mother and father could finally stop feeding them and let them eat on their own.

Their mother and I were more powerful than they were at that age and we did most everything for them. The intention was to keep them alive long enough for them to learn to do it for themselves. Both my daughters are now adults; they would be offended if I tried to dress them every day, feed them their meals, hold and move the mouse as they surfed the internet, brushed their teeth, or did anything else of that nature. They might not get offended if I cleaned their rooms though. I am so not going to!

The whole point here is that children, at some point, obtain power over their own being and start doing things for themselves. Trust me, neither of my daughters could ever be accused of being puppets on a string. Sometimes, we as parents, know better ways of doing things and make suggestions, but, in the end, it is up to our children on how they use that knowledge. I can't force them; I can't grab hold of their hands and make all the finger movements for them. I don't have shoes, built on top of my shoes, where I can stick their feet in and make them walk as I walk.

Why, would anyone think that God, being omnipotent and omniscient, would make us, his children, likened unto puppets? The best that could be said from a creation perspective is that capacity was created inherently within us and we must learn to master it.

If God is, in fact, all-powerful, then why is there so much suffering in the world? Is he obligated to fix it? You have the same power over the suffering, which you must grow into, so you fix it! What do you want him to do, place your feet upon his feet and walk you around? Collectively, the world should be powerful enough to fix its own problems. I wonder why we are not collectively doing everything we can to those ends.

As my daughters became young adults, they stopped wanting parental input. They learned to do most everything on their own and they continue to learn new things every day. Albeit, from time to time, my children still love when I help them out, it is not a matter of them being incompetent. If the church, here on Earth, is supposed to be the power of God, then why is this power of God not helping from time to time?

How many times did Jesus tell us to do it? Before moving on, I will point out two such scriptures of the many.

"O unbelieving and perverse generation," Jesus replied. "How long shall I stay with you and put up with you? Bring your son here." (Luke 9:41 NIV)

Within the context of this scripture, which I have not quoted in full, his disciples could not heal a man. The implications of Jesus's words being that he will not be with them long so they better learn how to do it.

> By this time it was late in the day, so his disciples came to him. 'This is a remote place,' they said, 'and it is already very late. Send the people away so they can go to the surrounding countryside and villages and buy themselves something to eat.' But He answered, 'you give them something to eat.' (Mark 6:35-37 NIV)

Within the context of the scripture, Jesus is saying that his disciples should feed the multitude, but they thought he wanted them to go and buy food. This is evident by Jesus saying "you give" and not "you buy". As an example, Jesus then fed the people himself with what he and his disciples had with them; two fish and five loaves, multiplying it.

True, these things are only religiously relevant when you believe in God or a higher power. We are taking the bible as being true as a complete document, whether believed real or not, and should be bold as stating these things as biblical fact.

If, at this point, with all that we have covered, you don't get the message that God is not only knowledge, but wants us to be knowledge as well, I have failed miserably. The bible verses I have used have failed miserably. God wants us to have knowledge and be faithful in and to that knowledge! I can do no more to convince you and I shall return to my opening topic.

If we know to do something, and yet, do not do it, then unto us, it is sin. Being ignorant is one thing, refusal is quite another. If gaining knowledge is the remedy for evil:

along with the remedy for ignorance, poverty, sickness, hatred, and so much more, why is it that we do not seek knowledge? If we know we should seek knowledge, but do not, is it not a sin as well? Does it not stand on the same ground as not doing what we know we should be doing? Therefore, why should it not be counted as sin to remain ignorant? True, we are not going to write another commandment: thou shall not be ignorant, but we don't need to as it is already an ordinance of the law.

To bring all this writing about knowledge around to my book's main theme, I will ask you, the reader, if these things do not count as knowledge. DNA, the recipe for all life, is not to be considered worth knowing? Are stem cells so well known that we can afford to ignore them? Is it just too bad for the people dying from cancer that we can't help them? Is it not our problem that most stem cell research is stalled because of moral complications? Are we guiltless because this mess is not settled and stem cell research is not fully supported?

Perhaps the biggest contested aspect of embryonic stem cell research, next to the soul, is should we be playing God? This atheist could, and should, ask, "Does your bible really pronounce you to be gods and demand knowledge of you?" The importance here is not that we become arrogant, know everything as gods, but that we don't sit on our arses and do nothing about human suffering.

I will look at many of these issues throughout this book, but the above is still reasonable, faithful and legitimate questions to ask. I can only speak for myself, of course, but I know better. I am, therefore, compelled to be faithful and learn about the problems. I will never be an expert on stem cell research, but I can do my part to advance support for the experts on stem cell research.

The last thing I want to hear when entering the Pearly Gates is, "Wait a minute, you knew better, but you just sat there and did nothing? What should be required of you before you enter?"

> That servant, which knew his lord's will, and prepared not himself, neither did according to his will, shall be beaten with many stripes. But he that knew not, and did commit things worthy of stripes, shall be beaten with few stripes. For unto whosoever much is given, of him shall much be required. (Luke 12:47-48)

Chapter Two

Modus Operandi

[T]hat the acts that were done in those days, were the subject of those words; and in the Greek, which (in the scripture) retaineth many Hebraisms[sic], by the word of God is oftentimes meant, not that which is spoken by God, but concerning God, and his government; that is to say, the doctrine of religion. [Theologia]

— *Leviathan:* Thomas Hobbes

Several evangelical ministers use the term modus operandi in their description of God. Some say that God's modus operandi is faith. I will detail faith and reason in the next chapter but that will not stop me from introducing my own philosophical concept.

Somewhere in this book, perhaps in several places, an overview of the arguments need to be established. We must also ask what the basis of these fruitless arguments establish. The answer is nothing! Although we might extend these findings to cover some moral issues later.

God has been taking some incredible hits of late. With book titles, such as *God is Not Great* by Christopher Hitchens, first referred to in the last chapter, and *The God Delusion* by Richard Dawkins, to single out two powerful works, we have seen an outright attack on God. It is important to critique both books as having little or nothing to do with God, de facto, but instead, are the religious aspirations of man. Almost exclusively, what are depicted as problems with God are nothing more than problems manifested by the things people believe about this God. Therefore, to single out one of the above books, the world would have been better served with the title *Religion is Not Great* and point out this religious deficit than blaming it on God.

I am, however, convinced that God does not mind these hits, as they are not really directed at Him, but at the many religions that claim to embody Him. The same way as my description of Him, which could just as easily be Her or something otherwise indicative of a god-like entity, then what we have thought to address this persona as. In keeping with biblical tradition, I will refer to this deity as He, or Him. There is a huge difference between God and the religious manifestation of God. For the sake of this book, I will only deal with the possibility of there being a real God and leave the religions to fend for themselves.

To place a little bite into that paragraph, we should examine at least one piece of content in the book: *The God Delusion*—I read the hardcover version and acquired this case on page 311. I will not take a direct quote, but, instead, paraphrase it.

An older girl was babysitting a Jewish boy, Edgardo Mortara, and she took it upon herself to baptise him in the name of Jesus; herself the age of fourteen. (The Mortara Case, 1858) Upon telling her parents what she did, it fell into the lap of the Catholic clergy. They took it upon themselves to remove this now "Christian" boy from his

Jewish family and raise him in a Catholic upbringing. True story as the facts bear it out! It was claimed that they had the right afforded by his baptism, willingly or not. Richard Dawkins is exactly right! This was a real problem! He was, however, incorrect, in pointing at whom was at fault.

What we see written are scriptures like "as many as heard, and believed, were saved, then baptised" (Acts: 2:41, 8:13, 16:30, and 18:8). An even larger context here from the book of Acts. "What is to stop me from being baptised? Do you believe? I believe! Then nothing!" (Acts: 8:36-38) These scriptures are paraphrased, but they are nonetheless there. These scriptures indicate one must first believe, and then be baptised.

Then [indicating after an event] will I sprinkle clean water upon you, and you shall be clean: from all your filthiness, and from your idols, will I cleanse you. (Ezekiel 36:25)

He that believes [primary] and is baptized [secondary] shall be saved; but he that believes not shall be damned. (Mark 16:16)

There are no scriptures indicating otherwise. Baptism does not save you! Believing saves you! Baptism is a cleansing symbol only. A symbol of having your sins washed away. Not, as the Catholic Church would have you believe, that your parents' sin of conception is washed away. No, if your baby dies before she is baptised, she will not go to hell. Your child is not even mature enough to commit sin, as per the biblical definition of sin. There are no such scriptures in the bible. In fact, being baptised as a child will not save you from hell if you grow up to be a non-believer. (Biblically speaking.)

There are no scriptures in the bible that condone any person being baptised under the age of consent, against their will. Baptising small children was a means, created by the church—not God—to keep power over the people and ensure repeat business. It was surely not the will of God!

Who is at fault for this horrendous act of abducting this child from his parents? Religion! Not God! In other words, it is what man says about God and not what God says!

Religion asserts that our laws come from absolute and supreme authority, placing them beyond challenge. I am not what one would call religious. I identify as Christian, non-denominational. By choice, I take the sacraments at an Anglican assembly, but I identify as Christian while serving Him in an Anglican parish. I believe in a deity, not a religion.

Religions are what man believes, transposed onto their God. They do not reflect the perfect love of God in a non-prejudicial manner. Us and them! We must come to the realization that placing religious laws beyond challenge is not condemning God's one law of love.

People, the world over, look at what man says about God in judgement. Imagine a cult, using the name of God to promote hatred. If you type in your search engine the words, "God hates fags", the first website it directs you to is, in fact, godhatesfags.com, home of the hate-cult Westboro Baptist Church. They walk around holding hate signs in the name of our Lord.

It is important to take no heed of anyone who uses God and hate in the same sentence! It is not too hard to see why God is taking flack! Ovid in the Metamorphoses, of the god Cupid, sums it up best:

Then from his quiver Cupid took two darts:
One kindles love, one hate in mortal hearts.
The first, sharp-pointed, with a golden head,
The other dull, and blunt, and tipped with lead.

The same could be said about picketers at abortion clinics. They would do more good in the world if the signs read: Your sins are forgiven, and you have life eternal; go in peace. That, as far as I have been able to induce from the bible, is the will of God. I think the Apostle Paul says it best, "I can do all things, but all things are not expedient."

If you don't know what that means, then you are not alone. When the world judges the signs of picketers, it does not judge the picketer, or their ignorance, but the God they profess to love. A God, to whom, many are supposed to be an expert. Yet, people fall short of His love for humanity because they lack their own love for humanity?

I will look at love shortly, and return to the abortion issue later in this book.

As I hold out hope for both faith and reason, I must, above all, be diligent in pointing out the most common mistakes made in our thinking, within our two brain configurations: belief and logic (or faith and reason as they are often called). Before setting up systems to work with, that is closer to the truth in either science or religion, I will examine one mistake, which is commonly supposed. The mistake has been written about throughout literature for centuries now and is exemplified in *Knocking on Heaven's Door* by Lisa Randall, where she wrote this passage:

> The problem is that in order to subscribe both to science and to a God—or any external spirit—who controls the universe or human activity, one has to address the question of at what point does the deity intervene and how does He do it. According to the materialist, mechanistic point of view of science, if genes that influence our behavior are a result of random mutations that allow a species to evolve, God can be responsible for our behavior only if He physically intervened

by producing that apparently random mutation. To guide our activities today, God had to influence the ostensibly random mutation that was critical to our development. If He did, how did He do that? Did He apply a force or transfer energy? Is God manipulating electrical processes in our brains? Is He pushing us to act in a certain way or creating a thunderstorm for any particular individual so he or she can't get to their destination? On a larger level, if God gives purpose to the universe, how does He apply His will?

The problem is that not only does much of this seem silly, but that these questions seem to have no sensible answer that is consistent with science as we understand it. How could this "God Magic" possibly work? (Lisa Randall Page 55-56)

I was not going to quote that much of her book, but these questions were riveting and vital to answer. I also wanted the "God magic" part to be read here. These are all excellent questions and Randall has a very interesting and well-written book. With no criticism to her, or to anyone else, who says that God must be doing anything at all? That is an assumption of the religious! Curiously, it is also the assumption of the atheist! Not in asking about creation, but when refuting God as creator, or His existence at all. Things like: why does God allow suffering, earthquakes, sickness, and so much more to continue? It's the base assumption of atheists when they condemn a belief in God. Science has the same type of problem to overcome! I will deal with these same types of scientific problems in the following chapters.

Why do we think God must be working all the time and taking care of us? He loves us! So? Can't He be lazy? Do you know how many people there are to babysit? Can you even fathom doing everything for every dumb ass on the planet, night and day, for all eternity? Why do you think big corporations have so many employees? The CEO's cannot do everything themselves! Even Moses, at the suggestion of his father-in-law, appointed elders of the people as officers over them. They were set up rather like officers over thousands, officers over hundreds... and the harder social matters were brought directly to Moses. For reasons I will not get into, if one man cannot rule the earth without the need of implored aid, then why would we assume that God would ever want to? That says nothing about being able to.

Omnipotent and omniscient are two of the attributes given to God in an "all or nothing" strict fashion. They are widely misunderstood in my opinion, which is why I chose these two attributes to single out. Both attributes are used as a tool against religion as a reason for supporting a no-god-theory. The argument is made for no other reason than some misunderstood concept.

Commonly, believers accept these as facts, but don't understand the whole of their entailments. Even theologians have stumbled on the concepts of these attributes, which I have witnessed not just once but many times. In light of all the suffering in the world, Jesuits have begun to theorize that God created the universe, but is not all-powerful and does not know everything happening in it. Wow, even the faithful, who were once the defenders of God and religion, are stumbling on this very important point.

Here lies the greater fallacy as I have come to understand it. Being all-powerful does not mean you *must* use this power. Having all knowledge does not mean you *must* correct, or order, everything. Combining the two attributes, we see the same logic hold: knowing everything and being powerful enough to do something about everything does not mean one must. Does it? This would place God in the position of being a puppeteer of the world: not only knowing what you should do, but also forcing you to do it. Worse, as puppeteers suggest, we would never even need to know, believe, or decide anything. Our lives would not have any meaning—neither for us, nor for God. If we are free will agents, which theology professes, then we need free will, which includes learning knowledge and having power over it!

One cannot defend both faith and reason without stepping on toes, and that hurts, sometimes. All we have left of the argument is faith and reason—reason is not proof, strictly speaking. Reasoning is used as a means of developing proof, but it is, by no means, infallible. Maybe we should examine the prospect of a deity with both faith and reason, which, in times past, was called philosophy.

The first thing we should do here is to grant perfection to any deity, suspend disbelief, and properly examine what is possible, differentiating it from what is desired. If we state that God is perfect, then it automatically follows that everything He does will be perfect. What's the problem with perfection?

Well, a couple of things. One, too many believers, either directly believe, or have had preached to them by someone who directly believes, that Adam was created perfectly and his sin caused his imperfection. Really? Two objections! First, if he was perfect, then he would have never sinned! Oh yeah, there's that ugly fact! Being perfect deprives you of a sinful nature. Second, there is an inherent problem with perfection, in and of itself.

The first conundrum—man was created perfectly—is way too long to argue. The second conundrum—perfection—has a very logical and indestructible explanation. Imagining yourself as a perfect being is the only requirement for figuring this mess out. Everything you make is absolutely perfect. This might give you great pride in things of little importance—like building your home without a flaw.

Just think for a moment about something different from inanimate objects. Think about another living being, with whom, you will interact with at some point on some level. Does making him or her perfect solve any interaction problems? Whether you are a male or a female, just imagine creating your perfect physical and emotional mate—the perfect specimen. The perfect specimen for you and your needs. Now create this perfect being to be madly and uncontrollably in love with you and only you. Feels pretty good right?

Problems? Can't think of any? How about the ugly fact that this perfect soul mate only loves you because you created and programmed this perfect love for you into them? It is not genuine, but completely artificial—not unlike artificial intelligence. Call it artificial emotion. How does that love feel to you now? They did not choose to be your perfect mate, did they? In fact, you forced yourself on them! You created a copy of you to love you.

The second ugly fact is that they don't even know any better. Being perfect and doing everything perfectly has a set of drawbacks. Huge drawbacks!

Think back to a time when you were first falling in love with someone. You never met this person before. They never met you before, either. They gave you that look and things began to heat up. Your heart raced and your face was sore from the constant smiling. You hung on every word they spoke. Even the mention of their name sent your pulse rate soaring. Strangers, now lovers! Does it sound surreal, or is it real? Neither one of you created the other, so the emotion that is building between you is real!

For comparison, check out the angels of Heaven. It is said that God created them to be perfect, but this begs two questions. One, why did it not please God to limit creation to perfect angels, who are said to worship him night and day without ceasing? Two, why is it said that one-third of these angels turned on God? If they were perfect and given free will, then free will to do what? I think we should concede that there is more here than the scriptures are saying. Serve God and live forever in perfect conditions, or serve evil and live in horrendous conditions. Chose love or hate?

Are these biblical stories created to raise our thinking to a much higher level? A higher meaning, perhaps? Creating a choice between good and evil, and free will to chose, would be no different than flipping a coin if no provision was made for a genuine property of that nature.

Look at it this way, things change when you create the perfect specimen from above, and that perfect specimen falls in love with your friend, instead of you. If you are astute at all, you will see that this cannot be done. They were created with perfect love for you! Giving them a choice of loving you or your friend is to program a fifty-fifty chance of them choosing you. How does that make you feel this love is, in any way, more real than without a choice? This leads to so many variables; one cannot track any part of the creation of angels, which includes a genuine nature.

By genuine, love is understood to be self-generated and freely applied. True, these are just words and man creates words as analogies as needed, but we can't deny that these analogies are needed. Creation will not give you self-generated anything, but natural selection will. When you think of genuine, think of diamonds. They are self-generated, by interaction in the earth naturally. Humans create artificial diamonds too! They are worthless! They also have few, or no, flaws! If you had the choice, wouldn't you rather have a genuine diamond?

There must be some way to avoid these complications of attaining love that is genuine in nature. To this, there is only one answer: let it be self-generated and freely applied.

This would give another, totally different, Modus Operandi of God: devise a way to create a universe, complete with life, without doing anything to influence the outcome. Then allow whatever creature, faith, and love that evolves to be accepted as a genuine, albeit, an imperfect love toward Him. Let it come into being on its own and applied to our belief in a superior being. Faith as a necessary means of learning anything would become selected for with certainty—next chapter. Both love and faith are highly predictive of natural selection.

We often hear people claiming God used evolution to perfect the human race; poised as a question. "How do we know God did not use evolution to perfect the human race?" The question is pointless as we are far from perfect. Perfect can be created perfectly. We should, instead, ask, how do we know that God did not use evolution to obtain genuine in nature?

The gods, according to every mythology, were plentiful. This is the most likely way for divine lives to become manifested with evolution as a driving factor. At some point, some single individual concluded that only one god is needed to perform, and, by extension, perform the necessities of every god. Abraham is credited with spawning the three major monotheist religions of Judaism, Islam, and Christianity, all from I Am That Am, signifying eternal oneness. Being true, it is the most probable evolutionary outcome that some form of love evolved, then the big question can be asked: would you rather have a sloppy, messed up love you could feel as the genuine thing, or a perfect quality of meaningless love? Genuine, or artificial?

Believing in a superior being, or God, gives meaning to life. It allows us to not answer the impossible questions, oftentimes being stated: as God only knows. Beside religion being a major problem, believing in a god is harmless. Problems only arise when you make your beliefs out to be God's will, which are problems that go way back in time. We may as well be devil worshipers killing each other in the name of hate, instead of embracing each other in love.

Examine what would happen if God really did exist and everyone knew this as fact because it was proven. If He appeared to everyone and talked with us, would there be any more problems? We may not sin any longer. However, freedom would become eradicated. Choice would cease to exist. In fact, the meaning of life, at least for many, would cease to exist as well.

My wonderful editor made a great point here on what I just wrote. "It would cement their faith." I have a whole chapter dedicated to faith and belief, but, must defend here this perfect comment. Belief would not need to be created, at all, because knowledge of God would hold as real. Believing something without proof is what theology considers faith. If you knew, first hand, everything, then you would not need to believe as your knowledge would be cemented. Knowledge that is cemented does not evolve or grow...it is stuck.

Faith gives meaning to life and requires believing in something greater than oneself. In a perfect world, God would not want Himself proven as real; neither would we want this proof. Belief is needed. If your knowledge is cemented, then where would we have the ability to entertain other concepts? How could we choose other than what is known to be true? It would not allow for free will. It would not allow for genuine.

This leaves man with many options of presenting himself with unknown gods. We can make the astute observation that God cannot be evolved. However, religion can become an evolved property of human nature—what man thinks a god entails. Things like questioning natural events such as a volcanic eruption could lead one to assume it was the work of a god of the underworld. If every action needs a cause, then what is the cause of lava flow? If I pour water upon the ground, then someone must be pouring lava upon the ground.

Taking religion as an evolved nature can, and has been, postulated scientifically. Somehow it was needed as selection requirements for our survival, possibly on the back of some other survival advantages. Adding false gods to these beliefs give a persona for actions and morality. Realizing that one real God can take the place of many gods, and be everything to everyone, glorifies God.

What attributes would we give this God? Creation! We are made in His image! He is the perfect specimen of which we fall short! The problem is that if evolution is true, and it is, then we must have evolved God from our image, based on religious requirements. Remember I said religion could become evolved, but not God, per se.

I will, strictly speaking, treat the scriptures as true. A reminder that these scriptures are facts of the Bible as noted above. Following this line of thinking and putting it into practical conclusions, we should question anew what the scriptures say.

"He did not abhor the virgin's womb" (Te Deum, Book of Common Prayer—based upon several scriptures) would be my first query. Being a virgin was not a good thing? Asked another way: Why would He abhor being born from a sinless womb? Unless it has another deeper meaning. One possible answer is that He did not abhor being born into the descent of man from animals. That is, the scripture, "Taking our nature upon Himself" (Hebrews 2:14) and thus becoming the same species as we are to save us. Blasphemy? How about the biblical fact that no man has seen God and lived? How do we actually know what God looks like?

Beloved, now we are the sons of God, and it does not yet appear what we shall be: but we know

that, when he shall appear, we shall be like him;
for we will see him as he is. (I John 3:2)

Another scripture says we will be given "a new, glorified body" (Philippians 3:21). If we were created in the image of God, then, by the act of creation, we are glorified already. What if this is a means of acquiring the true form of God, instead of the evolved form of humans? This would allow for natural process to evolve genuine properties.

What about "when the fullness of time was come" (Galatians 4:4) as another scripture. It could be read as "we have not suffered enough" or "we had not learned to repent." It could also be read as "we were still immature as a species" and saving us within the lifetime of Adam would have been lost on us. Perhaps, spirituality, as we know it, had not developed as a quality in our ancestors yet (I Corinthians 15:42-44) and needed a trigger to set it in motion when the time was right. Less blasphemous?

I am Christian by choice, but, more than this, I believe in some form of a deity. It gives me hope for humankind. Christianity is the one perfect form of a three persona God, or a trinity: The Father, the Son, and the Holy Spirit; all in one God. It is also the highest form of God, which could be made in our likeness. We see ourselves as three things. These three things will be considered in more detail later in the book when I examine the soul, or mind of man; faith, reason, and their ilk.

For now, I will just sum them up. One, we have bodily form. We have motion, which is directly derived from the Latin word anima, from the Greek anemos dealing with air or wind. Two, this animation gives rise to soul. We get animated, or have movement. Three, we also have spirits, or are spiritual in nature—having two meanings. Spirit traditionally has been used with the meaning of wind, or breathing, to inspire. It also has another meaning, that of "to think." It is taken from the word for man: *Manti* meaning "spirit" or to "think". This forms a trinity, making us Body, Soul and Spirit, but says nothing about separate entities. Read another way, we have form endowed with animation and independent thought. Another trinity?

For God to make Himself like one of us, He would need a human body as well to become completely as one of us. This would be true whether we created God or He created us. He would need an earthly vessel to interact with us in our earthly vessels upon the Earth.

With this view, hypothetically, not only did God create mankind, but mankind created God as well. This mutual creation would allow for the common ground of mutual acceptance. Hypothetically!

This does not negate the possibility of there being a real God. Does it? Looking at the Bible, as a whole, we see that God does not intermingle with man until man has at least developed love, faith and a belief in gods. This is the point most prominently needed to become a genuine attribute in man towards this God. Interacting before love and faith developed would taint this genuine nature. According to science, ancient man already performed ritual and had some moral fibre, which includes the extinct Neanderthal.

Brain-wise, nothing could be accomplished with man until he had achieved a higher consciousness. Scientifically, the Garden of Eden is replaced by another line of thinking:

> Over time, in the crucible of the hot African savannah, far away in time from the Eden of rain forest, an exchange was being made— reproductive agility for mental agility. (Chip Walter)

It could evolve morally into a more complex version as it is told and retold adding in the gods of our beliefs. Disobedience to the tribe caused Adam and Eve to be ejected from the clan and roam into the wilderness causing this famed encounter of Genesis, Chapter Three. From here, it became disobedience to God, ending in a life of harsh farming, instead of hunting and gathering.

In sum, none of these things are concrete proof of there being a real deity. Neither are they disqualifiers of a real deity. However, there is enough of a reason to believe in a deity, from unasked questions alone, that most people will not need to give up their faith. I know I haven't!

Problems only arise when you unrealistically believe your God to be the only God. When you take him out of the one God nature, and place Him as superfluous to your own prejudices. In other words, stop doing evil in His name! The world is watching and judging.

Chapter Three

A Faithful Phenotype

The body is for food and the most divine part is for wisdom, the motions of the stronger part prevail and increase the power of their own kind, while they make the soul dull, slow to learn and forgetful, and bring about the worst of diseases, ignorance.

— Plato

Food is the diet of the body. Knowledge is the diet of the brain. The question remains, how does the brain ingest knowledge? I must define something indefinable, and I must do it in a manner that is understandable. First, a shaky definition must be established. Language, at least as an artifact of knowledge, is limited in scope and definitions are sometimes poor. How far back do we need to go before we assign a cause and effect relationship? The atom?

Both knowledge and belief are artifacts of language. Realities are purely designated by if-then relationships.

Atoms stay together due to an if-then relationship known as causality, or cause and effect.

If I were to place a definition on causality, it would be as follows: if-then is the act of being real and performing real consequences without the knowledge of how that reality exists or how it performs the real act, or action. An atom does not know it is an atom.

Curiously, the definition of "believe" is the same, or close to it. To believe something is to accept it as true without the knowledge within the if-then supporting that belief. The knowledge within is unknown, but believed. Language, in this respect, is poor: we have no single word, nor set of words to explain this process. It is due to the way the evolution of language works.

Innate instinctual concepts drive language. Other innate instinctual concepts diverge to explain selected innate concepts. We can only carry so many innately instinctual concepts relating to survival. Intuition is awareness of undiscovered knowledge, which is innate within the brain cells. Knowledge cannot make sense to us unless it satisfies the senses, and this, to us, is intuitive thinking. When something feels off, we say it is not intuitive. The brain does not feel as if it is true. It must become learned and accepted as true before it can become understood—our awareness facility. Information senses, as opposed to natural senses, is the product of understanding knowledge. We don't say, "That makes sense," for nothing.

By placing one of the above definitions on top of the other, we can see a correspondence and a divergence. We may never have words for a proper definition. Let's try placing the definitions together and see what happens.

If-then is the act of being real and performing real consequences without the knowledge of how that reality exists or how it performs the real act, or action.

Plus.

To believe something is to accept it as true without the knowledge within the if-then supporting belief.

Equals.

To believe the act of being real and performing real consequences without the knowledge of how that reality exists or how it performs the real act, or action, by accepting it as true without the knowledge within the if-then supporting the belief.

What about the atom? The atom is too far back of a starting point to even ask that question. However, if one were forced to make a statement, one would say the atom does not know, but must believe. The reason being is that without proof, requiring knowledge, if-then falls in a state of acceptance without proof. It is meaningless though! The only starting point we must consider is that of cells upward. Notably, brain cells. It is the only place where true belief can be established as a starting point with any real meaning. This will become clear when I enter proof of a soul elsewhere in the book. For now, I ask for you to partially accept it.

Due to the above-mentioned language restriction, this explanation may fall short too. Let's transfer the atom belief from above, upon that of a brain cell. If one were forced to make a statement, one would say the brain cell does not know, but must rather believe. The reason being is that without proof, requiring knowledge, if-then falls in a state of acceptance without proof. A brain cell accepts something as true without knowing why. The acceptance of action without knowing why is belief.

If-then can be divided into its two components. *If* takes place and a separate act of *then* takes place. We formally call this causal or causation, or cause and effect. Why did *then* happen? Because an act of *if* took place! Thus, we can see how knowledge would evolve from belief.

First, hold it (believe) as true so it can be examined. Why did *then* happen? You can look to see whether *if* took place. Did *if* take place first? Does the *then* always follow the *if*? What other conditions cause the same *then* to occur? If only one set of conditions cause the if-then to occur, then the if-then in question must be true—proof. It then enters the environment of the brain as proven. Logical knowledge would evolve from a state of acceptance, without proof—belief. I doubt this would happen the other way around.

In the chapter dealing with the soul, I will add to this theory but, for now, we are going to focus on other concepts.

To being the concept, which would become embedded within our learning brain, would be both faith and belief. They have become an innate feature of humans and are selected for naturally. The default brain is belief! (This concept is from a paper published by Harris, Sheth, and Cohen, Annals of Neurology, February 2008, Functional Neuroimaging of Belief, Disbelief, and Uncertainty). It may seem at odds with many theories, but the fact is, through science, we have found belief is the resting state of the brain. Natural processes would support the evolution of that outcome definitively. By the way, faith and belief are not as interchangeable as many evangelical ministers preach. This fact will become clear as you continue reading.

I could cite several examples and arguments, but one or two should sway you to concede. If you walk on the ground, and this would occur naturally, then you would believe the ground supports your weight in the form of unproven knowledge. Having belief in something is to acknowledge it as fact without proving it.

In other words, you just accept it as true. Therefore, accepting something as true is belief, and acknowledging it by action is faith. Walking on the ground is your faith that the ground is there and will support you as you believe it will. The two properties are relative in nature and are expressed as accepting and doing what is accepted.

If you act upon a body and that body obeys your action, then it will follow that you will acquire a belief in your action abilities. You will believe you can act upon a body. This too would occur naturally in nature. You believe you can pick up a branch and then you pick it up. You now have a belief in agency as well. You might object to this as being knowledge, but consider this. You don't know you can do this until the first time you try. After doing it, you now believe you can do it again. Proof, thus knowledge, would only come after several successful repetitions of picking up a branch.

You can't express it as knowledge until you know something about it. You can never know something about it until you examine it with other known properties of the universe. You just blindly accept it as knowledge due to no other reason but that doing it produces the same result. That sounds like belief-knowledge to me. It also sounds like faith to me. Both faith and reason would evolve from a strict if-then belief system and I will cover both.

Naturally, your brain evolves to be in a belief-knowledge state. You believe things you cannot even test. You believe things you cannot explain. Some of your "knowledge" in belief form would be true, but some things would not be true. It makes perfect sense to me that the brain's neutral state would be one of belief. Belief naturally takes the first habitation of brain function. The very word "reason" says it all. I believe this happens and it is true, but what is the reason for it? Reason would evolve from belief. Faith would be selected for by natural causality—kinship to natural selection.

As an ancient document, only, we even have a record for the selection of faith in man within the pages of the bible. Hebrews could be considered the record of selection. (Hebrews 11:1-2) states: "Faith is being sure of what we hope for and certain of what we do not see. This is what the ancients were commended for." Then it goes on to give examples of faith in men, who were selected. The King James Version used "convinced of what we do not see" and could be construed as blind faith indicated by the "do not see." I think it references better as "even though we don't see them, we work toward them." Them, referring to effects—results— that you work toward.

I envision faith evolving as the natural by-product of doing—directly from believing. Doing can be selected for at every level of life. If a single-celled creature did not eat, it would starve. It must "do" to exist. Believing that this other object exists and can be eaten would become belief, eating the object would become faith—the act of doing what you believe—the higher up the evolutionary hierarchy we climb. "Quod non agit, non existit"; *whatever does not act, does not exist* (Leibniz). "He who worketh not, eateth not" (Proverbs). Doing would be the drive for the selection of a Faithful Phenotype ©2010 Bastarache.

Genotypes and phenotypes are not an exhaustive list. In what might be Richard Dawkins best work, we are introduced to an extended phenotype, which includes our surroundings shaping our phenotype as well as us shaping our surroundings. Why not a faithful phenotype? The genotype is the collection of genes holding the information to form the phenotype. A phenotype is the body that is created by the genotype. An extended phenotype is influenced by niche change. A faithful phenotype would be a phenotype that does what it believes for the good of its survival—selected for by acting upon naturally occurring incidences.

Incidences will be better explained in the next chapter. For now, we can accept an incident as something produced by natural affects—the incidence of light from heat waves. Light now has a purpose if it is acted upon.

Any reader might see a flaw in this hypothesis and challenge it. Let's do just that. If-then is a place of knowledge you can legitimately challenge. You can contend that causation is true, whether you believe it true or not. You can contend causation would ultimately be the prime starting choice of evolution, because evolution works by causation. If-then causation predicts that knowledge would evolve first. Then, through some unknown event, belief must have evolved after—no one has yet produced an acceptable account.

Belief, on the other hand, has no means of becoming selected for or evolved. If you already know, then why the need for believing? There is no legitimate reason for belief to ever evolve, unless you call it a happy accident, or "god of the gaps". I would be placed in the position to concede. Concede, I would!

Then, I would say, let's examine causal knowledge. Here, I can revisit the atom. If one atom has one proton and two electrons, it is unstable. If another atom has one proton and no electrons, it is unstable. This would be true to causation in if-then form. If the two different atoms interacted, it would balance both out—the atom with two electrons could give one, in a chemical interaction, to the other atom and form an automated molecule. Automated life, as opposed to animated life, would have evolved. We would be unaware robots, without mental complexity. Neither faith nor reason would have evolved.

Awareness of knowledge is a better resolve. An atom is unaware of the knowledge it contains. Awareness advocates the known. As Descartes, the French philosopher, put it, "As if they could be aware, without intermediation, of what happens in places far away from them."

Automated life requires a superimposed awareness. It requires the impartment of a soul to make it aware. Animated life does not require a superimposed awareness and the impartment of a soul, it is self-aware and self-animated. Substitute organic matter over inorganic matter. Organic matter has the ability of interaction with the environment. Single-celled organisms are limited. They can become aware of causation and the effects of causation: through the chemical signal (awareness of food), then eat it as food. Awareness could evolve first, but reason could not evolve first. The act of awareness is not the act of knowledge. Both belief and awareness are independent starting points. They don't conflict with the theory. If a scent triggers the signal, then it is food. The scent can be said to be awareness of the food. Awareness can be considered the perception factor.

Multi-celled organisms begin to fit our needs better. If a multi-celled organism senses a chemical signal not through smell, but through changes in light, it behaves like a predator, then things must be examined. Both cannot be true. That predator cannot smell like food. One can be true only. You can "hold" one aspect as true, while "examining" it closer. The act of "holding" is the act of belief. The act of "examining" is the act of reason. If you hold neither, then you have nothing to examine.

Before knowledge can become known, it must first become awareness. It must be held within the organism in some form. The form must be accepted as true, or false. One must accept something before one can examine it for content. You can accept a wrong before examining it proves it wrong. You can accept a right before examining it proves it right. Until it is proven right or wrong, it must first be accepted as right or wrong. If it is not accepted as right or wrong, then nothing can be proven of it. The act of accepting is the act of believing until it can be proven right or wrong.

Before moving on, we must concede to three choices. One, we can choose to accept it as true, act to examine it as true, to the end of attaining the knowledge about it. Two, we can choose to accept it as false, act to examine it as false, to the end of attaining the knowledge about it. Or three, we can choose to reject it altogether and remain ignorant about it. The rejection of true or false acceptance would become disbelief and would need to be qualified. Mostly, we believe it to be true, exercise faith to examine it as true, to the end of obtaining what can be known. The reverse cannot be said. Know something is true, examine it for content to prove it is true, so you can believe it is true. Why believe when you can know?

This cannot be destroyed by postulating that knowledge came first in species development. If knowledge came first, then how did this knowledge learn to believe? How could "hold this as true", or postulation, come into practice if knowledge deals with if-then facts? Knowledge demands it to be true or not true and does not allow for examination of "may be true". It will not allow for something to be held as true or false while being examined for true or untrue characteristics.

This would describe a faithful phenotype. A phenotype that developed an acceptance mechanism leading it to act on the acceptance, produced by awareness, until it could become known. A phenotype that acquired belief, developed faith for the acting mechanism in discerning the known, by means of reason. Apparently, we evolved mechanisms to seek the known properties of cause and effect by means of awareness and acceptance.

Sentient beings would accept belief as a default state early in history and seek to solve some of the misconceptions. Here we enter philosophy.

The Greeks were most famous for their philosophical works. Philosophy stems from sophy—directly derived from the word sophia—meaning wisdom. Wisdom, here, means to analyze a held concept. We also get the words sophistication, and sophisticated. Everyone understands sophisticated to mean something that is hard to explain or something that has complicated details.

Sophists were the ones who gave wisdom by study and teaching. Socrates, Plato, and Aristotle are perhaps the most famous. They were masters of philosophy. Their works can be best quoted by "Among the answers they explore: knowledge as perception; knowledge as *true belief*; knowledge as true belief plus an account (i.e., a justified true belief)"—The *Theaetetus*, Plato. (The quote comes from the introduction to the works by Francis M. Cornford) It follows from this that belief would naturally be examined for knowledge with wisdom or sophia.

Wisdom would break into two different meanings. To hold and reason, being one. To make the best use of, or application of what is known, being the second. The second is where I attained my definition of wisdom. The first meaning could be translated as reason. Both meanings are different than knowledge itself.

I think this is enough of an overview. I clarify these points in the chapters on the mythology and soul and will readdress them later in the book. For now, we are set to examine disbelief, and fact versus opinion.

First, we need to examine synonyms, which are replacement words that have the same meaning as the word you are replacing. This is not true in the strict sense. It is believed that the words belief and faith are interchangeable, as they hold the exact same meaning. As I have shown above, they are two different aspects of the same concept. Compare and equate, according to my thesaurus, are interchangeable and both have the exact same meaning. Compare, means to check for the same result or components. Equate, could mean to check and balance out the components. Are they the same? Slightly different! The same holds true for accepting, holding, belief, and opinion—they are close, depending on what you mean by the words. They are interchangeable enough that I will use them as such.

A replacement word for opinion could be theory. As I have shown elsewhere, theory is of God's designing, or understanding God's design, derived from the word Theo. I believe this belief is the same as I believe this theory. Theory takes reason into account and is the reason for the slight difference when applied to topics. Theory predicts the best probable course of events leading to a known outcome—a logical opinion, a logical belief. They are often correct, but sometimes wrong.

Opinion, on the other hand, would be defined as your belief in the power of a theory to explain the probable course of events leading to a known outcome. The same, but slightly different? Both revolve around belief. It is like saying I believe this belief. Once a theory is proven, with every fact covered, it enters the domain of real knowledge as factual. It no longer matters what your opinion of it is, or whether you believe it or not, the proof is unchangeable. Scientists believe in their theories, thus work with the theories, gathering information in support of the theories, until facts prove the theories correct. Thus, scientists, believe, just as much as anyone else in the general population. Atheists also believe—in the lack of God.

There is no such thing as unbelief, unless it contains a qualifier. I do not believe Y because of X. Unbelief is a quality of doubt. Doubt is the qualifier.

In order to have the true negative of belief expressed, a different supposition must be made. A phenotype must be selected for that does not have the property to accept something as true or false. To not believe something is to believe it to be wrong. Since belief is a default state, unbelief is impossible without the qualifier of doubt. Don't confuse this with not believing something. To not believe something is to not accept it as true. Not believing has a visible qualifier. I do not believe X! X, must be proven before you accept it as true and, thus, believe it true. By believing the proof as true, you allow it a default state within the brain. The more information you obtain about topic X, the more acceptance you allow in your brain as support of the initial belief in X. One can only be said to truly know, when one knows everything, in complete detail, about any topic of concern, X in this case. Anything less is to believe. Any negative belief: unbelief, disbelief, unbelievable, non-belief, must have qualifiers—doubt, refusal to accept, accept something other than...

From the above, belief is the neutral brain state, to believe something does not need to be qualified. You can qualify a belief by saying "this is why I believe" something to be true, but it is not necessary. I believe evolution because of the thousands, upon thousands of pages of facts and proof that I have read on the topic. If I had not read these facts, I would have never believed it could possibly be true. I can't say I know evolution is true because I do not know everything there is to know about evolution. Nor does anyone else! I believe in a God for another reason!

Subjective Truth

Lying is the most common habit of every organism on the planet. Lies are needed for survival. Honest people are the worst because they think they never lie. One would become frozen in space-time, if one never let go of an occupying matter. You are chasing food. If you lose that food, you could become paralyzed, unless you had a mechanism for letting that occupying matter go.

The lie? I will survive! I was not reliant on that food for sustenance anyway! It was just available, so I chased it! The truth? It hurt your meal plan! You might not survive! You are disappointed! Lies help to overcome matters, which occupy you, so you can move on.

We lie about everything to make ourselves feel better. To give a meaning to the things transpiring in our lives that are beyond our control. God took her to be with Him is one such potential lie. We say this when someone's life was cut short. Do we know this to be factual? Evolution is true; therefore, God does not exist is another potential lie. Do we know this to be factual? Everyone does it! It's not my fault! You know this to be factual? How? Lies are subjective! Vox populi (voice of the people) often carries the day.

Mammon—imagine me trading metal for food. You want to give me some piece of metal, no matter how precious, which I can do nothing with except look at, in exchange for food, my sustenance? Money is a complete myth; you want me to take paper for my time? Yet, my atheist friend, it is accepted as real. Is this different than a wafer and drink of wine? Only in quality and not in kind! Money is not only the universally trusted currency, it is also universally accepted as truth by the voice of the people. "Because I and my companions suffer from a disease of the heart, which can be cured only with gold" — Hernan Cortes, Spanish Conquistador. Apparently, it is a sickness, too!

Strongly agree, somewhat agree, neither agree nor disagree, somewhat disagree, and strongly disagree, are all answers poised on a personality test. They describe opinions.

True, false, not enough information, all the statements are correct, and none of the statements are correct, are often seen on IQ tests, searching for your knowledge. They seek what you know to be factual. They describe knowledge.

Let's examine this under reductio ad absurdum (reduction to absurdity)! Imagine talking about squares. One could say that squares cannot be reduced to absurd portions. Draw a square on a piece of paper. One must account for the thickness of the ink, thus, it is not a square in two dimensions. It has three dimensions if ink thickness is properly accounted for. What about a cube? It fits better as a descript. One can say that a cube can be reduced to the smallest possible cube. Is that true? No! At some point in the reduction, one must concede a *point*. A point is spherical—a three-dimensional dot. How do you get a cube from a sphere? Alas, how do we know that a sphere represents an atom? How about a quark, which makes up the main ingredients of an atom? Are they spheres?

Truth is more like three-volume-dimensional relativity. This is the main reason for including a chapter on physics. Three-dimensional: yours, mine, and factual—reduced until it is not true anymore. If we consider string theory here, then the final, true shape may not be spherical, but donut in shape. One should be able to apply the same principle to religion, politics, pro-life, and many other topics. Theist and atheist have nothing to do with factual reality. These religious war books that become best sellers are based upon belief exclusively. Not one fact! Faith and reason, on the other hand, are based upon fact; we all have faith in one form or other. We all have reason in one form or other. These religious, political, and pro-life battles are based upon opinion only.

One can read, in any work on evolution, that "Organs have not evolved with a purpose," but, when an organ evolves, it creates a purpose. The unplanned purpose of a heart is to pump blood. Some might, wrongfully, add, it endows us with feelings too, but this is only an indirect consequence of the heart working harder under some conditions. The same can be applied to the pro-life/pro-choice argument. Where does the truth start and end? I will return to this in the chapter on pro-life.

Reducing something until it is absurd is a hard thing to do. It works well on some topics, but not well on others. At some frame of time and place, we must establish boundaries. We can say things like, "You can reduce a cube to infinity if you treat the cube as a separate subject." When you include dots, it changes the subjective topic. Agreed! How does this logical conclusion agree with what truth is? It makes truth subjective, doesn't it? Truth is subjectively treated! Vox populi (voice of the people) often carries the day.

As soon as you take an object into the brain, it becomes a brain represented object. Looking at it makes it a subject for the brain—thus making it the subject of inquiry. Subjective thought can evolve, while objective thought can remain. The difference between subjectivity and objectivity.

Here is as good a place to comment on this as any other place in the book. Unless you have all the information available, you cannot presume all human experience produces the same human product. This human, the author, is different than another human, the reader, due to extenuating circumstances. We have enough similarities (life) to be the same species, but not enough life experiences to be the same human product.

We can, at least, carry a lesson over to the rest of this book. Judgement! God does not judge anyone who does not judge others. "Judge not, that you be not judged." (Matthew 7:1), expounded in (18:32), where a man was forgiven, but forgave not his own servant "should not you also have had compassion on your fellow servant, even as I had pity on you." (Matthew 18:35) states "Likewise shall my heavenly Father do also unto you, if you from your hearts forgive not everyone his own brother their trespasses." We can add yet another very clear scripture here, "You judge after the flesh; I judge no man." (John 8:15)

Justification is produced within a faithful phenotype to answer these absurdities, or fallacies. We justify ourselves in our sins to make truth subjective in nature. We fail to extend it to others. I qualify, he or she does not! Look at the abortion issue discussed in the chapter on pro-life. Several scriptures refer to God doing the justification. Subjectively, we cannot! Rather, I think we can, but refuse to!

Why can't we look at another person and say, I don't agree with what they are doing, but I don't have the information needed to judge them. The truth for them might be justifiably true. Countering this, we could say most people have no idea what they are doing so truth has no meaning to them. This is my truth because this is what I want! You have no idea what influences another person utilizes to make a choice between these two resolves because you don't have enough information. How far does the truth reduce and still hold true? What is truth?

These are the only brief considerations I will include in the formation of a faithful phenotype. Much more evidence can be added, but we must move on and draw some extended conclusions.

I believe this logic of what constitutes truth applies to every aspect of life, including religion. We should strive to build better arguments, ones that will not crumble when pressed with the tiniest amount of scrutiny. We must endeavor, in our attempt to devoid the world of evil, to search for the greatest truths. We must search the darkest corners of the Earth and shed the brightest lights possible upon them until these dark evils are vanquished. These bright lights must come from someplace and what better place than the hearts of men and women all over this world, from every religion, from every philosophy, from every materialist, and from every place in time: past, present, and future.

Instead of using the words faith and reason, we can substitute the words opinion and fact. There is a slight degradation of opinion in some sense, but we shall ignore it, at least, for now. That is, an opinion can be true or it can be what you believe is true. We can, with this premise, examine the reality of God.

Blaise Pascal, known for Pascal's Law of Hydraulics, as well as for his work with probabilities, was theologically famous for another law. "If you gain, you gain all; if you lose, you lose nothing. Wager, then, without hesitation the He is." This is the conclusion of the wager, famously known as Pascal's Wager. It was based upon probabilities, which the Bible destroys quite nicely anyway. Whenever they can't prove God exists, they offer this paradox. The wager is thus: if there is a God and you believe, then you are safe. If you don't believe, then you are condemned. If there is no God and you believe, then no foul. The biblical rejection is in the Gospel of Matthew:

> Many will say to me in that day, Lord, Lord, have we not Prophesied in your name? And cast out devils in your name? And in your name done many wonderful works? And then I will profess unto them, I never knew you: depart from me you that work iniquity. (Matthew 7:22-23)

Apparently, one cannot do works in the name of God just in case there is a real God! Some people place their faith in Pascal's Wager as a safe bet, but it affords zero truth.

There is absolutely zero proof or factual evidence that God does not exist. Not one single bit of proof that there is no God! Zero! If there were factual, duplicable proof, then more books would be written trying to disprove this factual proof, than written trying to convince you He does or does not exist. Including intelligent design! Who would write about an intelligence guiding nature if it were proven there was no intelligent designer? Lack of proof keeps these fires burning.

On the other hand, there is zero proof God does exist! Zero! Yet, one often hears more than one minister claiming that something or other is proof the bible is right and therefore God does exist because He wrote the bible.

Whether you add them, multiply them, divide them, or subtract them, you get zero! The only thing left is one must choose to believe one of the two: either there is, or there is not, a God. In fairness, one does not need to choose at all. However, that is a different argument. I think a lesson in fact versus opinion, and theory versus proof is needed.

A fact is something that is proven to be true. It must be duplicable to be fact. You must always get the same results every time you duplicate the process. Thus, it becomes true knowledge. No further details should be required of us for this definition.

There are several memes on the internet about truths. One meme, shows two people looking at the number six from two different directions. One person says six and the other says nine. The caption says, don't think that you are right when there is more than one way to look at things. Ugly facts are not consistent with opinion.

Facts are more akin to spherical bastards, as coined by Fritz Zwicky. It does not matter how you look at a fact, or what direction you view it from, it is spherical in nature, where every direction looks the same. A spherical fact is a complete fact. Many people view facts as opinions and still claim themselves to be right. A fact is a fact and if you view it differently, it does not make you right, in your opinion. It makes you factually wrong. Relating to the number six, there is only one fact. It looks different upside down and resembles the number nine.

The difference, or at least it was when I went to school, is as follows: a fact is something that is true and proven to be true and must be accepted as true. A theory is the expression of an unproven idea, which fits the underlying facts most closely. Sometimes there is more than one theory fitting the facts, neither one with enough evidence for supremacy. Opinion, then, is the holding as true of one unproven theory over that of another unproven theory. This is much the same as faith in a creator versus faith in evolution. Evolution is the correct, fact-based postulation, but it does not follow as being proof God does not exist.

Absence of proof is not proof of absence. Scientists use this term to account for the lack of evidence in the fossil record. Not being able to discover any fossils that fit the transmutation of species does not mean that species did not evolve. These missing links are never considered problems in evolutionary thinking. The same holds true of a deity. Absence of proof is not proof of absence.

Theists are considered believers of divinity. Atheists are considered unbelievers of divinity. Monotheists believe in one divinity, while polytheists believe in many divinities. Universalists believe in one or many deities in search for truth and meaning, combining theology with philosophy. Pantheists believe everything to be divine, while agnostic takes another route. Agnostics correctly establish that nothing can be proven—ever—to accept or reject the existence of a deity. This puts me in the awkward position of being an agnostic-theistic-Darwinian.

Yet, everyone still holds their opinion to be fact! That is a perfect fact! Does it mean you are right? If you say you love pizza more than any other food, it makes it a fact. However, there might be some foods you never tried, which might challenge your current favorite. This shows that opinions can change as new information becomes available. Sometimes, whole ideals must be replaced and, sometimes, whole ideals must be altered to fit the new opinions held as facts. If you say that everyone loves pizza more than any other food, this is not fact, but opinion. Your opinion! It may be the majority opinion, making it a fact as well, but still formed of opinions.

When it comes to the things you love, then you are right to use them as self-facts. That is, so long as it is self-consideration and you accept that other self-facts apply to other people's individual tastes.

Let's first clear the air about the whole argument and its mockeries, but, for both science and religion. First and foremost, there is no practical way to either prove, or disprove, the existence of a God! Yes, a statement!

It is as much a fact-based statement as it is a philosophical one. Both boil down to what you believe, not what you know. Any argument, therefore, does not stand on terra firma (from the Latin terra—earth, and firma—solid giving solid earth). The only real terra firma is that no proof can be given either way.

Let's leave this terra firma and examine the quicksand of reality. Scientists claim their craft only requires knowledge all the way back to the point of the Big Bang and no further. A Belgian astrophysicist and priest, Georges Lemaître, to explain the expansion of the universe by need of a big bang, introduced this cosmological model. Questions before the Big Bang are not required to answer this current universe model we abide by. That is, de facto, true for this universe. It will never answer how the Big Bang came into being unless pre-Big Bang conditions are examined.

To not ask these questions will never solve the Big Bang model. However, when pressured, most scientists claim this question can remain unanswered and still produce the answer of evolution creating life. So, evolution in, creation out. I agree! Natural selection can completely explain our existence! It does not prove God does not exist! How is that fact-grounding proof? Refusal to speculate on the unnecessary becomes a defence of stubbornness.

Scientifically speaking, the evidence for a big bang is colossal. If light takes billions of years to transverse the universe, then it takes billions of years before seeing light from very distant stars. That directly equates to time being more than ten-thousand years old. Both, relativity and special relativity have been proven on so many points of space-time and gravity. There is even a complete formula of all the ingredients of the universe. Many aspects of evolution have been proven to be true (de facto) and are widely used in biological medicine. Also used are quantum encryption, atomic clocks, and so much more. All indelible proof of self-assembly in the universe, as well as the evolution of species.

Yet, science has not discovered how a primeval atom came into existence, nor how it created the Big Bang. Many, but not all, have used this as proof, there is no God. These things prove evolution is true, but they do not prove there is no God. For all anyone really knows, God could have created the universe using a primeval atom. As I read, in amusement, on the internet: *the universe could be in a bottle, in some science lab, where some student got a "C" on their science project* - unknown. Is this terra firma? Actually, right down to the creation of the Big Bang, not accounting for minor misunderstandings of the evidence, science is climbing onto solid ground.

You might ask yourself, why, with all of this evidence, does he still believe in God? As the reason for faith is unveiled, we will see that faith is needed—something needs to be believed, including our penchant for God's, or other religious, beliefs. This holds true for science as well. No, it is not serving two masters to serve both faith and reason. To seek truth by any and every means possible is to serve one master.

When a religious argument takes place, almost always, without exception, the question arises about why the Big Bang needs something to explain it—God. I was in such an argument one day with my brother and those were his words, too. Playing the devil's advocate, my words were, "Where then, did God come from?"

He exclaimed, rather proudly, "God just is and always has been."

"Maybe, these prima materia have been and always were," I replied.

"You can't be serious!" he said.

Why would one accept that God can just be, but that, a prima materia cannot just be? This brings us back to the terra firma of no proof!

One day, I almost put my car into the ditch. I was listening to a Christian radio station and I heard some minister talking about the atom. He made this point, "The reason science could not figure out how atoms were held together was because God was holding them together." First, he got the idea wrong. Atoms are well known and the statement was originally, "Can't figure out what holds sub-atomic particles together" not the actual atoms. Second, what kind of question is this anyway? Why would anyone in their right mind create something that made them a slave to it? God continually holding "atoms" together would make for one busy God. You don't think He would create a universe that was self-sustaining? Including sub-atomic particles?

Science is about knowledge, as its name suggests; it is, in fact, the Latin word for knowledge. Knowledge is based on fact, or evidence. There is strong evidence that a big bang, in one form or another, has happened. Fact!

Any theories are about how and what happened, not if it happened. Several theories about how this might have happened do not negate this fact. In this sense, science is like religion. Taking the Big Bang as being true here. Every theory of how it happened has become a religion and argued over, critiqued, by the other camps. The two major examples being standard particle physics and string theory, which we are not going to go into great detail about. This is analogous to different religions arguing over whose God is the biggest and badest.

Does this mean God does not exist? Does this mean the Big Bang did not happen? Creationists have taken this to mean science is wrong. If scientists can't agree on exactly what happened, then their evidence is wrong! No! The evidence is correct!

Assessing that evidence, like assessing religion, is a harder task. Models are used to tell a story about the facts and the Big Bang is such a model, not theory. Not only do camps get set up within science, but rather sadly, atheists have started a new religion, one that excludes a deity. I wonder if they collect tithes and offerings, and do some good with the money collected? Just what the world needs is more religious fuel to an uncontrolled fire.

Science makes close to the same mistake as "the god of the gaps," in intelligent design thinking, with their "happy accident" hypotheses. Occasionally, in books on different topics, one sees this happy accident explaining how some quality arose, i.e. mind is a happy accident of higher brain activity—consciousness. It is my estimation that there is no such thing as a happy accident, only missing information. Incidence explains this away. One non-related incidence, naturally occurring, can influence another naturally occurring incidence to alter the effect, or be treated as a double effect creating a separate cause.

In other words, two naturally occurring incidences create a completely different cause or effect to happen. An example would be of atomic structures. Protons, thus an atomic nucleus base, were naturally formed. Separately, an electron was naturally, but independently formed. Combining them made electrical forces possible. Electricity was not a happy accident. As tempting as this is, one cannot explain away the unknown by calling it a happy accident any more than calling it the "god gaps". My opinion!

Maybe I am too old and opinionated. Maybe, I don't hold enough opinions, or don't have the ability to form opinions. Maybe, on the other hand, I seek knowledge more than what could be arrived at from opinion alone: I want to know the truth. Opinion is predictive!

We have conservatives and liberals. Both divide into right-wing and left-wing. Left-wing conservative or right-wing conservative. Left-wing liberal or right-wing liberal. We have God Hates Fagots, to welcome, my cleansed brother theist. In some countries, you must define atheist as Christian atheist or Islam atheistic. Islam has their peaceful majority and the hateful minority toting terrorism, instead of Westboro Baptist Church.

Then we have pro-life. There are pro-life advocates and extremist anti-abortionists. We have "faith in our truth" not, in "universal truth". The grey line being our truth is always the only universal truth.

You can tell when opinion dominates any topic. Watch political debates. The person opposing can hardly get a word in edgewise. Interruption after interruption is seen and it stems from simple facts. We, as a whole, do not naturally listen to conflicting opinions. For example, if someone opposes the view or opinion you hold, you will not let them finish a sentence.

This is not an intentional action in most cases. Instead, the interruption is a mechanism your mind uses to avoid anyone else's opinion from interfering with convincing everyone you are right. When anyone starts talking about facts, your mind automatically rejects them and interrupts the discourse. The same is true of faith versus religion. The same is true of any moral discussion on abortion, medical research, humanitarian issues, prejudice issues, and women's rights. It is also true of scientific theories that are new.

There is a bottom line that is drawn, whether anyone wants to accept it or not. Everyone uses belief and reason. Atheists use belief as much as the so-called faithful. They believe theories that only have explanatory power, yet are unproven to be absolute fact. Every year, one sees theories being overthrown by newer, better-informed theories. No one yet has the right to use the term known, in the strict sense of the word, for holistic ideas when only diverse parts are proven as fact.

Belief must be utilized. You can either believe there is no God, or you can believe God exists. You can also refuse to believe anything about either and remain ignorant. Likewise, you can believe in God and evolution at the same time. You can believe in both faith and reason!

I must reiterate here, that I only had one chapter. The Faithful Phenotype ©2010 was meant to be a more detailed book on the topic of how faith could have evolved. I likely won't finish editing and publishing that book. I took some main conclusions and used them here as it was needed in this work. I also added religious connotations applicable to this work as needed. Having gaps does not mean that the knowledge of these gaps is missing by the author; simply that it is needed for a larger work.

In the following chapter, I will create a universe without using a primeval atom and tie it into the universe we have. I need an end to establish information and the best place to start is at the beginning. Then I will take us on the journey of faith, reason, and the soul in search of knowledge for the truth. This truth-seeking knowledge will inevitably lead man to the cure of all disease and open critical moral issues on embryologic stem cells—what this book really covers. We cannot properly understand moral issues until we understand the nature of the human species, including our belief in a higher power and, if true, what that higher power expects of His creations.

Chapter Four

The Information Gap

The unwillingness to consider Creator as governing by laws is probable that as long as we consider each object an act of separate creation, we admire it more, because we can compare it to the standard of our own minds, which cease to be the case when we consider the formation of laws invoking laws and giving rise at last even to the perception of a final cause. [sic]

— Charles Darwin

It might seem odd; to include physics in a work on morals and stem cells, but it is an important subject, even when discussing the soul and absolute truth. Absolute truths must be produced from reality. The universe is our reality. It also helps us question evolution, creation, intelligent design, morals, and stubbornness.

In trying to give a complete story in one chapter, it leaves us with complications of flow. I will try to give it the best flow I can, but several topics must become integrated, along with the explanations and summations, that it proves impossible without interruption of flow from time to time. I will try to deal with topics clumped together before illustrating the whole picture.

I will attempt to create a coherent explanation of how the universe came into being. More, I will do it from a starting point of nothing. We need to see how to get information from nothing and what information really is.

The number one quote from every single science book or paper I have ever read is this—we don't know! How can you convince anyone the Big Bang model created life if no one ever produced a coherent story anyone can follow and concede to? Therefore, I will not use "I don't know" as an excuse. After all, I only need to produce one simplified, tangible model that has explanatory power, although not necessarily technically precise, as an *elementary* explanation. Read the preface to this book if you haven't already, as I follow that content here.

How Many Ways

First up, will be a coherent starting point. Richard Dawkins famously stated, "There are more ways of being dead than there are ways of being alive." He was, of course, correct in that summation. This leads common sense to dictate there is only one way of being alive and an infinite number of ways of being dead. There is one flaw in this type of thinking, which I should point out. The flaw is that *one* equals *one way*. Alas, 8-7=1 also holds true. As does 1+1-1=1, 1x1, or 1 squared, and more curiously -1x-1=1.

From a mathematical standpoint, there is an infinite number of ways to get 1. Poetically, there are an infinite number of likely realities within an infinite set of possibilities. Personally, I see no reason to question why the universe is the way it is. There would undoubtedly be some other form of universe, which sustained some other version of life, in which some other form of human would be questioning, if not this universe we currently abide in. That is the basis of string theory and not something we will get into deeply.

Having an infinite number of ways has one saving grace. The more complex the ingredients needed, the more complex the model needs to be. No one assumes there were 1,000 ingredients needed to cause the Big Bang model and I am not assuming this either. This somewhat caps infinity, but does not exclude a few different ways it could have occurred.

This book is about stem cell issues. It is also about the fight between faith and reason. I am not looking to change anybody's mind, but we need to see if any proof for, or against, God does, in fact, exist. In keeping with the first few chapters, we should see whether scripture can be carried over here and compared to science. This one scripture seems to fit the mathematical model I am about to explore so I will quote it.

By faith, we understand that the universe was formed at God's command, so that what is seen was not made out of what was visible. (Hebrews 11:3 NIV)

If it is not made out of something visible, then it must be invisible. It could be taken as something from nothing. Another scripture, which I won't quote, says there was nothing, then there was something. This one quality seems to be the hardest quality to attain. Something from nothing. This was among my mathematical examples above so I shall use this $-1 \times -1 = 1$. It would be set as a negative multiplied by a negative giving rise to a positive. Equally set up as nothing multiplied by nothing giving us something.

Define Causation

Before we move on, it is necessary to define nothing. We need to understand what is meant by nothing! It is also necessary to define negative versus positive values. As a thought experiment, we could define something or nothing in terms of cause and effect, or causation. We could say a cause is a positive attribute and an effect is a negative attribute. Remember that thought experiments are just that. The definitions would be as follows.

Take an apple. An apple is an effect, not a cause. Take a hot oven. The heat in the oven is an effect, not a cause. Place the two effects together and you have an apple pie. The apple pie is the result of two effects producing another effect—the pie. The two effects become degraded in status as two causes—apple and heat, thus, the pie was the effect of two causes. Are there really any truly defining lines? Cause and effect are arbitrary terms until qualified.

Commonly, in science, they are singular in nature—one cause, one effect—but, they are by no means limited to singular entities. In other words, you can have two causes to initiate one effect. Conversely, it is possible to have two effects converge into one cause. They can also have their names transferred to define other effects or causes. This proves these terms are logically arbitrary, but it does not prove these terms are naturally arbitrary. We shall examine it under logical conditions only.

A cause is something of real substance, which has an effect on the production of direct outcomes. A primeval atom would be considered to exist, therefore a positive, and be the direct cause of what it produced. It would be said to be the cause even if it only produced effects and not other causes. It would be a form of matter in pre-matter form. Substance. Positive value.

By contrast, an effect, not having any direct existence, would be considered a negative. There is nothing concrete, of matter, or of substance, like the primeval atom for it to be manifested by, therefore lacking an agent of cause and effect or causation. There cannot be only "effect" without having something to effect upon or interact with. One cannot have a gravitational effect without having matter to act upon. If matter did not exist, then gravity would not have anything to interact with so gravity would not exist. It would not exist as a cause of attraction, although arguably, it might still exist as an effect upon nothing. So, an effect without anything to effect would be taken as a negative value, or no form to become a cause agent. Remember this is a thought experiment! Cause would require substance and be positive, while effect would not require substance and be negative. Effect cannot be causality. Alone! What of two effects? What about double negative?

A Testing Standard

First, we need a gold standard, one with great predictive power to judge any thought experiment by. I have applied natural selection principles to the development of the universe below and this requires definitions. Charles Darwin used natural selection as a description of his theory; he did not use evolution. Natural selection carries the idea of something being selected for naturally. Evolution is said to run from simple to complex in nature. Without starting at simple, complex cannot form. Something needs to *occur naturally* (an incident) before it can become selected for as a species standard. Applied to physics, something must occur naturally—an incident— before it can become selected for as an ingredient of the universe. *Nothing* is natural.

Evolution, on the other hand, is the changing of things by influence, directly or indirectly, on what already exists, by what already exists. Matter cannot be formed from sub-particles unless sub-particles are present and there is a sanction for changes under fluctuating conditions.

Natural selection and evolution do not mean the same thing, but they are meant to be combined into an idea. The evolving of things by incidences of naturally occurring events into something sustainably different by means of selecting naturally for what can exist, over what cannot exist, by specific causes and effects under changing conditions. A mouthful I'm sure!

This is the gold standard, which we shall judge by. Darwin's dictum was not "survival of the fittest". That statement was added by others. His dictum was organisms that could change best under changing conditions would survive better and supplant the organisms that could not change.

After this gold standard, then, we see the only qualities needed, are for incidents to occur naturally and be acted upon. If we are going to claim nothing as a negative effect and an incident, then we need to examine nothing. Moreover, we need two nothings or two effects without causality. We need to examine if it is possible to get one cause out of two negative effects. We need to integrate mathematics into this mess, but we can at least make the mathematics painless.

The only thing people love more than physics is mathematics! Especially algebra! No, wait. Don't stop reading yet! Complicated algebra! Now you can stop reading and say you tried. Or, you can do, or do not, and see the answer is easy: it is always *something*.

Let's try a few algebra equations so you can get the hang of it. A+B=C translates into something (some thing) plus something equals a third something. This is the premise of which algebra is built—something or some number can be represented by a letter symbol.

Is A something? Do we care what A is as long as it is something? Is B something? Do we care what B is as long as it is something? As long as C is something completely different than A and B, do we care about the exact information? One more time! D=C–E and F. Something [D] is now different than something [C], because something [E] and something [F] were subtracted from it, leaving some other thing. I would ask you to understand that removing or adding something to some other thing causes it to change into something different. Mathematically, the universe in question would become expressed as [(-A x –B = D) – Cc] our double negatives creating a positive effect minus the changing conditions (Cc).

Whatever can adapt to change will move to the next level of change. Clearly, then, we only need to look for two incidences or two "somethings" to occur, leading to changing conditions. Incidences would be considered the same as variations under natural selection. Variation naturally occurs in species. An incidence of a longer ear is a variation.

Seeing that I have brought up two incidences, I must, at least, point out it could be construed that the universe is a coincidence. The word coincidence has been polluted and transgressed with time. It has become tainted as superstitious from its original form. The original meaning was closer to that of more than one incidence coming together to create a specific effect or result.

In physics, we could express it as having an up quark and a down quark joining forces to create something tangible—coincidence. Quarks are an elementary particle that is important for matter. Separately, an incidence of the creation of an up quark and an incidence of the creation of a down quark working together as a co, or co-incidence in the incidence of a stable particle. Let's treat it like that and see how far we can travel in our effort to create a universe on selection factors only.

Define Nothing

Let's define nothing for our little thought experiment and see if we can find any hint of a second nothing. Since I have chosen to use the double negative, I may as well start with the word *nothing*. In school, it is demanded of us to blindly accept the conclusion nothing postulates— complete absence, end of story. This is an idea placed upon an absence of information. When we say nothing, we are concluding a lack of substance or information about a concept. Realistically, there is no such thing as nothing!

When you hear, or read about, scientists talking about there being nothing outside of the known universe, what they are saying is that they have no information—ergo, there is nothing. We shall use the term, nothing-absolute, when referring to this premise.

Other times, scientists are not referring to nothing-absolute, but the nothing that exists in outer space—ether, which is now called dark matter, background radiation, and dark energy. Nothing, after all, is made from the words: no and thing. This nothing-absolute I am referring to does have a few observable features or informational qualities, which, at least, hitherto have gone unmentioned.

Nothing-absolute contains an absence of heat for one thing. Technically, there is an absence of cold as well. In addition, it contains an absence of forces, pressures; both positive and negative, and energies. It is even throughout. That is, there is nothing any place one chooses to take a sample for testing. The list could become very long, but we need to include an absence of a beginning and an end. That is to say, that the size of nothing-absolute is absolute, in terms of space or volume, and time.

Our conclusion should be that nothing-absolute makes the first great negative contribution to our formula. It also makes the perfect effect-conditions for a beginning—that is, you have one incident for each attribute mentioned above. It has an attribute/incidence of eternal. It has an attribute/incidence of no forces, pressures, energies and so forth. It has an absence of cause, but not of effect. That is one negative entity and now we need a second negative entity to multiply by.

Heat, after much contemplation, seems to fit quite well as a second negative entity when examined close and under the same conditions as nothing—no thing—was examined. This might not be intuitive, but it is still within the realm of possibility. Nothing is not intuitive either, which is why we are expected to just accept it as true in our early schooling.

Pure heat, or heat-absolute, has no temperature set without a contrasting point of reference. It is even throughout. That is, there is no difference in temperature—temperature does not exist—any place one chooses to take a sample for testing.

In order for a temperature to be set, there would need to be another temperature to contrast with or an existing energy. Calling it heat-absolute, as mentioned above, might help. Heat is also absent of a beginning and an end, which means it is not in a closed system and cannot build pressure to create energy to do work. That is to say, the size of heat-absolute is absolute in terms of space or volume, and in terms of time, much like nothing-absolute. The same things can be said of heat-absolute that can be said of nothing-absolute. Heat-absolute, then, has an absence of everything that nothing-absolute has, so we could call it heat-nothing-absolute.

Nothing is nothing until it is something. Hot nothing is nothing until it is something. Hot, an after-product of language, cannot even be used until qualified as contrasted with cold. Cold nothing and hot nothing are arbitrary after-the-fact terms of nothing. Both nothings have negative effects as they have no substance. A substance would be considered a cause. I will leave off here while letting this settle into your mind, but we will return to it later.

Define Heat

Unfortunately, most people do not understand entropy, heat, temperature, and energy. Anyone can visualize this misunderstanding by the videos on social media claiming one can heat their homes with one candle. They get a lot of views though. As Yoda would say: Do this, we must. Let's get it over with so we can start the exciting creation of a universe.

Entropy is a thermodynamic quality that measures the fraction of the total energy of a system that is not available for doing work (New Lexicon Webster's Dictionary, 2017). It is commonly understood as a measure of disorder—the dimension of energy divided by temperature. In other words, temperature and energy are in a relationship. Since this whole heat versus temperature relationship is mixed up in almost everyone's minds, I shall quickly examine it in layman's terms.

When you turn the burner of your stove on to heat a pot of food, the burner becomes extremely hot. The burner can be measured in temperature and will glow red in color. Let's say the temperature is 1000 degrees. All temperatures are given in centigrade. Question! Does your whole house instantly become 1000 degrees or is it just the burner? The answer is not yes, or, I don't really know! The answer is no!

This is because you don't think about the diminished capacity created by the air around the heating unit. Heat, then, is more akin to a field. The closer you get to the burner the hotter the temperature of the heat. The heat has more energy associated with the more rapid movement of waves, or frequencies of waves, the closer you get to the energy packets of origin—the burner.

Just like a magnetic field gets weaker the farther away you move from it, the weaker the heat field gets the farther away from the source. Both heat and magnetism radiate away, as does gravity and every other field known to man. Fields and waves are in the same type of relationship as heat and temperature. I will build our universe out of nothing but waves when I soon enter the complete story.

If you can't understand the following, my advice is to not give up. Just accept it and move on. Heat is less understood by the masses than I would like. Heat, temperature, and energy are the same things, albeit, different ways of talking about the same thing. The heat of the heat is its heat. The temperature of the heat is its energy. These are both the exact same sentences. It could also be written as the temperature of the heat is the amount of work it can do—its energy. How hot the hot is, is the hot it possesses. Or the hot of the hot is its hot.

The holistic concept of hot, or heat, breaks down into smaller sub-concepts of temperature and energy. What is taking place is that we talk about hot being a different rate of heat as its temperature. 1000 degrees of heat versus 100 degrees of heat, worded as the temperature. We take one temperature of heat and call it more energetic than another temperature and call it energy—it can do more work. To talk about heat as energy is even more confusing. Adding to this, I am asking that we should consider heat as being nothing—no thing—in its pure form.

In terms of the relationship between heat and energy, there would need to be some particle to create the energy needed to create the heat, which negates the need to create particles by postulating the Big Bang model altogether. One could argue if particles—primeval atoms—existed to create a big bang, then there were particles to do the creating without the Big Bang being needed.

In other words, we say the gasoline caused the fire to create the heat and smoke. We don't say some fire caused the gasoline, which then caused the fire, in positive terms versus negative terms. It might not compute logically for you but heat, in and of itself, is an empty or negative entity, but that is only because we naturally treat heat as a by-product. Before matter and energy came to produce heat, there must have been something to create that energy and matter. This postulates a cause—a primeval substance, which would be a negative multiplied by a positive.

Also, remember temperature and pressure are in the same relationship as temperature and heat. It is a three-way—indeed many more way—relationship. The relationship is such that one cannot take the heat of a candle and heat an entire house. You cannot get more energy than the energy supplied by the candle. The relationship is not there. Understanding the relationship of heat, temperature, energy, and pressure a little better, we can venture forward.

I am about to start the story, which should take a few pages, but I need to remind you this is built on the theory of natural selection, evolution, and algebra based on the occurrence of incidences. We have defined negative attributes from two forms of nothing-absolute to use and somewhat understand cause and effect as a relationship. I will not, for the most part, be using any algebra or calling out any natural selection. However, the whole story is concluded from these things happening and you must not forget to remind yourselves of this fact while reading.

Creation, By the Skin of a Balloon

I always find using visual aids is the key to understanding new ideas, especially in cases like this one, which is a thought experiment. We have lots of onions. We have Spanish onions, sweet onions, red onions, so after much contemplation, I have decided on balloon onions. I am going to use only a balloon, and an onion, analogous to waves—forces and fields—to explain everything starting with the double negatives or double-nothing. Onions are, after all, made with spherical layers and give a great visual effect, spherical layer upon spherical layer. The balloon also has great properties for a visual explanation.

I started with nothing for a very good reason—absence. Absence, not of effect, but absence of cause. There is no cause of nothing-absolute, but nothing-absolute is effectual. It has the effectual nature of a cooling system. It can be converted from an effect, in the negative, to a cause in the positive. It caused the cooling.

Heat-absolute has an effectual nature of warming up, but no substance. To get heat to drop in temperature, one must have a complete lack of heat for the cooling process. There is no cause of heat-absolute, but heat-absolute is effectual. It has the effectual nature of cooling. It can be converted from an effect, in the negative, to a cause in the positive. It caused the cooling by losing heat. Thus, the nothing-absolute, that space is expanding into has an effectual incident of cooling, added to the effectual incident of the heat-absolute diminishment creating temperature, the cause of space itself. This is how the double-negative becomes a positive value. Negative one, multiplied by negative one is not negative one. It becomes positive one.

Straight into the balloon we go. Take an imaginary balloon, place it to your mouth and blow. Now imagine what happens! The air from your mouth—heat—cools off into absolute cold and no longer exists. Did that imaginary balloon appear before your mouth as a real one? No? Therefore, it is not even possible to create a universe from nothing. Right? Wrong! We missed something, partly because I haven't brought it up yet. Quantum mechanics and absolute-zero!

Postulating this "nothing happens" is not restricted to my little made-up story. A primeval atom would cool to nothing if there is not something to contain the heat. Possibly, the first physicist to question the validity of ignoring absolute-zero, or more exactly the temperature of space, which is 2 degrees Kelvin, was Mark Jagg.

I am not a physicist and my interest came from a different question.

I will not mention every available theory, just the ones that are not commonly known to the masses. Reinventing Gravity: John W. Moffat, has influenced some of this model I am composing. Namely, the suggestion of gravity being the same force as the strong nuclear force et al.

The first thing created by this coming together of effects would be the first set temperature of absolute-zero. Temperature did not exist before the smallest temperature was set, only pure heat-nothing, and pure nothing. To keep things simple, let's just say that the smallest set temperature reflects the smallest quantity or quantum, from which the word is derived. Again, for simplicity, call quantizing a first cause created by the two effects of nothing-absolute, one hot and the second cold in properties. Effectuated cause. As soon as the heat wave cools, it forms a barrier of a minimum temperature energy. This minimum temperature energy is now a cause for stopping further cooling. The outside edges of the pure heat cool faster than the inside. The hotter inside waves of heat now bounce off the leading edge causing the leading edge of heat to retain energy.

The leading-edge temperature set as absolute zero forms a containment because time, for the first time, becomes involved. Call it quantum time for ease of explanation. Below absolute-zero matter will not exist. At time-absolute-zero, it is held long enough for another wave of heat to hit it, thus forming a quantum containment, not unlike the skin of a balloon only in quantum form.

I take a quote from *Quantum Theory Cannot Hurt You:*

> Absolute Zero [is the] lowest temperature attainable. As a body is cooled, its atoms move more and more sluggishly. At absolute zero, equivalent to -273.15 on the Celsius scale, they cease to move altogether. (Actually, this is not entirely true since the Heisenberg uncertainty principle produces a residual jitter even at absolute zero.) (Marcus Chown)

Now take a real balloon and blow it up. Imagine the fiber of the balloon is this minimum temperature energy known as absolute zero—the leading edge of the released heat, or your breathing into the balloon. Now that we have formed a barrier we can note two things. First, the barrier is not ridged and expands the same way as a real balloon. Second, being a barrier, it allows for pressure to build up. Remember that the heat, the temperature, and the pressure are in a close relationship with the energy, thus matter. When pressure is referred to here, don't think 100 psi., think quantum pressure. Pressure can only build if it is in a closed system sustained by something.

> The uncertainty principle developed by Werner Heisenberg, one of the chief architects of quantum theory, implies that no particle ever stays completely at rest but is constantly in motion due to a ground state field of energy constantly interacting with all subatomic matter. It means that the basic substructure of the universe is a sea of quantum fields that cannot be eliminated by any known laws of physics. (Lynne McTaggart)

Now imagine the balloon is filled with spherical waves like an onion—infinite in quantity. Every layer is moving outward hitting the balloon and being sent inward again. Every hit of a wave stabilizes the balloon skin and causes it to "exist" in quantum. These waves of heat energy are now hitting this barrier—the absolute zero quantum barrier—and acting as a pressure to expand the nothing barrier of space, being different than our nothing-absolute, which space is expanding into. This "containment" is what blows the balloon up. The waves hitting this barrier are then reflected backward from their original direction while conserving energy, which brings us to describing wave function in simple terms.

Waves in one dimension are described as being wavy lines on paper. Think of the spikes on a heart monitor. Two-dimensional waves are best described as waves on water and are circular in shape. Three-dimensional waves are best described as spherical waves and thought of as filling the spherical balloon with airwaves, much like the layers of an onion. Only the airwaves want to oscillate inside the balloon. That is, they want to move from the center outward before hitting the barrier and then moving inward again. For the universe, it is enough to have the waves reflected back in on itself to produce tangible effects, or selective properties.

Having a wave pressure of heat forcing the expansion of the universe does not prevent the same wave pressure from slowing the expansion. The wave hits the quantum-barrier and is deflected in on itself causing a slowing down of expansion, known to be the effect of gravity.

Remember the levitating vehicle model in the preface of this book, and keep your thinking simple. The wave travels the same in every direction, thus spherical both outwardly and inwardly.

The deflected inward waves have conserved most of their energy but have lost energy by leaving some of their energy to keep the quantum barrier stable. This is fine as long as all energy is accounted for. This reducing the amount of energy they have while returning to their starting point of time-zero means they are less energetic moving inward then outward. This would allow for a rapid expansion followed by a slow down, but it never ceases.

The running front of our balloon-universe would, by default, set a minimum temperature too. The coldest anything could get before it would stop existing. This is currently known as zero degrees Kelvin. It would be the first time a temperature, thus an energy, was set and allow for different temperatures of energy, or different energies.

We could say each onion layer has several billion thinner layers. Billions upon billions upon billions of waves can produce billions of billions of billions of energies—which are infinite in our model here. Each wave in our universe has a choice of becoming a force (remaining a wave) or an energy particle. Each wave can keep its heat-wave energy and move freely inwardly or outwardly as a force. Or each wave could collapse upon its own heat-energy becoming a smaller particle of energy. Like collapsing one layer of balloon wave onto another layer of balloon wave. The outer layer would act as a containment upon the inner layer. It would be like crinkling up one balloon and stuffing it within another balloon.

The wave of the outer balloon would constrain the energy of the inner balloon, creating particle of energy. Consider an infinite supply of waves to crinkle into quantum packets. The same energy as the wave, only on a more minute scale: the quantum scale or Planck scale. These behave as quantized energies. The Planck scale is 10^{-33} and translates to 0.000000000000000000000000000000001 for smallness. The same can be envisioned as the thickness of waves per part in our balloon onion segments.

This small ball of heat as an energy particle would become smaller and more energetic but still be too large as we will soon see.

I need to deal with two things before we move on—waves and energies. Waves are usually described with water. Throw a pebble into a pond and you see waves of peaks and valleys. Peaks can become added together to form larger peaks and valleys can form larger valleys when added together. They can also cancel each other out as a peak fills a valley. Water is solid. Heat or energy waves are not. Neither are gravitational waves, magnetic waves, or God particle waves—Higgs field waves. Waves in these formats can pass through and cause an effect, or not cause an effect, as required of them. Combining, cancelling, and passing through, with or without effect, are all possible contenders—non-effect being an effect of its own, however different.

Remember, I wrote about changing conditions? As the universe (our balloon) gets bigger and bigger, conditions change. The heat and pressure, inside the universe, drop so sustaining high levels of energy become impossible. Mass, discussed in more detail later, becomes a huge problem. The universe can no longer support the mass of these rather large energy particles and the energies must decay.

The first large energy particles are an incident of the creation of energy from heat waves wrinkled up. Decaying would be caused by the effect of diminished capacity—the continued expanding and cooling of the universe. This would lead to the creation or occurrence of smaller energies. It could select for incidences of different energy particles as well.

The bigger energy breaks into smaller, different energies with different properties for selection to act on. Similarly, these new smaller particles become too massive to stay together with the diminished capacity or changing conditions of the now bigger, cooler universe and they decay into many smaller energies again.

Different energies, as noted before. With more energy particles available, selection can work on keeping particles of energy stable by combining them at each level of decay. When the particle energies are of sound enough mass to remain supported by the present conditions of the universe, the sub-atomic particles can form atomic structures.

The standard model of particle physics has such a model, which I will add here. I must point out we have been partially successful in creating matter out of nothing but nothing-absolute. After reading the current model, we can pick up at the wave again and deal with forces and tie them back into particles for a full vision of a complete universe.

Without references or citations; majorons are, according to one theory, believed to be a more massive particle than the Higgs Boson. Majorons, at an earlier time in the denser universe, were the particle of mass, but as the conditions of the universe changed, they became too heavy and decayed into the Higgs Boson and two neutrinos. As energy must be conserved, the extra energy was released as the neutrinos. Neutrinos are now free ingredients for interaction, but I won't go into that.

The new mass was the Higgs Mass until it too could no longer be supported by a less dense universe and it decayed. As energy must be conserved, and there is choice of particle or wave, the Higgs particle, which is also known as the God particle, decayed. It took on a wave function to confer mass and, in doing so, released the lighter particles we have today.

First, visual aids help when trying to understand something new, and we are trying to keep with our levitating vehicle model from the preface. I will express things by means of the number one example of entropy used in books on physics—coffee.

If you take black coffee, add cream and then mix it, it is said the process will never unmix. This is known as entropy, one of the laws of thermodynamics. Pages of literature are written on how they can never become unmixed. These are the details wherein the devil lives and we said we would avoid them—so we are going to do just that.

We can, however, see something else happening that can help us understand our mathematics.

Add your cream to your coffee while hot and mix it. Leave it for a few days in the fridge and check the mixture again. Without a doubt, there will be an almost solid mass of white on the surface, which is the fat from the cream. The hot coffee started off black, turned a light brown, then when it cooled, it separated again. Not completely true! Take the white stuff off the top and look at the coffee again. Even though the cream separated from the coffee not all of the cream was removed. The coffee color is now dark brown and not black. Some ingredient from the cream remained and it is evident from the brown color of the coffee.

To further the analogy, imagine the fat from the cream as being solid matter, the remaining brown color in the coffee being dark matter, and the coffee itself as being the dark energy. You now have a visual aid to apply to the Higgs Boson.

The Higgs Boson decayed because, like our coffee, it cooled. The creamy color coffee was no longer supported in the same manner that the Higgs Boson was not supported. The boson, a particle, was decayed, but the wave function remained to confer mass to the other particles much the same way as the coffee remained with some color left by the remaining cream. I cannot cover every ingredient in a work such as this, but it applies to every particle and force in the universe at some level or other. The same coffee story applies to the majorons from whence Higgs particles cometh. It also applies to gluons of the strong nuclear force in the following paragraph.

Remember that the first wave responsible for collapsing an energy can be maintained as a wave function—majoron wave holding the first energy particle remains as the Higgs wave. This will hold true even if several decays took place. Different ingredients being left over is the main point here.

This brings us to our little friends in the quark family. The Higgs particle decayed into up quarks and down quarks and other fragments of energy that I will not go into. Now, we can use our algebra again to see what happens here. $(A + A + a + B) = 1$. Add the ingredients and we have up-quark + up-quark + down-quark + Gluon—the new name for the force holding them together = proton with a charge of positive one. Up quarks have +2/3 charge and down quarks have -1/3 charge so $2/3 + 2/3 + -1/3 = 3/3$ or 1, plus the gluon force holding them together.

Neutrons have two down quarks and one up quark, so, $-1/3 + -1/3 + 2/3 = 0/3$ or 0 charge and are considered neutral in charge and it is represented in an algebraic formula as $(a + a + A + B) = 0$. They collectively form the sub-atomic nucleus of atoms. There are six flavors of quarks: up quark, down quark, strange quark, charm quark, bottom quark and top quark; none of which we shall visit the devil over.

Electrons are made up of another independent material, or energy, and I will only vaguely cover these in sparse detail. Electrons are more akin to probability clouds. Imagine thunder clouds with the potential to produce lightning strikes. You can't tell where or when the strike will take place. The only thing you can say is that there is enough energy in them to produce an offset discharge within the cloud, which produces a strike. How much energy, or where the energy is, is unknown until the lightning strikes.

In the case of electrons, you don't know where or when, but you know the potential energy is enough to balance a proton. Generally, this is taken as an electron having the perfect energy to balance a proton.

As electrons are considered probability clouds, not too far akin to wave function or fields. They are negative in state. There is no reason to suspect a wave of negative value could not particle-form to balance a positive state in another particle. That is a little more speculative than would be generally accepted. Improbable, but not impossible. We now have atomic structure, which fits physicists' current body of knowledge in a vague summation. I will sneak in this small quote:

> In the beginning of the twenty-first century, we have expanded the scope of our thinking to the point that we now envision matter as made of, inter alia, leptons, which include electrons, muons, neutrinos, and, furthermore, six different kinds of quarks, each in three colors; the notion of one more type of particle seems straightforward. But, in 1930, all matter was presumed to be composed simply of electrons and protons. (Gino Segre)

More Formations

Under natural selection, an incident of a positively charged up quark and an incident of a negatively charged down quark selected for each other in a positive self-sustaining state charge of one and evolved into a proton, along with a force discussed next. These evolved from previous cycles of incidents and selection factors. Other, none mentioned particles like electrons would also be self-sustaining and need no meddling influence to hold them together. The gold standard shows a complete universe could become filled with particles. We can turn our attention to waves and forces, which will interact with what we have already established.

Perhaps explaining it a few times in slightly different ways would help in our understanding. Back to the choice of either collapsing into smaller, wrinkled energy particles or continuing as a wave in full inward or outward motion. Wave here should be understood in terms of wave function, force, or field all being related and the same. Different wave temperatures can now behave differently or cause an effect upon other wave energies, including wrinkled particle energies.

There are basically four forces: the strong nuclear force, the weak force (responsible for nuclear decay), gravitational force, and the electromagnetic force. I will use only one wave or force to describe everything until the conclusion. We only need to see waves in action and natural selection at work.

These deflected waves—the ones traveling inward—lost some energy. The law of "Conservation of Energy" was formally called "Correlation of Forces" circa 1800 and previously. If they remain waves, they can act as gravity waves. If the same waves cause another wave to collapse into an energy particle, then the wave can become stronger due to the size surrounding the smaller particle. We can call this the strong nuclear force. *Note: Because the conditions changed, they would have different properties and can be rightly called different forces.*

Outwardly moving waves are still present and must become included. They still fuel the expansion of the universe. We can call some waves forces, but it does not need to be exclusive. There are both negative and positive forces, but we are not considering them in this model.

Any waves still considered outwardly moving will still place an effect, thus cause, upon the universe. As matter, in whatever form, is now present, along with inward moving

- 87 -

forces, outward-moving forces or waves have something different to act upon. An outward moving wave can act to slow down the inward moving products in their new formation. Thus, particles can freely move anywhere in the universe, not just outwardly.

Waves can act as matter builders.

To give you a visual of this, think of waves in winter, as each wave reaches the shore, it freezes and pushes the ice (matter) into higher peaks. As these waves slow and collapse into quanta particles, any inward or outward moving waves act like gravity and give viscosity to the universe.

Viscosity is the effect the Higgs Boson places on matter after decay. Viscosity causes resistance to movement or makes energy "feel" heavy. At the three levels discussed above: majorons, Higgs and current state, we could say the first level, before majorons, waves travelled through the universe like we move through air. Second level energy particles moved through the universe like we swim through water. In the last level, the Higgs effect or the Higgs field, energy swims through the universe like we swim through honey. Viscosity! Mass! According to Kant, a German philosopher, matter exists because it moves in the opposite direction of force, or opposite motion between two forces.

As space is slowed down, energies form called quanta, which are speed restricted. We are no longer calling them wrinkled energy particles, but quanta. Because waves can now act directly upon the quanta, and the speed of these quanta have become frequency or energetic waves and not force waves, they can't move as fast. In other words, the fast-moving waves act as a viscous medium slowing clumped energetic waves of tiny packets—our quanta.

We can therefore say that a wave packet describes a particle that is travelling with a range of momenta. But the De Broglie equation implies that we can just substitute the word 'wavelengths' for 'momenta' in the last sentence, because a particle's momentum is associated with a wave of definite wavelength. This in turn means that a wave packet must be made up of many different wavelengths. Likewise, if a particle is described by a wave with a definite wavelength then that wave must necessarily be infinitely long. It sounds like we are being pushed to conclude that a small wave packet is made up of many infinitely long waves of different wavelengths. (Brian Cox, et al)

This was Einstein's insight with his constant squared. You either have an energy-frequency speed of 300,000km/sec through viscous space, or you have an inflation-wave speed of 90,000,000,000—the energy that goes into creating matter. It is not written about this way in physics, of course.

At a certain speed, the quanta become massive enough that all the energy forms a mass, proper, and holds true to that speed limit. All the energy moving faster than the speed of light as waves become heavy enough to form the mass of $E=MC^2$, which is the speed of light squared—it equals 90,000,000,000 units of energy for one quanta, or one unit of mass, by the time it is reduced to light speed. I will not compute the different energies and masses, plus the different stages of matter. It is important to think back to the constant change and the three levels I previously wrote about.

Mass is energy! How does energy become mass? Energy can do work. Energy can move or lift weight— excluding here the effect of gravity—and it is this weight that constitutes matter. The more energy added together, the more it can lift or move—the more work energy can do.

It can lift its own energy or has the capacity to move its own energy. If we say that energy can lift or move one gram of its own energy, then that energy is said to weigh one gram at rest. This is different than mass under the effect of gravity on Earth where the weight of mass is affected by gravity. The average person here on Earth might weigh 150 pounds, but, in weightless space, you only weigh your energy mass. Energy mass, then, is defined by how much work a sub-atomic particle has to do classed as its own weight. The weight effect of mass is endowed by viscosity and momentum.

While using the word momentum here, it would be expedient to cover its uses and meanings. Moment of time, derived from movement, motion, or move, is one meaning and it relates to the theory of relativity—both Galileo's and Einstein's. Also, it happens to be a direct measure of size as in minute (my nute) as well as minute (min it), regarding a small unit of time. Momentum is the measure of "falling", understood to be the effect of gravity here on Earth or how fast an energy particle moves.

Both as an energy particle itself, and that energy particles movement through space-time. Momentum is in a relationship with speed and time—all related to relativity.

This begets the necessity of examining the word relativity. In every sense, it has the reference of related to. Galileo's relativity was to contrast your non-movement with someone else's movement, or the movement against that of a fixed object. Einstein's relativity was relating time against movement, to that of another person's movement or time, or that of a fixed object. Time and movement are related to one another, as is speed and the size of an object—the mass. It is the same sense that temperature and heat are related along with energy, which could be equally called thermodynamic relativity.

Relativity means related to. Momentum means movement in speed related to time. Conversely, to move in time is related to speed. Now, we understand a wave can affect both movement, or the rate of falling, and the frequency of particle energy in relationships rendering time.

We do need to consider the creation of time from the expanding and collapsing of a universe first. Outward moving waves are expanding the universe. In theory, the reflected inward moving waves should collapse it again. It is important to remember the inward moving waves lose energy. In either case, waves do not need to obey the speed of light as a limit. They can, however, create the limit. As soon as matter energy is factored in, this becomes more likely, because, when an energy particle formation latches on to another energy particle formation, it would drag it along with it. This would result in the energy particle formation becoming very massive—and a slowdown. This is a well-known fact.

Take expansion of the early universe as very fast with no speed limits without matter. This is known as the inflationary period. The creation of particles would not only stop the speed of expansion and collapse, it would set a speed limit. The speed limit is the start of time, or rather the stop of time as time stops at the speed of light. Now wave momentum energy that is acting upon particle-energy is transferred to slowing down mass. As mass slows down, time speeds up. Our inward moving waves attract matter, outward moving waves slow it down, and the slow down causes time to become set by the speed of the matter in question. This is where all that energy gets converted into mass.

Waves, or wave fields, can collapse other waves into balls of energy, which act like our strong, nuclear force. Waves can slow these quanta, acting like our current Higgs field, giving them viscosity of mass. Waves can act like a gravitational field attracting matter and acting to slow the expansion of the universe. This leaves out the weak nuclear force, which could be explained by other means, which have not been discussed here. The electromotive force is created by interaction of charged particles. Movement and time are subject to another aspect of creation.

Space-time

A law which applies to everything, including space-time, is conservation of energy. It is one law that is impossible to get around when we look at any of our big bang models.

Momentum now has two forms. One form is called energy. The energy contained within the small pockets of particles, which we concluded were quantum energies. The momentum of the energy is contained within the pockets. However, the pockets still move through space. This second momentum is the movement through space of these quantum particles. Therefore, the law of conservation of energy needs to be explained.

A particle can move through space at the speed of light with a time of stopped. Time is stopped. The momentum is high for the particle. High speed, which supports energy. If the particle slows down, it loses the ability to absorb more energy, which prevents an increase in mass. The lost energy must be accounted for. This is the relative relationship. Time being stopped.

If the momentum of this particle slows, then the energy of time speeds up to allow for conservation of energy. It maintains an energy balance as energy can neither be created, nor destroyed. Longer periods of time use more energy than shorter periods of time.

Slow momentum uses less energy than fast momentum. If momentum is slow, there is more energy for longer periods of time to use. It becomes balanced. As one rises, the other falls, thus the conservation of momentum energy is satisfied. The slower things move, the longer it takes them to move. Space-time relativity!

Before continuing, I should detail time as an effect. Time is a man-made analogy for movement. Directly related to movement, as mentioned when I wrote about relativity being related to, or in a relationship with every other thing I could think of writing at the time.

Since all movement is multidirectional: outward moving waves, inward-moving waves, and collapsing waves; we must solve this puzzle. Outward waves define the expansion of the universe. Inward waves are the waves causing effects. They create fields, energy, and matter. As these inward waves become the universe we know, they are free to travel in any direction but the main direction is still, primarily, expanding.

The speed and direction of movement are two things. One, its direction is always away from a starting point. Two, the speed at which objects move around in relation with one another can only be tracked by how long, in momentum, it takes them to move. For ease of clarity, our forefathers placed the term of time on tracking movement. Heaven forbid we should say it takes ten momenta to move ten momenta. Technically, we do say this. It takes ten units of minutes to move through ten-minute units of space. Since movement through space is one directional, then time through space is one directional, thus space-time. The one direction being expansion from the Big Bang.

There are no numbers in any physics' literature I have searched through so far, so I must compromise and make them up. My best guess would be by factors. I submit the number of 10,000 as the gravitational speed effect factor on matter. We already established speed of energy into matter is $E=MC^2$, which is the speed of light squared, and that it equals 90,000,000,000 units of energy for one quanta or unit of mass by the time it is reduced to light speed and stopped time is created.

From the speed of light being divided by a factor of 10,000 twice, this also gives a good approximation of thought. 300,000km/sec moving the decimal point four times gives 30 kilometers a second, the actual average speed that the Earth orbits around the sun. The next approximation is very close, too. Moving the decimal point four more times gives us .003 or three-thousandths of a second, which will be explained better in the chapters that follow, is our cognitive thought process. That is, what the human brain sees as thought time, or cognition time.

Time is stopped at the speed of light! Time to us is the momentum of mass below the speed of light. Matter forming, as I have indicated above, results in a slowing down when traveling through the waves of viscous Higgs energy. Waves also want to make matter come together with speed.

On Earth, our speed, thus time, works as the division of light-speed by a factor of ten-thousand in our orbit around the sun. Our time is unique to Earth. This is why our supplied numbers work out as well as they do. Gravity and gradational time apply to us by these numbers because we gave them these numbers from Earth measurements.

Different waves have different effects on matter. Some waves act to give matter-energy viscosity, which holds them together as mass. Gravitational waves act to attract mass, and the strong nuclear force waves act to bind sub-atomic particles. They are all waves (fields or field waves) and they are all moving. Moving, as per none other than Albert Einstein in his theory of relativity.

According to the Theory of Relativity, movement is both time and gravity. We fall toward the center of the Earth and it makes us feel heavy. Our ability to stand and walk while this falling occurs is a matter of the brain. We travel in a straight line around the bent orbit of the sun.

These are all proven and well-known facts. Speed affecting time is also a proven fact. Now, we need to see where momentum and time come into play.

Dimensional Space

Any creation from any means whatsoever, would lead to a three-dimensional space. If one were to send waves, again, remember the term field applies to every direction, then a spherical dimension could result. The sphere would be three dimensional. I use a sphere, but it is only known that space is expanding in every direction from a starting point, not that the universe is of necessity a sphere in shape. The collapsing wave of gravity, then, would result in a spherical shape naturally, at least as far as clumping matter-energy together is concerned.

Thus mass, when it's clumped together creates a displacement around the object of a spherical nature and distorts the straight momentum of bodies orbiting them. It is this orbiting effect, which we judge our time here on Earth. The real picture of momentum is that time differs on every planet and is more relative in nature.

Secondly, by space expanding the same in all directions, a three-dimensional space is created. Don't confuse this with the concept that space is flat, which refers to something totally different. This is not quite true! Gravity is movement. Time is movement. Slowing down is movement. Magnetism moves, heat and energy move... We see four dimensions, collectively, which can be stated as: forward-backward, up-down, left-right, and movement—in all its forms.

Volume is composed of three dimensions. A point is said to be of zero dimensions. Length is one-dimensional, or one-directional. Area is length by width and is two-dimensional, or two-directional. Volume is length by width by height and is three-dimensional, or three-directional.

The dimensional quantity is based upon how many directions add together—which should be self-explanatory—to form the dimension in question. There is no fourth dimension, which can be logically added, because the physical demands of space are met. Any other claims of dimensions are either, superimposed or extra-imposed.

In technical terms, the word homogeneity is used. Homogeneity of time, gravity, position, and mass, or Higgs field, to name a few, are all superimposed or extra-imposed upon the three dimensions of volume.

Sitting in your living room, everything looks static. Remember, everything is moving, including the whole house, which is moving with the Earth. With that movement, which we consider as treating space as stopped, we have the wall in front of us, the wall behind us, the two walls on either side and the floor below as well as the ceiling above, we consider to be volume. This entire volume is filled with diverse waves or fields. By the mere fact that the house is moving with the Earth, solar system, galaxy, and universe, momentum, thus gravity, is present within the living room.

When you get up and move to another place within the volume of your living room, you are, in fact, moving through the extra dimension of both gravity and time. Since you are made up of matter, your matter is moving through another dimension of space called the Higgs Field. Not only that, but you are also walking through the dimension of electromagnetic fields. It seems our entire volume of space is filled with every kind of extra dimension you can account for with both particle physics and string theory. This gives us n-dimensional space.

When you consider volume as three-dimensional don't forget to consider gravity as three-dimensional, time as three-dimensional, and the Higgs field as three-dimensional. Every force, or field, has overlapping dimensions with your volume dimensions, superimposed because the maximum of three has been established in volume.

Since we humans utilize observations, we can account for our lack of understanding space-time, and our ability to seize it for our own purpose. We can demand that space is stopped and we are moving, or we can treat space as moving, wherein we are stopped. We can and do treat space and time both ways. The number one problem in trying to understand the Theory of Relativity is getting one to understand that time and space are relative to one another based on movement within our volume of space— the universe. Too many people condemn physics because of these invisible particles and fields, which I have just shown to be real and active dimensions within your very own living room.

Now, in the life of our universe, we can officially bind things together. Gravity attracts the lightest element created so far, that of hydrogen, and places them under a great wave pressure, that is, gradational pressure. This causes them to become liquid plasma and they can then bind into different atoms with different atomic weight known in the Periodic Table of Elements. Everything, from the air we breathe to the food we eat, comes from the explosions of stars. It is done by conversion:

> The answer to this conundrum is that the W particle steps in to save the day. in a stroke, one of the protons in the collision can convert into a neutron by converting one of its up quarks into a down quark, as specified by the branching rule in Figure 11.2 Now the newly formed neutron and remaining proton can get very close, because the neutron carries no electrical charge. (Brian Cox, et al).

This whole story I have just composed is 99% accurate within the current particle theory of physics! The only thing (the 1%) I have added to the story is the hardest starting point to advance: the double negative. Every other detail is taken from relativity, quantum mechanics, and field theory.

> The victory over the concept of absolute space or over that of the inertial system became possible only because the concept of the material object was gradually replaced as the fundamental concept of physics by that of the field. Under the influence of the ideas of Faraday and Maxwell the notion developed that the whole of physical reality could perhaps be represented as a field whose components depend on four space-time parameters. If the laws of this field are in general covariant, that is, are not dependent on a particular choice of coordinate system, then the introduction of an independent (absolute) space is no longer necessary. That which constitutes the spatial character of reality is then simply the four-dimensionality of the field. There is no "empty" space, that is, there is no space without a field. Dr. Jammer's presentation also deals with the memorable roundabout way in which the difficulties of this problem were overcome, at least to a great extent. Up to the present time no one has found any method of avoiding the inertial system other than by way of the field theory. (Albert Einstein)

While this does not diminish what I have written about, it does mean there are several more ways the universe could have manifested, as there are several more ways to get one. Everything else stated above has been proven true of this universe, albeit, I have provided you with a simplified summation. If you had problems understanding my story, you should at least understand these words: the whole story worked out perfectly, through natural processes, without the need to postulate any form of guiding hand, preplanning, or the tossing of any dice.

One can only postulate the finite beginning. Scientific literature has a few postulations. A pre-existing primeval atom, which means this atom, pre-existing time-zero, must be the god of creation. Creation being finite—has a starting point—created by something infinite, understood to be something pre-existing before the finite of time-zero.

> Lemaitre powered onward, and in 1930 he further proposed that our expanding universe actually began as an infinitesimal point, which he called the "Primeval Atom" and that this beginning represented, in an allusion to Genesis perhaps, a "Day with No Yesterday." (Lawrence M. Krauss)

Quantum foam is a second postulation. This would make the pre-existing quantum foam the god of creation. Infinite before the finite time zero.

We also have string theory, whereby, a pre-existing donut-shaped dimension, wrapped with string, erupts by the strings breaking and forms the finite starting point of our universe. Therefore, as per string theory, this string dimension is the god of creation—infinite, due to pre-existing time zero.

I can picture many ministers—inclusive term—claiming none are true, because God spoke the universe into existence. This is also a scientifically based starting point of time-zero. It was the sound waves that started the act of creation. Sound waves are waves that contain energy of different quantities, thus qualities, and are fair game of possibilities. Possibilities are different than probabilities.

None are known to be true! None can be proven true to a 100%! All, can only be examined back to time-zero and not before! Why reject acquiring knowledge as far back as we can attain? "God said, let there be lights in the firmament of the heaven to divide the day from the night; and let them be for signs, and for seasons, and for days, and years." (Genesis 1:14). This requires studying the stars to learn the seasons and times. Notably, signs! But, signs of what? Magical horoscopes? Or signs of creation? Signs of how the universe came into being are very much akin to evidence by observation. In fact, the word miracle connotes signs and wonders, not magic!

If we insist on God, I am not nice enough to allow any tampering to gain the desired outcome after the point of time zero, or anything that is not self-sustaining.

I am of the opinion—not fact—that, if the universe were to come into being a thousand times, in a thousand different ways, things would turn out the same. A planet would form; life would form; cognoscenti or cognisant would evolve, that is sentient life; agency would evolve into animus; animus agency would evolve into gods, then force would evolve from agency in physical terms as knowledge proceeded. It took until 1621CE, when Kepler transformed soul into force.

Information

This leaves only to comment on information. Information is an after-the-fact word humans use as a measure of consciousness. The base word is form. As in the spherical shape of the Earth. The form is spherical! The form of the universe is space in every direction, or volume. The form of gravity is attraction on mass. The form of mass is its compressed energy. If gravity acts upon mass, then it can be said that gravity is informed of the existence of mass by its interaction with it.

We say gravity has information about the universe. As does the Higgs field, electromagnetic waves, and every other particle and wave. It does not follow that the universe is consciously working toward creating anything, nor guiding anything. Information has become synonymous with knowledge. Every field or particle might know where every other field or particle in the universe is, this is known as entanglement, but the universe does not think or have consciousness, or plan, or use morphic resonance.

There is an interesting book called Morphic Resonance, written by Rupert Sheldrake, claiming the "nature of formative causation." In short, once something is discovered in the universe, the universe responds by making that information available to a multitude of minds. This makes "regularities of nature as being more like habits than immutable laws".

Quantity holds information known as Quanta. Quality also holds information known as qualia. The quality of energy in quantity is real. It depicts, not only how much—quantity, but also what type—quality. In the words of Albert Einstein:

Everything is energy and that's all there is to it. Match the frequency of the reality you want and you cannot help but get that reality. It can be no other way. This is not philosophy, this is physics.

Along came man! We acquire forms from observation and it becomes our information. Because we now observe information, we acquire knowledge from form. We know form exists. We know movement is also information about our universe and this becomes knowledge, too. Information from our universe is one directional—that is, from the past moving toward the future. This predicts that when brain cells, or any cell for that matter, evolve, these cells will learn information in the relative terms our universe possesses—space-time relativity, and time-direction.

Brain relativity will evolve to cope with the conditions here on Earth. Your brain will naturally see things as space-time related, in both states as needed—space stopped, you're moving, or you're stopped, space is moving. Your memories will form space-time related or past to future-oriented.

Mathematical relativity will evolve within species as the need to compute distances and speed, thus time, in either catching prey or avoiding predators. This is known as a math instinct. Language will come into being as space-time related, explaining grammar or syntax, more expressly, the space-time ordering of words. Your thinking will be in space-time related concepts and you will be completely and utterly obliviously to it. You will evolve the hungry drive to seek out explanations of forms going from belief and faith to knowledge.

Information Requires Design?

Define information? Surely, any definition I place on it will fall short. To convince you, and for my own sanity, I will write out the mathematical expression of information. This way you can just glance at it to see information is everywhere and, by doing so, you will know what information is.

First, I will look at the actual word.

Forma, Latin—form in English, includes many ideas: formal, former, formalize, formalities, inform, information, concept-formation, deform, uniform, formation, preform, perform, reform, reformation, conformation, conform, informant, formattable, format, formable, cruciform, terraform. While far from an extensive or complete list, it illustrates to things in common as it pertains to language. First, they are all derived from a common holistic concept—that of form. Second, they are all sub-concepts—smaller portions of the holistic concept—altered to express different uses of the whole.

Information is made up from the word "form" or "inform", which says a lot. It implies that knowledge is gained from the form in question, and would be expressed as, "What is 'in' 'form' of this object?" Or, "what 'form' is this object 'in'?" The "ation" is an expression of query. What factors or qualities does this form have? That is information!

An up quark has a different energy, therefore different information, then a down quark. The difference in energy is the information within the quark. Quarks can become combined into protons or neutrons, making the information different in ingredient. The ingredients are both quanta and qualia—quantity and quality in form. The information becomes written as an energy-information formula:

(energy state + energy state + energy state + field-energy state) = combination of energy information into a sustained, information structure. An atom!

(up-quark + up-quark + down-quark + force) = proton, which is the minimum for the information in a simple atom.

The same can be written out for neutrons. In long notation, for a more complex atom, we will then have:

(energy state + energy state + energy state + field-energy state + energy state + energy state + energy state) = complex atom.

(up-quark + up-quark + down-quark + force + down-quark + up-quark + down-quark) = complex atom. An atom containing a proton and a neutron combined by a force or forces.

I won't write out the long version, but adding another energy-information state will show a stable atom:

(up-quark + up-quark + down-quark + force + down-quark + up-quark + down-quark) + electron = complex balanced atom.

Different atoms have different quantities of protons and neutrons, thus different information quantities and qualities to form information states. They also require one or more electrons.

Now, this information, complete in detail, can combine into molecules of different matter. I will not write out any long notation, although it would be interesting. Most readers will remember learning chemical equations in high school. These shorter and familiar equations will suffice it to give enough information from here on.

$(O + H + H) = H_2O$ or the combination of information combined into a molecule of water—oxygen, and hydrogen. The same can be said of CO_2—carbon, and oxygen, becoming carbon dioxide.

The question should be posed another way. If an oxygen atom and a hydrogen atom did not form water, then what went wrong? Here is a case where divine intervention would be acceptable. They have the nature to form, but disobeyed that nature.

Acid, which is well known under other names: sugar, salt, vitamin C—ascorbic acid, behave to exchange work for energy to do the work. They are chemical motors. The same applies to alkaline substances: they all behave to exchange work for energy to do the work. They are chemical motors. Think alkaline batteries. If chemicals did not form because work was not accomplished, then it could be truly called divine intervention. Some unknown influence must be stopping them. Energy exchange is completely natural from physics. The question is not who did it, nor why it happens that way, but how does it happen?

Creationists claim God is holding everything together. The intelligent design advocates claim additional information must be inserted, every now and then, to correct for unforeseen problems—in flagrante delicto (blazing offence). Empiricists know it happened because it exists as such and they try to understand how it happened naturally. Empiricists seek the how, not the why or who. If there is a gap in our knowledge, the gap is in the how.

Another form of acid is deoxyribonucleic acid known as DNA. The different DNA composites would have different information structures and would be combined into larger information structures. It would build energy-using machinery. These information machines would build bigger information machines by combining the information into a self-sustaining entity. Any information would become duplicated upon reproduction, asexually, or a clone of itself as it is referred to.

The information from sexual reproduction divided, like with like, and recombined into a single information organism. This applies to every means that goes into creating a living, transmutated cell. If information can be combined, then this argument will never hold up: the new information added to cause transformation of species must be created whole by an act of design. Ergo, intelligent design answers this gap in the evolutionary process.

There is no gap needing to be filled. The information is there. We have not found where that information is and intelligent designers conclude it must be missing, ergo, super-added by an intelligence. This I call tampering and voids any genuine nature. Plus, it is unnecessary for any competent intelligent designer.

If hydrogen and oxygen were available on Earth, then water would surely form. When you take every element into consideration, then every possibility—within the formation restrictions—can and did form. Quod non agit, non existit, "whatever does not act, does not exist."

The starting point of most intelligent design advocates is how life started on this planet without forethought. Interestingly, based on quod non agit, non existit, someone has written a book on how life, through electromotive forces, might have arisen.

The Vital Question by Nick Lane, is a must read! It will likely become the most famous postulation on the origins of life. It predicts that any system can be built as long as the system uses energy and performs a task to maintain energy flow.

Thus, whether electromotive force: electron-motive, or proton-motive, self-assembling units of agit productivity— doing something productive—can and will evolve. These units can also become stable, combine with other units and form more complex molecular motor life forms, built by motor proteins.

Life is defined as, whatever does not act, does not exist. The step by step information may be missing to our intellect, but that doesn't mean that step by step information is missing to our universe. Someday, someone will find it!

How Intelligent?

When one calls upon intelligent design as the means to evolving organisms, one places caps on intelligence. It is not intelligent to create single-celled organisms, which take thousands of years to amount to anything. If an intelligence is guiding natural selection, then this intelligence does not know what it is doing and must learn.

Every book I have read on creation and intelligent design falls into the same dilemma. When a gap is present, they call it "God of the Gaps" intelligent agency. For sure, an intelligent agent will explain the things we have not yet come to understand. However, it does not mean we will never come to understand them. It is a human, natural tendency to afford agency to explain any and all phenomena. I have a separate chapter on agency, or soul.

Every book I have ever read on science falls into the same dilemma, only it is not a dilemma. Casualty—cause and effect—is agency writ large. The agency of the Big Bang caused matter—matter was caused by the Big Bang. This is still agency as much as I shudder to write it in these terms.

For science, the agency does not need to be intelligent. The agency only needs it to be present naturally. In science, finding these naturally occurring causes of the acting agency steps in evolution is difficult. There are gaps in knowledge but it does not mean whole theories are wrong.

Looking at intelligent agency as an answer does not make God real. It does make God look bad. If, as we believers contend, God is perfect, He need not fumble to get things right. There is no reason for Him to start the process. There is no need for Him to intervene from time to time, and adjust for his previous mistakes. Clearly, He does not need to add chunks of knowledge to DNA, which would not occur otherwise, to cause the transition of organisms.

In fact, granting God created everything, granting Him perfection, and granting Him all power, one must ask why He needs to adjust for anything? If magic is called for, then one must also ask why six days?

I can read, therefore speak, the first chapter of Genesis in six minutes. Why not a creation time of six minutes? The scriptures do say "God said" and not "God did", don't they? Perhaps not oddly, there is not one scripture written to support God making any of these adjustments to His creation. If God was the one who created everything, then He created it with the ability to become what it is naturally.

God or no God, science seeks to explain how naturally occurring processes shaped life in this universe. There are no gaps in nature. There are only gaps in our understanding of nature. How bad are you going to look when knowledge discovers how an occurrence took place within a gap that we attributed to "adjustments made" by not so intelligent design? Is the designer intelligent or not?

Chapter Five

Origins of Mythos

I would rather have questions that can't be answered than answers that can't be questioned

— Richard Feynman

At some point in this book, I will need to cover the following two points and relate them to our search for the truth. Mythology and religion.

While we often think of them as separate, they are related as both have evolved into our current understanding of nature. I cannot cover every minute detail in a work such as this since we have much to cover before we come to a close. We can, however, deal with larger chunks of information and relate them to our current stage of the human thought process. As we examine these steps, our eyes will open to the nature of man.

Mythology is a somewhat polluted word. Its subversion takes the form of wild stories or tall tales. Its origins are in wisdom. The word mythology is derived from the same source as mystic, magic, magi, myth, magus, and mystery. We should also include magari as a wistful dream, or the romance of what is possible.

The wise men from biblical fame were originally referred to as magi, who bore gifts of gold, frankincense, and myrrh. A quick pause here. All of the above-mentioned gifts are both singular and plural in noun. Gold refers to tons or ounces and it is all called gold by quantity. Same with the other gifts. Talking about turning stories into foolish stories, one should not miss this chance to examine interpretation alterations. The bible does not say, ever, three magi. Since these gifts are plural in nature, there could have been dozens of wise men giving just gold alone. The three must come from man. Possibly one for each gift, which is never mentioned in any case.

Jesus could have been very rich by these gifts. Keeping Jesus in extreme poverty helps ministers to keep people in extreme poverty by using Him as an example. This is a case where men interpret mythos to fit what they want it to say. But, I digress, let's get back to magi.

Magi were students of the world, or seekers of wisdom. Magic, considered as revealing wonders, was what they studied. Mystic was a means of expressing inner knowledge. Myth was the science of relating effects of nature. Mystery should speak for itself as we continue to use it much the same way today as in the past— trying to understand something that is not readily understandable. It also includes the terms: image, imagery, and imagination (i-magi-nation).

If we consider the Greek meaning of the word, one could include math. Math has its origins in "teachable knowledge". Method, holds roots in that word system and we get words like methodology, methodical, and even the scientific method, first advocated in Two New Sciences by Galileo—"Measure what is measurable, and make measurable what is not."

Methodological, readily translates into logical method, or a method of discovery based upon logic.

Of equal importance, miracle depicts signs and wonders, more akin to unexplained events.

Mythos is the Greek word used to denote a narrative. Myth, in its original meaning, meant to place facts into a narrative. As a whole, the meaning would be to uncover facts from within one's inner knowledge, or logic system, and combine them with the knowledge passed down from generation to generation. It would be to put them into a sequence of narratives that could be "reliably" and "accurately" repeated.

As an aside, here, I should clarify cultural learning from "gene" learning. Epigenetics, is now accepted as a means of genetic learning, over and above mutations in genes, called "gene memory".

If you introduce a mouse, say, onto an isolated island and it multiples for several generations, without the predation of snakes, say, it will remember, genetically, hundreds of years later, when snakes are introduced onto the island, that they are predators. The genes remember!

The same goes for learning new survival qualities. Independent of mutations causing change, change can become remembered by genotypes. This includes factors, such as, natural environment changes—famine—and niche change. The expression of genes can be influenced by environmental changes.

A "molecular memory" is thus stamped on a gene—this time, indirectly, by attaching the signal to protein. When a cell divides, the marks can be copied into daughter cells, thereby recording the memory over several generations of cells. When sperm or eggs are generated, it is conceivable these markers are copied into these germ cells, thereby recording the memory over several generations of organisms. The heritability and stability if these histone marks, and the mechanism to ensure that the marks appear in the right genes at the right time, are still under investigation... (Siddhartha Mukherjee).

The investigation may have been partially solved. In an article by Futurism (13 May 2016) titled *Memories Can Be Inherited, and Scientists Might Have Just Figured Out How: how our experiences get passed down to our children*. Scientists claim to have identified a process.

Scientists [Tel Aviv University] were able to determine that specific genes, which they dubbed, Modified Transgenerational Epigenetic Kinetics (MOTEK) are also involved in turning epigenetic transmission on and off. Switching on/off are based on the feedback interaction between RNA,s (which are inherited) and the MOTEX genes that are necessary to producing and transmitting the RNA through each generation. (Futurism)

This implies the act of cultural learning can become part of one's genome.

Accepting the above definition of mythos as close to accurate, one can see where religion and ritual, the second point, comes into play. A rite or ritual is the step by step process of completing a certain task, narrated as mythos.

In the rite of Holy Communion, the step by step narrative of feeding the mysteries of the soul is repeated from the Last Supper. Jesus is taken as the teacher of the rite and the disciples are his literal students. Mythos would be your minister reading the narrative while giving thanks to God and blessing the bread and wine. It is not called the mythos of Jesus, but the Rite of Eucharist. One could ask, "On what backbone is this process built upon?"

What about the step by step process of learning to chip stone into arrow tips, spearheads, scrappers or cutting tools? The rite leader would become a minister of knowledge; a magician, or mystic if you will, and his students would become followers of the rite. We can, and should, tie these two points together since they clearly relate to belief, wisdom, and knowledge.

Magic, in the past, was used to express wisdom—not hocus-pocus—and was held in great esteem. Doing magical tricks are not magic to you, but they are magic to the ones watching. Mystic was a means of expressing this inner knowledge. Expressing it to others was a form of teaching. The means of teaching was a step by step process, where if one omitted a step it could lead to disastrous results.

From this, we can understand that ritual is a step by step process in our earliest development. It should surprise no one that the mythos of "reliably" and "accurately" repeated information as a narrative would come into being from natural processes alone. Chanting, then, would be a means of repeating information until it became second nature or an adopted-instinct.

Rite and ritual being a step by step process of transferring information as reliably and accurately as possible would almost immediately take the undertones of religion. We have all heard someone use the word religiously, without reference to God. For example, he takes his morning walk at 6:00 am, religiously! It is not hard to envision rites becoming divine right, then a standard for higher beings—our gods.

Brain Relativity

Brain relativity has been suggested in the literature, but not fully concluded. I will transform space-time relativity into structural agency and deal with agency next.

"In mathematics, you don't understand things. You just get used to them," as said by John Von Neumann. Predators plot a course over the shortest distance between them and their moving prey.

Presumably, the prey, when it sees the predator coming, plots a course to lengthen the distance. This is within the field of calculus. The predator and prey do not consciously know they are doing complicated mathematical calculations. Their movements, and the math, are automatic. This is called the math instinct and it is very well studied, indeed.

I would like to submit innate mathematical brain relativity as being responsible for our math instinct. Everything moves within our volume of space. Time is movement. Calculating distances would evolve within the brain based on both the Theory of Relativity and general relativity. Every brain would automatically evolve with both space and time references to calculate movements within that volume of space. Space-time relativity.

This is shown to hold under scientific scrutiny even though it is not called brain relativity per se. I found the following paper to give some support: *Functional Neuroanatomy of Intuitive Physical Inference,* published in the Proceedings of the National Academy of Sciences of the United States of America [PNAS] June 29, 2016

Move, movement, immovable, momentum, minute, motion, emotion, movable, mobile, and moment, which is not an exhaustive list of the root word, express sub-concepts of action. Greek gives us movens—the mover, and motum—the moved. Unmoved mover, or primary cause. Movens motum gives living being, life force, or soul. Of note, altering the main word by changing vowels or consonants alter the word meaning. This gives sub-concepts, or different applicable concepts of the root word. This should be self-explanatory.

Brain relativity, in general, would evolve to track movement from past into the future because the expansion of the universe is the same and time is also past into future, which is the order in the universe. Why not make it the order of the brain function naturally? Instead, we profess it as being created, like the joke:

In the beginning, God said let there be grammar: and there was grammar! And then there was grammar issues, and they was bad.—(unknown).

Why not make it the order in math and language? Relativity first, and then brain relativity, a brain oriented under space-time by natural selection, and then finally, language relativity. Relativity would predict that when language evolved, it would evolve from past into future orientation.

We could say we added words together one after the other, but the order of them is important. This, in and of itself, would explain grammar, or syntax, being distinct from word meaning or lexicon. We would naturally say, the sun comes up in the east and sets in the west, because that is the naturally occurring space-time event. It is in the natural order of the actual happening, one word added to another grammatically correct word. Grammar is language structure, which would be structured space-time relativity as an instinct, known as a grammar instinct or language instinct.

Structure having a substantial influence. Space-time has structure in volume, which is the reason I included the creation of the universe in this manuscript. Therefore, mathematics dissects the structure of dimensions to calculate space and time events in an orderly fashion. You will never catch your prey if you see it running any other way but the proper way. Grammar dissects the structure of dimensions to calculate a verbal description in an orderly fashion. You will never describe an event unless you word it in a structurally ordered way.

Take those at face value as being true. Then ask this question, could events being directionally ordered naturally, become a means of faith-knowledge? The sun always comes up in the same place, plus or minus the tilt of the Earth at 23 degrees and your location. The sun coming up always presents day. The sun going down always presents night. These are belief-knowledge without the actual facts as proof. We see the sun moving, not the Earth.

What about cause and effect? Relativity would exert a cause to produce an ordered effect? In other words, could it be said that agency is also space-time relative? Agency could become the cause for space-time itself in belief-knowledge terms, could it not?

Think about how we all speak. With enough time, everything is possible. Could time have become an agent for thought purposes? What about separation of body as a natural consequence of the universe?

Bodies at rest versus bodies in motion? For that matter, what about myself as a separate body giving rise to "I" within the treatment of space-time? I am standing still and everything is moving. I am moving and everything is standing still. I am moving and another person is moving relative to some other point of reference, which is standing still. Are these terms space-time relative, plus an acting agent?

I already gave two examples of yes in two paragraphs of this discourse. Predator chasing prey as two distinct agents, and again, when I spoke of the sun coming up. We give agency to the sun by singling out its actions by whatever means it produces those actions. First by the gods, then by natural laws. First, the sun moves, then the Earth moves.

Speaking in terms of space-time relativity allows for agency and belief-knowledge. This brings us to question whether something is needed to separate holistic concepts. Logic or analytical abilities are needed. Logos, meaning word, also produces logic, logical, or literally to examine in detail.

Learning to speak in articulate digital form, instead of calls and cries would bring with it a means of thinking in articulate form, digitally, if you will. Holistic concepts could become separated into smaller, yet are still related in nature as sub-concepts. Like the small child who always says, "I am too big" even when they mean they are too small. What they really mean is that they are "too" size different. Being able to think digitally about a whole concept via language, seems to instill a power upon man. The power of analytics.

Slowly, we are building a case for how knowledge was realized within the homo-sapiens species. Ipsa scientia potentia est, directly translates into, itself knowledge potent is, or in proper English: knowledge itself is potent (or power more commonly referred to) as said by Sir Francis Bacon. I prefer potent as a direct translation as it leads nicely into a potential for gain.

So, knowledge itself is, and builds a potential, for gain. The more you can challenge the position of agency of current knowledge, the more potential you have of gaining more knowledge. To do things better. To understand our world better.

Agency

In the book: *Concepts of Force* by Max Jammer, the history of force is explored. It draws very good conclusions.

Problems? He does point out that other authors use the term agency, but does not draw this conclusion to fruitarian. Maybe it has been missed completely in the literature? He does not use agent the same way as I am going to either. His book does argue compellingly that God as a prime mover has become reduced to the force of natural phenomena. Agency and force carry close to the same meaning. A quick quote by Philo, a philosopher from Alexandria:

'He [God] has made His forces extend through earth and water, air and heaven, and left no part of the universe destitute, and by uniting all with all has bound them fast with invisible bonds,'

Philo postulates the existence of invisible bonds of forces throughout the universe, as does Stoic, another early philosopher.

It is not hard to conclude the same meaning of the words. Force is causation. Agency is causation. One says enforcer, as describing the actor upon the action of force. One says agent, as describing the actor upon the action of agency.

The preliminary focus should be on a few factors. Agent is a good place to start since we consider ourselves to be the agents of our own lives. Agency is the act of control over our bodily functions under "will" or automation/animation. This includes our thoughts that are roaming around in our minds coming to fruition. If we are the agents of cause in our lives, then, acceptably, there must be an agent of cause within natural phenomena or we would grant agency to many false gods. Lightning would have the agent of Thor, as well as the Greek god, Zeus. That is the agent causing the lightning. Animist: is the theory that all things have souls.

I must point out an obvious brain related effect here: we understand an agent causes an effect or affects a cause. This is all part of our ability to understand nature born from our universe—the reason I wrote the last chapter. The reason I mentioned brain relativity as an evolved property of evolution. If everything moves from past to present to future, then everything has agency not unlike our own agency. The first steps to learning would be to attribute our type of agency onto other types of agency. Including creation itself. Some agent must be the cause affecting the universe. Even today, as mentioned, we ask of our God why He allows suffering and how He created the universe. He is not the agent of your suffering.

I must take a detour here as this book is all about doing what is right. As is well known, the original bible was not written the way it appears in the English King James version. Ancient Hebrew did not use punctuation in any form: question marks, commas, etc. and it was written from right to left.

The translators added the punctuation marks as they saw fit. They were deriving them from what they believed to be the best interruption. For that reason, the English King James version could be very different. For instance, some passages we took for statements could, in fact, be a question, while some questions could be a statement.

Also, remember that cause and effect are vague, which I demonstrated in the last chapter. Allowing something to take place, can be construed as making something take place. Apply this to the next quote:

> Though He causes grief, yet will he have compassion according to the multitude of his mercies. For he does not afflict willingly nor grieve the children of men, to crush under his feet all the prisoners of the earth, to turn aside the right of a man before the face of the most High, to subvert a man in his cause, the Lord approves not. Who is he that says, and it comes to pass, when the lord commanded it not? Out of the mouth of

the most High proceeds not evil and good? (Lamentations 3:32-38)

That could just as easily be interrupted as "though he allows grief" because "he does not afflict willingly nor grieve the children of men" places a condition on it. You allow it, I allow it. "Out of the mouth of the most High proceeds not evil and good" can be interrupted as a question or a statement. Does both good and evil come from God? Or, both good and evil do not come from God! The latter makes it pertain to good only, but not both coming from God! The scribes that translated the bible and added punctuation, interpreted it as a question. We can rightly conclude the following: I did not create the mess you are in, but because you caused (allowed) it, I allowed (caused) it. Using agency instead, allowed me to alter the rendition, likely for the better.

Agency also transposes the movements—animation—into a completely separate entity. Our imparted soul will be considered at the appropriate place and time. Even today, soul is commonly understood as the agent interacting with the body and brain.

We can get the genealogy of this thinking by a quote from Plato. I quote *Laws* Book Ten:

Athenian Stranger: At this stage of the argument, let us put a question.

Cleinias: What question?

Athenian Stranger: If we were to see this power existing in any earthly, watery, or fiery substance; simple or compound—How would you describe it?

Cleinias: You mean to ask whether we should call such a self-moving power life?

Athenian Stranger: I do.

Cleinias: Certainly, we should.

Athenian Stranger: And when we see soul in anything, must we not do the same—must we not admit that this is life?

We can now examine mythology through the eyes of agency. We can see how it was considered to be placing facts into a naturally structured narrative—mythos. Some feel that our mythologies are all completely made up. Other thinkers feel that mythologies are somewhat fact-based, but altered into unbelievable fool's gold. Although, there might be real gold there to find.

There is something to be said for making things clear! This is as good of a place as any to make things very clear! I did not write the bible! I did not write the works of Homer! I did not write Egyptian mythology, Aztec mythology, Persian mythology, or any other ancient works! I am, however, an avid reader of all.

All of these pieces of work are of ancient origins, which means they are directly related to the thought process of the actual storytellers, and/or story writers. We can, at least, be real in our thinking and accept them as having some prescription of information we can tap into. We must be able to delve into these clues and *abstract* the information. This is what I will attempt to do in the following text.

The story of the fall of man in the Garden of Eden also, explicitly, deals with wisdom. As I have already written earlier "a tree to be desired to *make one wise"* and we must get wisdom from this. Calling the tree by its proper name of "the tree of conscience" might be helpful. Conscience is made of the words con, as in pro and con, plus, the word scientia, the Latin word for knowledge. To have conscience is to weigh the good and bad effects of your doings, which gives us knowledge of good and evil.

In the case of conscience, the bad effects (cons) are said to weigh on us as guilt. Oddly, when we refer to good, we never say pro-science. Correctly, then, it should be called "the tree of pro-conscience"! Not called "the tree of knowledge"! Realistically, it has nothing to do with knowledge, so should be shortened to the tree of wisdom.

This also brings us to the blame game. Adam blamed both Eve and God, while Eve blamed the serpent. How did Eve get blamed when it was Adam who was told not to eat of the fruit before Eve had even been created? The blame game is still going strong today and one only has to watch the news to see it. The blame game is derived directly from agency of cause. This biblical example is one of the best:

> The woman whom you (God agent) gave to be with me, she (acting agent) gave me of the tree and I (me agent) did eat. (Genesis 3:12)

Therefore, I would have never eaten the fruit if other agents were not involved. If you remember, Eve gave the fruit to Adam, and Adam was aware he was being given the fruit.

> When the woman saw that the tree was good for food, and that it was pleasant to the eyes, and a tree to be desired to make one wise, she took of the fruit thereof and did eat, and gave it also unto her husband that was with her (witnessing the act of the acting agent) and he did eat. (Genesis 3:6)

Even the most extreme critic of anti-religious thinkers can concede to agency being present—agency being selected out of the actual context of the situation, and agency becoming the blame game. This can be the moral stance, but does it need to stop at morals?

Conscience can also be taken as meaning to weigh your beliefs for true knowledge. The pros or cons of what your belief-knowledge is telling you.

This fits what wisdom actually does. If you can place agency on another person as a pro or con, then you can challenge agency in material matters as well. If you can blame another agent for some cause or effect, then you can challenge wrong beliefs, or semi-wrong beliefs. One can sophia out the actions of sophistication by any acting agents, by themselves becoming a sophist—material things included.

Ultimately, there are more meanings that we can muster from this story. Consciousness is derived from the same word. It has the con, plus the "ness" and serves as together-knowing. From this "vile" myth, we can draw the following. Eve ate from the fruit and nothing happened. Why is it that her eyes weren't opened?

Traditionally, biblically, it has been accepted by the reasoning since Adam was the one commanded, he had to eat it. This is not what this story actually depicts. It depicts together-knowing! I found this term "together-knowing" as one word, for the meaning of consciousness in the wonderful book: *Consciousness and the Brain*, Stanislas Dehaene. Using this term makes the job of writing a full explanation so much shorter.

"Together-knowing" depicts taking more than one person knowing the same thing. We could represent one person knowing as the single word one-knowing. So, Eve out, both Adam and Eve in. For those offended by Adam and Eve, you can use Dick and Jane, as long as more than one person is used. To go from one-knowing to together-knowing, all you would need is a trigger. The Bible uses a fruit. Not an apple as is commonly thought. This is how myth come into being.

Fruit has several meanings. One such meaning is the fruition of an idea. An idea growing into something tangible. The end product of an event, or an idea. A trigger is something that induces an idea. It is not hard to see getting something like, we ate of the fruition.

Imagine, explaining verbally, how you became wise. After several generations, you learn to write. Language evolves from Ancient Hebrew to a slightly different Hebrew and the writing must be translated. Then, try to translate these translated translations into Old English, which most people cannot read. These, in turn, get translated into ever-increasingly newer words until they are translated into modern English. The last English translation was the King James Bible, which most people can still read. Finally, they get translated into what we speak today in the New International Version.

Maybe, just maybe, we consumed the fruition of wisdom would become, we ate from the forbidden fruit—now considered a true myth, in the dirty meaning of the word, as ate an apple. This myth is expounded as Eve ate from the apple, and Adam, loving her and not wanting her to shoulder the burden of guilt alone, took the remnants of the apple and swallowed it whole. Thus, men have larger Adam's Apples, than women do. The myth might distract from the factual events containing some truth.

We will ignore the fruit and the trigger for now. We will examine the event with the details given.

Adam took the forbidden fruit and ate it. When he does, the eyes of them both were opened and they knew something. Something that was not a problem before their eyes were opened. This goes from one-knowing to together-knowing on the fast track.

What did they come to know? That they were naked? Wait! You're not wearing any clothes and you don't know you're naked? In another work, I wrote the trigger was a cognitive one, but we must also include an emotional one. Shame, after all, is classed as an emotional cognitive, not a cognition cognitive.

One-knowing understands you are naked. You have no clothes on. One-knowing also understands your mate is naked as she has no clothes on. Nudity of itself is nothing to be ashamed of as we are born naked. Together-knowing is a mutual understanding. Together, they both understood they were both naked and shamelessly so. After knowing this as true fact, does it, in any way, alter the situation? Who is ashamed to be naked in front of their spouse?

What if the shame was induced for another reason? What if our first modern ancestors were already in a state of shame for something else? The guilt of wrongdoing as one-knowing in each of them? They could have been banished from their tribe for some reason or other, which is unnamed here. Any act of mutual cognition, then, could trigger both logical thinking and shameful thinking at the same time. Once they realized that, they became together-knowing. In that instant, they would also become together-shameful. They would want to try to cover their shame of said incident from each other.

This does not automatically lead to body cover-up. It would be the added trigger for it. Together-shameful can be said, at this point, to be together-shameful-knowing, which makes it emotional-knowing or what we call emotional intelligence. Love, hate, fear, shame, and every other emotion falls under this title.

If I am in a shameful state, and I now know you to be in the same shameful state, then it would be together-emotional-intelligence. If I know the same as you know; together-knowing, in this one shameful state, then other states are now open to feel shameful of. For example, as we are both naked, what I want to do to your body right now could be shameful. I know that you know what I want to do to your body. In order to keep this hidden, I might just cover the visible evidence with fig leaves. Nakedness, secondary to the triggered shame.

It is one thing to just act on instinct and mate with someone. It is quite another to be seen by others as always wanting to mate. I can envision everything from the common "all you ever think about is sex," which most husbands will attest to hearing from their wives. Right down to "Hey, that's my mate you are looking at sexually." To keep other people from knowing what you are feeling, it would be best to adopt clothing. The main point placed on emotional intelligence becoming together-knowing.

There is another question to be asked. I have just shown that together-shame only became an after-the-fact product. Since I always question both sides of an argument to the bitter end, walk with me on this argument. If God created man by His own hand, then He must have created him in a precognitive emotionally-intelligent state. I have just exposed it to be scripturally accurate. Evolution would do that equivalent job too. Is there any difference in the presentation of a pre-state condition in the two choices?

We considered one-knowing and together-knowing, but it falls short of the complete truth. We don't consider consciousness quite this way. We take it as being sentient. This requires an additional step in as simple of terms I can muster.

One-knowing only states that you know one thing at a time of cognition. We must add here self-knowing in relation to knowledge. You know more details about your inner thoughts. So then, one-knowing does not get added to another's one-knowing to produce together-knowing. Self-knowing gets added to another's self-knowing to produce together-self-knowing. Shared-self-awareness-knowing.

Perhaps I should cover one more myth before moving on. We should establish that these myths do hold some form of correct information, albeit, in poor fact communication. The propagation of species. (Genesis 6:1-2, and again verse 4):

> When men began to multiply on the face of the Earth, and daughters were born unto them, that the sons of God saw the daughters of men that

they were fair; and they took them wives of all which they chose. There were giants in the Earth in those days; and also after that, when the sons of God came unto the daughters of men, and they bore children unto them. The same became mighty men which were of old, men of renown.

A quick analysis of these scriptures shows there were men (sons of God, so-called) along with other men—human species. Two different species! One group of men saw the other group of men had fair women and took them to wife. Sexual selection, if you will. These fair women would pass on their mtDNA (Mitochondrial deoxyribonucleic acid) to both their sons and daughters. With mtDNA, only daughters matter. If two distinct groups of early primates mated, then there would be no trace of mtDNA of the paternal group, only the maternal group.

The last part of that scripture is not talking about the paternal group or the maternal group, but about their offspring. "The same became mighty men which were of old, men of renown." "The same" belongs to "they bore children unto them" or the children, and "became" belongs to the evolution of the said children. In this case, the evolution is "mighty men" and "were" depicts place in time—past in this case. Their children became the mighty men of renown from time past. These scriptures (biblical fact) seem to be making distinct, the case for an improved species. Especially in the light of DNA testing. DNA markers actually prove these fossils are from a continuum of species with modification.

According to our models, however, the Neanderthal mtDNA [Mitochondrial DNA] did not trace back to this Mitochondrial Eve but went further back before it shared an ancestor with the mtDNA of humans alive today. This finding was immensely exciting. It proved beyond any doubt that we had recovered a piece of Neanderthal DNA—and it showed, at least with respect to their mtDNA, that the Neanderthals were profoundly different from us. (Savante Paabo)

As mtDNA is only transmitted through the female genome and never the male genome—only the sperm tail, which needs to do work has mtDNA and it is broken off after the penetration of the egg has started. The mtDNA is the genome of work or energy store and separate from the nuclear DNA, which is carried, as the name suggests, in the cell nucleus. All mtDNA in humans is passed down from females only and it is referred to in the literature as coming from one common ancestor known as Mitochondrial Eve. This is scientific fact, not speculation.

Scientifically speaking, Neanderthal mtDNA is missing from human genomes. If Neanderthal did breed with humans, then only female, modern humans would pass on any mtDNA. Neanderthal mtDNA would be completely absent from our genome. It is absent and there is no proof whatsoever. What would be proof of interbreeding is if nuclear DNA from Neanderthal were present in modern humans. Apparently, it is!

This indicates that male Neanderthals mated with female homo-sapiens and produced offspring of both sexes. These offspring survived of old and we are their direct descendants. Scientific fact!

Neanderthal Man by Savante Paabo is an excellent book on the topic of the Neanderthal genome and it is written by the scientist that broke the genetic code of Neanderthals. Well worth the read! The book points out that mixing of species happened more than once and I will take two small quotes from Neanderthal Man:

I had come to believe that although the big picture of modern human spread was one where the replacement crowd pushed other groups into extinction, this was not a total replacement. Rather, some DNA seemed to leak over into the groups that lived on, so much so that I started using the term I had picked up from somewhere to describe this process: 'leaky replacement.' Perhaps, I thought, the spread of Denisovans had also been a 'leaky' affair.

And
The picture that emerges is that there was plenty of mixing among several types of humans in the late Pleistocene, but mostly of small proportions. (Savante Paabo)

Both the scripture and science have similar postulations of early man. Point! How would the bible know to track the mating of the "daughters" of men—specific to human mtDNA—unless there was only cross-breeding of the male Neanderthals and the female homo-sapiens to record? Similar stories are to be found in many so-called mythologies of the world. There must be some accuracy to some of these stories, however distorted the stories are.

Perhaps, from our own arrogance, I should make a point clear. There are two theories from extinction. Replacement Theory and Interbreed Theory. There are also some minor theories that I will not mention. Possibly, all the theories apply to some portion. Replacement theory should be noted as of special value as it contends with arrogance. Replacement Theory implies that we removed them from existence, either by killing them or out-competing with them.

We do contain between 1 and 4 percent of Neanderthal DNA. Ergo, "we" replaced "them" as the thinking goes. After all, we exist and they do not! In flagrante delicto—arrogance! "We" do not exist either! "We" are now the product of both! The combined product replaced both the Neanderthal and the Pre-homo Sapient, at least to some measurable percentage. The same can be said of the Denisovans. This applies to the Interbreed Theory as well.

Charles Darwin left the notes he had gathered through the years and they have been published in book form. He, too, mentions crossbreeding:

> The facts of half instincts when two varieties are crossed as in Shephard dogs/Inherited habits: Horse/—is valuable it shows that new instincts can originate—strong argument for brain bringing thought, & not merely instinct, a separate thing superadded—we can thus trace causation of thought—it is brought within limits of examination—obeys same laws as other parts of structure. [sic] (Charles Darwin)

Possibly, the main reason for "us" transforming the way we did is from genetic alterations causing combined traits, habits, and instincts to advance.

When you really examine form in mythology, you realize our propensity to believe in God, or gods came first, then stories start to become structured around this belief system. Almost every myth has the gods fighting and they are called mighty.

Imagine that you were the first man and woman to gain full consciousness and could learn, teach and transform your world. Mighty "men of renown." What would your kin think about you as you solved problem after problem wisely, powerfully, and accurately? Would they call you the "sons of God", who married the daughters of men? Then you did the unthinkable. You taught them to do wonderful things for themselves. Things like talking in articulate speech, instead of inarticulate grunts and calls.

After learning how to communicate in articulated language, you would learn how they themselves came to learn speech. How would you tell the story to the next generation? How would this story hold quality wise when retold countless generations before the advent of writing? Would you be remembered as the gods of Egypt, or the gods of Greek mythology? Interestingly, the Greeks called the descendants of the "gods and man" heroes, or demigods.

Looking back at that last scripture, advances heroes in place of the men of renown. I think anyone would concede there is some truth in these mythologies.

It is easier to create simplified stories about happenings, than to remember the debris of facts under complex subjectivity. We teach our children how to tie their shoelaces using the example of "pesky wabbits". The rabbit climbed over and went through... Rabbits don't tie shoes, but they do teach children how to tie shoes themselves. One, if tempted, could call this, learning through mythology as opposed to methodology.

Demons

We have travelled as far as possible with the term scientia. Before concluding anything, we should not ignore the Greeks. In the Greek tongue, the word for knowledge is Daemon—information appearing within the brain—and has many forms. Demon is the common word used today. We also get demonstrate: to show or explain knowledge. Pandemonium means all knowledge confused or chaos. The evil connotation of the word, as all hell breaking loose.

Demos means people. Pandemic means all people—presumably to be thinkers. It would literally, in the original, mean we have demons in our brains. Thoughts, that is, in case you take it to mean devils. Biblically speaking, it does not have to mean a devil in your brain, but rather evil thoughts or demonic thoughts as it evolved into. These demons can be called schizophrenia, for example.

The same applies to democratic, as many or all in charge. Every normal person has voices in their head. They are your own voices, normally. If your brain is singing a song, silently, you likely hear the song sung in the voice of the group singing it. You might hear your mother or father giving you mental advice in their own voices with recollection. Normal. Abnormal voices are the problem and have been tainted as demonic.

From this, we can speculate the brain communicating within itself produces a normal active voice. Voice, whether in word or concept form. If a voice is active, then there must be an agent, or agency involved. As mentioned earlier, spirit was associated with the wind, to freely move around; to inspire. "From the root man, as in Sanskrit, mati (for manti) 'spirit' 'meaning' from man, to think:" A Comparative Grammar, Franz Bopp.

Several sources adhere to this concept of spirits:

Zosimus is quite correct. The Hebrew word *Adam* is from a root meaning "red," and is almost certainly connected with the idea of "red blood." In esotericism, Adam was the name given to the future humanity that first descended into physical bodies. The same denotes the first spiritual entities who clothed themselves in the red of flesh and blood. (David Ovason).

Let's clarify this. We call ourselves man, meaning to think. The thinking comes from spiritual characteristics of stuff freely floating around in our brains as if with the wind. As Jesus noted, "You can't tell where the wind comes from, nor where it goes and the same is the case with the spirit." Free-floating thought: we are not even sure where it comes from or where it goes to, it just happens in our brain. This is not indifferent from demon. Each thought seems to have its own agent. Is it that hard to see that one might attribute a free-floating thought to be the agency of God giving them some long sought after answer?

Speaking in terms of psychology and physiology, it is not hard to see that an act of nervation can cause a thought to appear from nowhere. If these thoughts are innate as instinct, and are belief-knowledge based, then what could we say about two or three conflicting innate ideas?

We would need to spirit or divine out the conflicts between them. This is what it means to think. Any other form of acknowledgement would be to just accept without caring. We can certainly see the process of critical thinking evolve within man throughout the millennia. Do we need a means? Nervation?

Most of the word-origin examples I use are either well known, or they have exceeding amounts of evidence to support them. I avoid using examples that do not have overwhelming evidence. I am going to use the next word, even though the evidence is poor, because it contains much revelation, even if it is not true of that word-origin.

Nous—Greek, Intellectus/intelligentia—Latin, mind in English. I checked every source I could find and came up empty. I must make my own summations here. Read them, then accept or reject them as you see fit.

Normally, I can find much on the evolution of words, usually starting with the Greek and/or Latin. I have an hundred-year-old dictionary, two newer dictionaries, and several online ones. I searched nous, nerve, neuron, nourish, without any luck. I also tried the Latin intellectus without any luck, either. I am going to try to expound nous—evolve it after the word move from above.

If we take a definition for nous as mind, which has an origin, we can enhance it to include other sub-concepts. Change the nous to nour, as in nourish, and we can see that not only does the body need nourishment, but the mind does as well. The mind absorbs knowledge. Is that a real stretch for evolving nous?

If we accept this transition, then the next transition makes some sense. Neur, as in neuron. A neuron is responsible for distributing information throughout the body and brain. Neuron, takes us to the word nerve, derived from it, and allows for sub-concepts of information distribution, control over bodily function, and, in short, mental nourishment. Mental nourishment is understood to be the feeding of the mind, or sense perception. Autonomous! Nomous, the last letters in autonomous, likely stems from nous as well.

I could be completely off the mark here and I won't feel bad if you reject this theory. It does make some revelation of sense, though. The concept of mind (nous) has been divided into sub-concepts relating to the needs of the mind and the mind's function by nervous activity. Nervous activity is known as nervation. Nervation also includes veins, which blood flows through, as well as the veins in the leaves of trees. Pathways for nutrition or information as in mind.

Theories

Telos means end result in Greek. Teleology studies the end purpose of something, and Theo means God in Greek. It is where we get the term theology, or things evident from design.

Lungs are created for breathing is one such statement. The statement is not totally accurate. Lungs evolved to move, or were created to move air, would be a better expression. It is in the movement that oxygen is exchanged. If lungs don't move, then lungs don't breathe.

In addition, lungs are not limited to breathing but are also used for the production of blood, which produces more movement. To move or movement was carried with anima, to animate something. There must be some force or agent causing movement. It must be for a reason (teleology) and it, therefore, must be imparted by another agent (theology). God, therefore, must have designed and imparted our agency of movement into body.

In Greek literature, it is known as a prime mover. The one who created all other movement. In religion, it is known as God creating the universe and everything in it.

This was the belief-knowledge state of thinking until the scientific revolution. A cause for everything was sought after, but, ultimately, ended with God. There was some progress made with this method. It is still the main method of investigating used even now, strictly speaking. There must be some cause before another cause or another effect can be measured. We have learned to give cause to natural laws.

> TIMAEUS: Now, let us state the reason why becoming and this universe were framed by him who framed them. He was good, and what is good never has any particle of envy in it whatsoever; and being without envy he wished all things to be as like himself as possible. This indeed is the most proper principle of becoming and the cosmos and as it comes from wise men one would be absolutely right to accept it. God therefore, wishing that all things should be good, and so far as possible nothing be imperfect, and finding the

visible universe in a state not of rest but of inharmonious and disorderly motion, brought it to order from disorder, as he judged that order was in every way better. It is unlawful for the best to produce anything but the most beautiful. As a result of reasoning, he found that among all things that are by nature visible, no work without intelligence will ever be more beautiful than one with intelligence, if we compare them whole for whole, and that it is impossible for something to gain intelligence without a soul. Because of this reasoning he fashioned the universe by implanting intelligence in soul and soul in body, and so ensured that his work should be by nature the fairest and the best possible. And so the likely account must say that this world came to be in very truth, through god's forethought, a living being with soul and intelligence. (Plato: Timaeus)

Theory is also derived from theo and theology. Theory becomes transferred from God causes "theo" to natural causes. Thesis means to put down or put forth. One puts forth a theory and tries to test it logically by reasoning or the tweaking of facts from observation. Usually, the observations come from nature, but we can devise ways of making additional observations. In the past, the theory was of God doing everything. Theo-ry—how did God do it? God does not sit there and spin the Earth. It spins naturally. Everything in nature works naturally. We must, then, be able to theo every law governing nature. In the process, agent would be replaced by natural cause and effect.

A theory gets tested until it fails. Ever since 1916, scientist have been testing Einstein's theory of relativity, our modern way of understanding gravity, space, and time. The theory of relativity has never failed, but scientist are still doggedly testing it. This process inspires confidence.! The more intense the testing that relativity survives, the more confidence we have in it, a scientific theory can be disproved by a single counterexample, but it can never be proven true because that would mean it couldn't be refuted; and if it can't be refuted, by definition it's not a scientific theory—it's faith, not science. (Joel R. Primack et al).

Since we are slowly learning the value of tearing our world apart, let's see what that science quote holds in store. First, and feel free to burn this book if I am wrong, one needs belief-knowledge of something before one can work with that same something. You must believe in your theory before you can ever think about ways to prove the theory true. Some ideas present themselves to the brain and seem good, but until you actually analyze them for proof, they are just something you believe. How can it be any other way?

Einstein may have gotten his theory from trying to understand a problem with light, but he also had to believe what he came to discover was true before he proved it true mathematically. This is the normal belief state of the brain. Belief is entangled with faith. We need faith in our theory so we can start to take the theory seriously and assign brain networks to work out proofs. Once we prove to ourselves it fits all criteria, can it become a real theory. It must be falsifiable, or it cannot be tested without prejudice.

Relativity is falsifiable, but it has never failed any test so far. Then what? The quote above said it could never be proven true because it would mean it couldn't be refuted. This begs the question, is anything true? Evolution, relativity, and quantum mechanics cannot possibly be true?

At some point, then, they must become belief-knowledge all over again, but with more information known about them. They can never become truth-knowledge. If they can never be true, then they must always be believed. How is this helping science progress? Take a look at the two following quotes: one from the year 1768 and the other from the year 2011.

This is not less unphilosophical, than if one was to doubt of universal gravity, because philosophers have hitherto attempted in vain to account for it. If we mistake not the matter much, the contrary has always been the opinion of mankind, viz. that every well attested fact is to be believed, although we are ignorant.(Robert Whytt. 1768)

[Daniel] Gilbert proposed that understanding a statement must begin with an attempt to believe it: you must first know what the idea would mean if it were true. Only then can you decide whether or not to *unbelieve* it. The initial attempt to believe is an automatic operation of system 1, which involves the construction of the best possible interpretation of the situation. Even a nonsensical statement, Gilbert argues, will evoke initial belief. (Daniel Kahneman. 2011)

A God theory can never be proven as true, or it is not falsifiable, so God is out. Evolution, after this standard, can never be proven true, or it is not falsifiable, so evolution is out? You might retort this is different. I know the arguments quite well and it is not different. Both knowledge and faith are standard mental equipment in all humans, if not all higher animals, and both should be sought for and developed.

With all of these separate topics I have randomly covered, I should at least try to come up with a coherent story so you don't feel like I have wasted your time reading this book.

In this seemingly random chapter, we have explored some myths, scientific facts, storytelling, established agency in a few forms. We have touched on cognition, together-knowing, one-knowing, and looked at how information is passed along as narrative, starting with the oldest forms—that of mythos. We have indirectly examined how reliably and accurately repeated information was transformed in language under the powers of being sentient.

Myth, used with the proper meaning, represented an exercise in knowledge. Imagination is widely acclaimed to be the best tool for investigating nature, even now. Ritual has become somewhat religiously polluted, but still holds true to learning. Today, these same exercises are replaced with different words.

Thesis or theory, replaces mythos. Pragmatism replaces unproven, but nonetheless true, knowledge. Pragmatism works like faith, in that, one cannot prove it's true, but it works, is readily duplicated, and has value, so it is accepted as true. We declare the elements of earth, wind, fire, and water as myths of another time. In truth, these elements were well thought out treasures that hold—at least the theory—on to the reality of everything being made up of the elements of the periodic table of elements. Maybe we have something to learn from mythology after all! I believe mythology was the precursor of our knowledge-seeking nature. At least, I am willing to accept that as a real possibility.

As far as I know, Aristotle was the first person to undertake any experiment. Not his idea and I don't remember the name of the person who made the suggestion, which is not important. Aristotle took eggs from chickens and opened one up every day to record the development of the embryo at one-day intervals. He even tracked the yolk after the birth of the first chicken to note that some yolk remained after hatching. The yolk was inside the body of the chicken, of course. Most of his work besides this seems to be solely the product of brainpower.

Others, before Aristotle did his experiment, dissected men and poorly understood the working of inner man as a read of Plato's Timaeus soon makes clear. Many followed suit from time to time by dissecting animals and human remains to explore how bodies worked. Some very bad ideas were floated about. The heart was the main organ of thought. The soul sat within the penal gland. The brain caused hydraulic action within the fluid of nerves, which produced several movements.

Man did not give up! Slowly, we discovered animation is the nervation of neurons and nerves and the cause of bodily movement as well as thought processes within the brain. Germs were discovered as agents of disease. Cells were discovered, along with the true properties of sex. An egg gets fertilized by a sperm and they swap DNA to become a mixed product of both contributors. Indeed, man has come a long way!

All of these processes were developed on the backs of other thinkers and doers. More, they all evolved from a single point of a sequence of narrative that could be reliably and accurately repeated, which, to this day, has set the standards of science.

If you cannot have your work reliably and accurately reproduced, by an independent laboratory, then there is something wrong with your theory or experiment. I can't help but have some fun with this. Science has its main standard set by mythos, the one thing it detests above all.

This holds true of all that is physically known about the universe. Does it hold true for the stuff of thought?

We did have some stuff of thought thrown into this chapter and we now need to see if it can produce scientia from thin air. Psukhein is Greek and means to breathe. Psykhe (Greek), psyche in Latin, comes from the goddess of the soul, or to breathe life. It means to put the breath of life into body, making animation or soul. We get the words physical (to direct the physical) as well as physiology the study of bodily movement. We also get the word psychology, the study of the soul acting upon matter or the brain. All of these are terms that relate to the soul, or the mind of man. How can we acquire agency of action without giving control of matter over to the control of non-matter? How can we understand having an observer within our brain? It seems to be an impossible problem.

Chapter Six

De Psyche

The soul is the same in all living creatures, although the body of each is different.

— Hippocrates

To clear the air, we should first examine soul, spirit, mind, heart, and any other, so-called, extra entity. They are all basically analogous, or interchangeable, terms. You can substitute anyone for the other. Mind is generally used by science to connote the happy accident of feeling as if some extra force is in charge of your bodily functions. Spirituality is used by religious thinkers to account for this extra feeling of control.

The same application is made by the term soul. The soul is an extra dimension of control. Religiously, to account for both a soul and a spirit, levels are sometimes set up.

The spirit is what transcends the body. The soul is in direct correlation with the body. Spirit influences the soul, which then controls the flesh.

Heart is said to be the center of the matter, a composition of feelings and actions, a control over the flesh. They are all close to the same in principle and function.

Examined with empiricism gives close to the same result. The body is made up of cells, some of which have control—neurons with neurites. They are chemical/electrical motors. They are animated by doing chemical/electrical work. The work is that of soul—anima. The work of these motors causes the animation to take place.

In the brain, the free floating of information caused by acts of nervation feel like superimposed activity and can be classed as spiritual activity. This gives three levels. First, natural bodily function, caused by acts of enervation. Second, seemingly willful control of these acts of enervation over bodily function attributed to the work of the soul. Third, the thought process seen as activity in the spiritual nature.

Religiously, the same can be said: bodily function produced by the soul and spiritually observed and monitored gives three aspects for one totality of form. As I pointed out earlier, at least in Christian belief, we have a Trinity. Why three? When divining the soul, I will deal with three as it seems to be a needed criterion to fulfillment. Possibly, a minimum.

Since we feel like we are actual observers of mental events, our first task should be to start with an observer. If we don't keep an observer making observations throughout, then it is nigh unto impossible to create an observer later. We need to do this with a thought experiment using real processes evolving one at a time. Unfortunately, this thought experiment is a book in and of itself. For the purpose of this book, we must, instead, settle for a brief summation. We could accept a lot less complicated data until we get some mechanisms set up.

I am going to use single-celled organisms for my model. Four single-celled organisms to be exact. Three will receive numbers and one will receive letters and numbers. 1, 2, and 3 for the subject and A123 for the observer. I promise it won't be too hard to follow.

Single cells have a form of sensing, called chemical sensing. Single cells, due to chemical sensing "know" some form of data. They know chemical signals and differentiate them from food and enemy.

Is that all? They could know same, as in the same species. Since this is just an exercise in thought experimentation, we can add other single cells species as being indifferent. They are not enemy or food. This knowledge, correctly speaking, would be if-then in nature. If I chemically sense this, then I move toward it and consume it as food. Simple enough, right?

1 gets the pleasure of being responsible for food, 2 gets enemy, 3 gets same or other species. These are all the same genius of cells, including A123. A123 gets to watch 1, 2, and 3. If A123 sees 1 changing direction and moving faster, it still has no idea what is going on. A123 would have to set its knowledge base according to how the other cells are behaving. After observing 1's change of direction and moving faster, Cell A123 could then track cell 1 and fact check. 1 is consuming food. Soon, with observation, cell A123 would be able to guess, with a high accuracy, what each of the other cells are doing, thus represented as its collective.

Further, if cells 1, 2, and 3 were watching cell A123 to keep within the collective, they might accept it as a watchdog. If cell 2 were to take off fast in another direction, then cell A123 would follow as fast as possible to also avoid getting eaten—cell 2 is in predator watch. Cells 1, and 3 would survive best if they, too, followed A123. A survival collective would become set. Cell A123 would observe the other cells and the non-active cells would follow cell A123 whenever it followed any other active single cell.

Simple, right? The observer single cell would come to know, in an if-then manner, exactly what the collective knew separately. If cell 1 moved, then move with it and get fed. If cell 2 moved, then move with it and be spared as someone else's meal. If cell 3 moved, then it could be the same cell type present and we should join them.

Conversely, we should move somewhere else due to competition from other non-same cells. They will not hurt us, but they will consume our resources. Single cell 3 would have the effect of more complicated data—present, but indifferent—which could become beneficial in the future.

What does this teach us about an observer? That observers are part of the process all along. In multi-celled organisms, there would be no need for other cells to follow the observer cell, would there? If cell A123 were to move, then automatically, the entire multi-celled organism would move. That is if we maintain cell A123 as observer. However, there are many more cells to observe and this might create a problem. The more complex the organism, the more complications it faces. Sex becomes a factor as well as more complex enemies. One cell watching three cells just won't do. Maybe a system of cells watching cells might help.

What if cell A123 continued normal operations, but another observer cell was added. Call this other single cell B456 because it watches cells 4, 5, and 6, which perform different tasks than cells 1, 2, and 3. Furthermore, we could add single cell C789 to observe the different set of tasks for cells 7, 8, and 9. Wouldn't this leave us in the same state as cells 1, 2, and 3 without an observer? That is, without a collective? The addition of another observer would be needed, right? Let's call it observer cell 1ABC. It would observe cells A123, B456, and C789, performing if-then functions of their operations, based upon information from cells 1 through 9.

Are we starting to lose control yet? Don't panic! I will not take us into infinity with this. I also don't see the need to assign any special task to every number of cell and repeat the explanation of the first few paragraphs. We only need to accept that an observer has the advantage of leading the entire collective.

We never need to exceed three levels either. We can have hundreds of levels if we want, but we can accept a minimum of three. Workers watched by one observer, watched by a second observer. The second observer can move the organism based on watching the decided output of the first observers. 1ABC only needs to see the decisions that A123, B456, and C789 made, not the input from cells 1 thru 9. Cell 1ABC would be observing the act of sex, because it would be observing cell C789's decision to have sex, based on cell 9's information. Single cell 1ABC would be viewing what the entire organism is doing.

The bigger the organism, the more systems it needs, not higher levels of observation. By this, I mean, not two-hundred levels of observers, but the maintenance of three levels. Senses evolve and three-tiered levels would suffice for each sensing system separately. Vision would become a system; hearing, taste, smell, and touch would become their own systems as well.

One observer can watch the picture from the observation of subsystems watching stimuli. We have an observer with soul vision! Not yet. Each sense system would have three levels and a subconscious level would need to observe the sense levels along with another observer watching sub-consciousness. We can have a sense observer, of sense observer. We can have a system observer of system observer. We can have a total observer of total observer. All too long to explore here. All conclusions of a faithful phenotype. Confusing yet?

One could, of course, object to this scenario as being completely crazy, even as thought experiments go. Single-cells don't have eyes after all. They can't do what we have just explored. Let's look to biology and see if there is any evidence this could happen. This does have some bases in nature when considering single-celled organisms:

> Each Volvox is at liberty within its own envelope; but it projects protoplasmic extensions which pass through its cuticle and place it in communication with its neighbor. It is probable that these protoplasmic filaments act like so many telegraphic threads to establish a network of communication among all the individuals of the same colony; it is necessary, in fact, that these diminutive organisms be in communication with each other in order that their flagella may move in unison and that the entire colony may act as a unit and in obedience to a single impulse. (Alfred Binet)

If we are ever to understand how our brains work, we must first build a hypothesis, then look for evidence to even remotely support it. Since I have already dug up some evidence for you, I shall start with that. I will build the system up one layer at a time until we finally have some form of philosophical hypothesis, fact-based, to learn from.

It might be better here to examine what has been known for some time now. In the eighteenth century, Robert Whytt, in *experiments made with opium on animals*, removed the brains of frogs, stuck heated wire into the spinal column "destroying the marrow" of the frogs, then examined the heart. With and without opium, the hearts of these frogs still beat, albeit at a reduced rate.

- 148 -

We can conclude a few things from this information, assuming the information to be correct. First, removing the brain did nothing to affect the heart. Second, if the actual "marrow" was destroyed, it would mean that the central nervous system was also destroyed. Third, the heart still beats, erratically, on its own for hours, which means that, independent of a nervous system, hearts worked and favored life.

Do we need to be more sophisticated or accurate? For anatomy, maybe, but for the search of the soul, we do not. I might add here it is not known what or why in the development of the embryo the heart cells start beating on its own. We will make the assumption that when enough heart cells become amassed they automatically sync and start beating as one unit.

If you are like me, you must know how all of this stuff could possibly work. I can only speculate, but fear not, no one really knows the answer.

It would be an excellent idea to define knowledge before moving onto the heart processes. Knowledge is progressive, so we need a starting definition. The letter key "g" on my keyboard knows it is the letter g and not the letter z. Every time I hit that key, the same exact letter is produced. The keyboard is not conscious but it has this knowledge—yet, it has no soul.

The same applies to the body and every cell in the body. If we can reasonably accept this as our starting definition of knowledge, it will make our search easier.

We need not be surprised that a primitive heart worked and favored life, even if it did beat irregularly; the cells knew they beat, unconsciously. Some irregular blood movement and a supply of oxygen to the body is better than none at all. This is evident and comparable to the final stage of killing the nervous system—bone marrow—in the frog experiment.

Having some form of better control over the beating speed and steadiness would become the first improvement in the heart. A nervous system would do this, but a nervous system would need to learn how and when to work at different speeds and force. These are known as heart rate and blood pressure. To achieve a steady rate would be comparable to just removing the brain of the frog and leaving the nervous system intact. Take note: this only applies to a steady heart rate.

If you become scared, the nervous system or, rather, a small portion of it, must learn the best heart rate and blood pressure to supply the required oxygen to the body. If you become sexually aroused, a small portion of the nervous system must learn a different heart rate and blood pressure to meet your body's sexual needs. A different learning must happen to return your heart rate and blood pressure to normal.

Any nerve control over the heart would need to be learned by the nervous system. The nervous system has knowledge that heart cells beat and the beat rate can be changed, as per our definition of knowledge. Consciousness of the changes is a different mechanism best dealt with later. Much of the brain's mind can be learned from this template so I shall follow it to a more completed state.

If, say, one nerve was to provide a steady heartbeat by electric triggering, a control device is created. This is not hard to imagine as even plants create electric discharge in photosynthesis. It fits the criteria of a single cell in nerve form. There is knowledge present: if electric discharge, then contract; if no electric discharge, then do not contract. That is one! Do we need to act directly on the heart? Can we act on that one nerve instead? Finally, can we have three nerves acting on that one heart nerve? This is the same story we started with, only it involves action and observation. You can have three or more nerves acting on one nerve and you can have another nerve observing.

Add a nerve for sexual arousal, one for fleeing from an enemy and one for everyday function. Basically, this leaves three nerve cells to watch: the normal nerve cell, the sexual nerve cell and the flight from harm nerve cell. Stupid question time! Does the flight from harm heartbeat save you? As long as your heart beats faster, then you are not safe in and of itself? Other movements are required, namely your limbs. Yes, your heart nerves should be observed by other nerves and the above-mentioned thought experiment directly applies.

Adding an observing nerve gives an advantage to natural selection. Nerve A123 observes nerve 1 (the normal state) nerve 2 (the sexual state) and nerve 3 (the flight state) and learns what they know. Having another higher observer 1ABC is again needed for the following. Nerve A123 detects rapid heart rate nerve 2 and nerve 1ABC observes copulation from A123 and does nothing. If nerve 3 was the end result of the nerve A123 conclusion, the nerve would observe flight from enemy.

It would allow nerve A123 action, but it would also allow for other activations as well. Such as look for an escape route. If the escape route system was nerve B456, then having a nerve 1ABC observer of nerve A123, nerve B456, and nerve C789 could coordinate an escape strategy. I know this got as complicated as the first story. Lesson? Apparently, having an observer early on is quite valuable, even in an if-then state of affairs.

It would not take too much to envision a nervous system capable of performing many coordinated functions. The entire system is able to observe the state of every nerve combination within its makeup. This is called our anatomic nervous system. Every species of multi-celled animal has one. At no point in this system does consciousness, at the level of one-knowing, need to play any role, strictly if-then computation with an if-then observer.

The observations are all electric zaps of communication in an if-then state. Which nerve cell fired determines which stimuli fired it. Which state is fired and when it is fired is the bases of that knowledge with observation. This is, in every respect, a psyche of body described as physical in nature; a self-created action performed from chemically generated electromagnetic acts of nervation, monitored by receivers of the induced stimuli. If we get zapped, then you get zapped. Simple enough?

The critical reader might object for one simple reason: there is not any real way for the organism to see what is happening. We are, after all, talking about nerve states in a heart created to induce more oxygen to an exerted body. Let's inspect the senses then.

There are, reportedly, a few dozen senses depending on how you count them. Traditionally, six senses have been the standard in popular culture: sight, smell, taste, touch, hearing, and the extra unexplained so-called sixth sense. Science counts differently. Something like twenty. Maybe we can gain some scientific understanding if we look at the eye. Although what is said about the eye applies to other senses.

We cannot just say that the eye has a sense of sight without saying it also has a sense of site. The eye makeup is such that the cones and rods see different aspects of vision. Cones detect color and are responsible for visual acuity. Cones also reside in the center of the retina only. The rods are more abundant and seat themselves around the cones. Rods make up our peripheral vision, track movement and are used as night vision. They, basically, see in black and white, or rather detect lightness or darkness.

How many senses can we get from this? The sense of color, the sense of movement, the sense of brightness, the converse sense of absence of light, the sense of focus, or attention, and the sense of shape. They also have a sense of pain related to extreme brightness or physical trauma.

We can learn the most from the sense of movement and the sense of focus, or attention. Rods track movement very well. Where there is movement, there could be danger. Rods don't see very well. They will detect a sudden shadow coming over you or a sudden flash of light accurately enough. They will tell you where the movement is coming from.

These are all very important for survival. To tell what direction the movement is coming from with any amount of accuracy the cones must fly into action. As soon as the rods detect movement, the cones move to the point of origin. Cones see things accurately.

This is the same thing as saying that they focus a sighted object clearly with detail, rather naturally. Not to be confused with depth perception and focus of vision, which the eyes also have. Both systems together make an object clearly and accurately visible. The cones alone make an object appear as an intelligible object.

Investigated differently, rods detect the appearance of movement triggering the cones to move to where the rods located that movement. The cones then locate the object and acknowledge what the object is with clarity. Is this not the same thing as applying attention to something? Albeit, in an unassuming nature. We cannot assume anything was paying attention. It is kind of reminiscent of applying our conscious attention to a thought. We can safely say "attended object" at this point. It is now up to us to decide if this "attended" constitutes the state predecessor of conscious observation.

Once the attended object becomes clear by the movement of the eye, placing the cones at an advantage, then color, shape, texture and other mechanisms or senses are made use of. A picture can be formed. Knowledge can be retrieved from the picture—friend or foe—which results in an action taken.

To keep track of things better here, we must catch what happened. The rods detecting the movement, had to have been observed by the eye muscle controllers, the nerves. The nerves then activated the muscles and moved the cones into place. Something was observing the eyes sense of movement detection. How can anyone avoid this conclusion?

In the brain, there is always something watching something. In this case, a nerve observing a rod detecting a movement. It does not work quite this way, but it is a good starting point of our theory.

Back to the picture for a moment. Now each separate cone has a chance to form an image. Or at least part of the image so the construction of the image can become whole. This requires one nerve watching each cone. It also requires a nerve watching the nerves watching the cones. This observation nerve would construct the whole from the separate parts. The science backs this up, but I am trying to keep it simple enough for any non-scientist to understand.

The time duration of the cones compiling the information is small, but detectable. It is not instant!

I consider this to be level one anyway, and the act takes however long it takes. The time taken would become the attended time. The attended time would be the time the nerve took to compile the information as a whole. If the movement were nothing concerning urgent action, then the eye would move on. This would be the case in an if-then situation. There would be no, if-predator-then-flee action. No "conscious" involvement, yet. However, if the eyes could not make out what was present, then added time might become a factor. There is something there, but I can't make out what it is. The time duration would be lengthened. What do we call the ability to stay focused? Attention? Abilities are selectable. Selection drives evolution. Mechanics become controllable.

Compare this to some actual known facts about neurology:

Those results suggest that, when we hold an image in mind, our brain literally keeps it alive in the firing of neurons in the visual cortex, at a subthreshold level, ready to be reenacted by a pulse of stimulation. (Stanislas Dehaene).

This requires an additional state. One state being yes, there is something there. The second state being no, there is nothing there. The additional state being, uncertain there is anything there. We have three states: yes, no, and uncertain.

By default, uncertain would lead to a longer act of nervation. There is a means at the eye's disposal to aid the situation. The eye can bounce between the cones and rods in hopes of picking up the movement again and refocusing on it. If nothing is detected, then the nerve cell in charge can give a weakened no answer. However, due to the length of nervation and the weak conclusion, the nerve cell would become hypersensitive to reactivation of that movement. Longer acts of nervation would lead to longer acts of attended-ness, along with more sensitivity. So long as we carry with us an observer at every level, then an observer nerve cell will also be fired longer and become more sensitive. It would learn that the twitching eye movement was to detect movement and refocus it. It would also learn to remain slightly more sensitive to the uncertain stimuli.

Add to this, the fact we have more senses to call upon and the case gets stronger. If you happen to smell a strange odour at the same time as seeing the strange movement, then your smell sense dictates you check chemical signaling. If you smell something different, all of a sudden, you automatically, uncontrollably, inhale deeply. Everyone does this naturally. It is an automatic method to inhale more chemical so your smell sense can identify it. It is also a means of getting more oxygen to your body if you have been breathing shallowly for too long.

If the smell is obnoxious, your automatic response is to stop breathing. If the smell is pleasant then you might trigger a response to fill your lungs and take an extra deep breath. This would be the same response your eye gives: yes, or no. It also postulates an uncertain response like the eye, if you don't know what that smell is, your senses mark it as uncertain and continues checking. This applies to all your senses in accordance with their properties.

We are back to the uncertain chemical property of smell as the uncertain structure property of vision. If you carry a level higher observer at every stage, then we can see that both systems, in fact, every sense system, has input to this higher observer. The higher observer can look at the two level one observers and look for any overlapping information. You "uncertain" something visually. You "uncertain" something chemically. Surely, you can grant longer nervation to the observing nerve cell keeping it in an uncertain mode.

To keep the experiment moving swiftly, we can add another sense. Hearing is quite sensitive to location as well. They say it is accurate to within a degree or two. If you hear a strange noise and the sound is within a degree or two from where your vision rods spotted movement, then your observer neuron has three points of reference: smell, vision, and hearing.

Alone, none can draw an inference, but together they conclude "bear" and flee. True? No! There is no together without an observer making an observation. All three senses are worthless in this scenario if they are acting alone as no one sense alone has detected anything but "uncertain" and no action can be taken. One needs a nerve cell watching a nerve cell or more nerve cells in certain cases. The observer, only, has the right to say three-support-sources-together and not the separate parts.

This brings up a few more points of interest. It looks like it is back to our A123, 1ABC cells to re-examine something. If cell 1, cell, 2 and cell 3 are separate entities along with cell A123, the observer cell, then what does acting together give us? We already supposed a mutual "collective" would be advantageous.

They would survive better if they fashioned a collective. To fashion a collective would be to grant oneness to the collective. To get "I" from being a separate cell is not hard to do. I move separately from my surroundings, therefore I am. Now, all of a sudden, we have other cells involved and they, too, must become "I" collectively. The rule is if cell 1 acts, every cell acts. We established this above. If cell 1 moves and every cell moves, then cell one sees "I" collective movement. If cell 2 moves and every cell moves, then cell 2 sees "I" collective movement. Cell A123 also sees "I" collective movement. Cell 1ABC sees "I" collective movement, only it sees it as a higher observer.

We now have two things: an observer claiming "I" and an attended object. So, "I" becomes the attending component. Does this not grant agency? We have managed to grow this into, "The agent is attending to the stimuli. I am collectively watching for some movement. The length of time the observer attends to a stimulus becomes the span of attention applied. This, made evident by the prolonged nervation of "uncertain content".

Most readers, by now, would grant this to be the reason for agency of attention. I, the observer, am paying attention to the stimuli, while allowing for my brain, my body, and my soul, becoming the properties of the highest observer. Any highest observer in the brain can say, I am observing my other observers, thus my thoughts. I would only grant its place to be the predecessor for agency of attention. It is, after all, only if-then in nature and holds no consciousness.

Something is missing! One can add another product to the mix and make it more believable.

Free will

There has been much ado about if-then! It is made to seem as if there is never a choice given. I partially agree! If everything is if-then in nature—causal—then choice would never evolve as free will. However, there is a challenge we could make. If a single cell were to move until it hit a wall, then it could move no more. It would perish. Are there any other factors? It could reverse direction. It could move to the left or right along the wall. Or it could stay put and perish. If there was only one choice, then causation would dominate the automation of life.

Remaining with sight, we see a rabbit being chased by a lynx. There is a tree directly in front of the rabbit and it must go either left or right of the tree. If not, other factors interfere, then it is considered an indifferent choice. The rabbit will survive with either choice. Randomly, it could choose one direction over the other. So what?

Randomly, another choice could be made. It could also choose to gather more information to access the situation. This places more choices, thus more control over the choice. At some point, choice will have meaning.

We have an instinct called fight, flight or freeze response. It takes place in the amygdala. Here is a prime example of choice. We can say if-enemy-then-flee. We can also say if-enemy-then-fight. We can also say if-enemy-then-freeze. We must allow for if-than and not only if-then. It would be represented as if-then-than and responsible for choice. In the longer mathematical form, it would be if-this-then-fight-rather-than-flee-or-freeze. The starting point of free-will. Free will can now evolve into something.

To give you an example of how this works, think of this story, you are walking through the woods and come around a tree. Standing there is a grizzly bear. For many, their first instinct is to flee, some may fight the bear and others will drop and freeze. None of these thoughts are planned. The amygdala, which is, in essence, our reptilian brain, chooses the best course of action for the ultimate chance of survival.

This is a minimum assessment, which saves a mere few pages of detailed explanation involving other co-factors. They can be explained, if I had more space to allocate to this subject, but they only add to the concept of free will being a small percentage of free, unexplained by other interferences. Commonly, one to three percent of actual free, in free will, is accepted as viable. That is all I would ask to be claimed.

Add this context to the above context of observer and we have a closer picture of what is happening in our brains, which we consider to be a separate entity. I, the observer, am paying attention to the stimuli, while allowing for my brain, my body, my soul, and my choices, becoming the properties of the highest observer. Any highest observer in the brain can say: I am observing my other observers, thus my thoughts, with free will to apply over them. We are getting close to seeing a soul manifested through natural processes.

Not Relativity Again

Circa Galileo, minutes were divided into minute-minutes. One could say twenty minute-minutes after the minute. This would be twenty seconds past the minute mark. Possibly, seconds are a derivative of simplifying words. Instead of saying minute-minute, it could have been described as second minute, as opposed to the first minute. After use, the minute could have been dropped, leaving us with the single word of second, referring to the second minute division. It is defined as the second division of an hour. The first division being minutes. We further divide seconds into tenths, hundredths, and thousandths of a second. We even have nanoseconds.

We need to examine every possible threat to this observer of observer idea before we can permit ourselves to concede to it. An additional delinquent is the space-time relativity problem. Remember I used the factor of 10,000 divided into the speed of light to give the speed the Earth moves around the sun?

I further explained, that using the factor again gave us a relative conscious speed state of .003 of a second. The speed of time our brains see the world. The number does not need to be exact, it only needs to be faster than a second.

Based on Libet's work on the speed of neurological firing and conscious perception in the brain, we have a lag time for conscious perception and conscious action. This gives us the perception that we act consciously, when we, in fact, do not. Our brains automatically act and our consciousness steals the glory.

Assign the special features of space-time relativity into this conclusion and it conforms nicely. We move through time as well as through space. Space-time is not present-oriented; it is past-future oriented. How can we get a present sampling? Firing a synaptic gap is like taking a picture: it freezes time, but time still moves on. From above, we see that an act of attention fixes a moment in time in the neuron as stopped. The neuron "holds" activity while it attends to it. This act makes it present tense to the brain, thus humanity.

It produces the feeling that present tense has a quantity and quality. A second firing of the same scene would freeze that scene into a different frame of time. By default, the first timeframe would be in the greater past tense than the second timeframe. In an observer of an observer of an observer brain state, how would that look? It would all look past tense. How would we make it look future tense? How do we review the past? How long does present feel?

I had all this information written out and upon doing a first round edit, I decided to delete almost twenty pages from this chapter. Explaining it in detail was too long and too complex. Some of it dealt with the mathematics of nerves.

If you are interested in all of the how and whys, I recommend you read about these topics in a good book on biology. For our purpose, in this book, however, all we need to look at are these facts. Observation levels need to be dealt with as do time intervals. Let's start with levels. To start, we only needed to conclude small numbers of cells in three different levels of observation. There are billions of neurons in the brain. There are not billions of different concepts, so we can have many neurons for the same purpose. I will not number them, nor letter them. We can just accept this as true, which is the main stance with science.

Some cells specialize in memory. Pages could be written on memory here, but I deleted most of them and even those pages didn't delve into the topic completely since it is inexhaustible. We only need to consider that memory does exist in neurons. I wrote the first timeframe would be in the greater past tense than the second timeframe. Even short-term memory would do its accounting in sequential storage.

Take ten memory cells as frozen frames of time. Small numbers are easy to work with, although we have billions of these frozen frames in our lifetimes. Conceivably, we could have ten present state events stored in memory of a single, longer event. These would all be low-level cells. They can become ordered in space-time, by having an observer cell "hold" the order in which the events were recorded. To review the past in a past to future picture. Place a number on order. Cell 1 was the first to store, cell 2 was the second to store... if the observer cell wanted a replay, it could naturally fire the memory sequence 1, 2, 3... giving the event a time construct of past to future, but under current present state conditions of reflection. This would form memory recall in a space-time format. Space-time here, is understood to be past to future orientation of all time and movement in the universe.

There are more than two types of memory, just as there are more than five senses. Sequential memory and reflex memory are two types. I just described sequential memory. Sequential memory is the basis for short-term, or working memory, much needed for the selection of brain formation and function. As Aristotle noted in his work on memory, "Acts of recollection, as they occur in experience, are due to the fact that one movement has, by nature, another that succeeds it in regular order."

Long-term memory is more like habitual learning: this always happens the same way, with the same outcome— store it indefinitely. Once long-term memory becomes established, it can continue to work as an aspect of autobiography.

Once this space-time format is achieved, it does not take much to project into the future. Oh, this is happening again. Just like the last time it happened. How did that end? I predict it will happen the same way again. The order of things!

How long is present in our brains? To avoid the math in any great detail, we must estimate as timeframes.

It takes one timeframe to store data in one neuron as present. A second neuron would take the same timeframe.

This accounts for the several first-level observers. The second-level observers would take a longer timeframe to store this data because several lower level observers need to be recorded. Any third-level observer would require even more time to watch the events unfold as shown by the second-level observer, because several second-level observers would be involved, too. To shorten the time requirements, under normal conditions, the highest observer would only receive a summation of what happened. This fits well with the theories floating around in the scientific literature.

Let's look at some of the information available.

I don't have time to treat this topic concisely, but if we add memory, the problem diminishes. If the stimulus-observer takes snapshots in past, but ordered sequences as noted above, then the observer of the stimulus-observer only needs to remember the order of the stimulus events long enough to place the order in correct time orientation. This is known as short-term memory or working memory. It runs against the grain of some older thinking:

> Memory, as a vision into the past, offers less utility than reasoning; we have more frequent need to look before than behind; it is a kind of intellectual refinement to contemplate the things of the past as past, and without making them serve in the explanation of present facts. Therefore it seems to us probable that memory is not a primitive, but a superadded fact; it has sprung from reasoning at a time when the struggle for existence became less imperious. (Alfred Binet).

I say memory offers the same utility as reasoning. We don't need to understand every aspect of brain functioning here. We only need to understand what makes us feel like souls are needed. Memory is the main component of reasoning! If you have no memory at all, then how are you to reason events of any kind? Memory, then, must be primitive and not superadded. Structured memory must have become selected for a good reason. The effects of space-time relativity are as good a reason as any.

Once long-term memory is established, then one can look into one's future, based upon past predictions and plan. One moves their past event prophecies into future event prophecies accurately because space-time order is preserved. All animals have this capacity on greater or lesser scales, but with man, it has been expatiated to envision lifetimes.

Consider now, driving your car. A neuron fires yellow and, at close to the same time, your foot muscle neuron fires moving to brake. Does level three observer need to see why your foot is moving to the brake so it can take control? First observer sees yellow, knows it will be red soon from stored data—when you learned to drive.

First observer initiates foot and second-level observer sees I will need to stop at that light so I am applying the brake. The report the third level observer sees is future tense. I must be stopped in the future for this light because time will continue to move forward until I get there. Thus, after action is already taken, at about one-third of a second, conscious delay, your highest-level observer receives a report and takes action as if the action being taken was its own response to a future event. Does an observer of an observer of an observer fall apart here? Do we get future tense action in the present?

Two modes of thinking need to be clarified because I have, up until now, ignored them. The two modes do not affect the observer of an observer, or soul hypothesis under our current scrutiny. The two different modes are thinking fast and thinking slow.

Making thoughts slow can prolong them causing the sensation of a prolonged present tense. It allows us the

- 164 -

illusion of present tense, which last about a second or so depending on what actions the brain is caught up in. I am against the "illusion of mind" theory as I cannot reconcile needlessness in nature. I have attempted to show our mind is real, based upon an observer of an observer in real neurological terms—brain watching brain. When I say the illusion of present tense here, I am not using it as an unknown answer for an unknown function. You can't stop time! The best you can do is to slow it down and treat it as present. The treatment of applying attention and closely examining the content of a moment causes the illusion of present tense. Different!

Intuitively, one would think that making thoughts faster than they happen would freeze them long enough to keep the past/future event stable as we observe it. Physics can only make time relative not freeze it. There is already a lag time when the first neuron fires. You cannot even count to 75 within a second, let alone 75 thousand. The lights in your home (western) cycle at 60 times a second and you can't tell. 500 milliseconds are half a second. Around 300 milliseconds is where conscious thought starts to take effect and increases from there.

They are referred to as system 1, our fast mode of thinking and system 2, our slow mode of thinking. It would be too confusing to use these terms as we have already used the terms for brain systems of sensing. I will take the initiative and suggest type 1 and type 2 thinking.

A brain system can work at the faster speeds of type 1 thinking. Therefore, most of your thought process is done automatically by observer systems, type 1, and the results are reported to a higher observer type 2 system. That is, this type is slower and the systems within works slower, but still of the observer of observer nature. The observing system within the type 2 gets to work on a 75 millisecond firing time, in a 300 millisecond plus environment. I am thinking this would make it looked stopped or present tense and enable us to reflect upon it. Does this not resemble your "soul" or "mind" as we understand them to be?

My analytical skills are limited and I would not be able to build a higher system without getting lost. Imagine using terms like A(ABC1) (C789ABCC123) to describe the acts of all higher levels of observers. I cannot do it. Likely, some readers would close the book at this point as well.

We can follow along if we grant systems in the brain along with system observers. Systems would be like separate brain modules—the language module has already been postulated, for example. The language system would also use sight, smell, hearing and other sense inputs, which in and of themselves would also be systems. These systems would have observers watching the system data. They would be degraded to sub-conscious observers watching other sub-conscious observers watching data-observers. They would follow the same steps as our little cell friends only in systematic forms.

Sub-conscious systems would be reported to higher conscious ones and an additional observer can watch what the lower level observer system is viewing in knowledge form and represented shape form or even language form. We would actually be viewing the going-on within the brain. This would be the Cartesian theatre, with an observer watching the action. The additional if-than of choice control would also become established.

This is all due to the fact that a larger system can observe more data than the smaller nerve cell groups of senses. Observer systems can still attend with agency. By this time, it will have grown enough to become full attention of observer agent. It would include working memory and long-term memory, known as retention of observer. It would still be automatically done by the brain with the highest observer receiving a report.

Some readers will understand all of this and accept it without all the minute details I have been withholding. Possibly the best book I have ever read on neurology bequeaths us with this quote:

> For instance, a "shadow" expert decides that it can account for the dark zone of the image—but only if the light comes from the top left. A "lighting" expert agrees and, using this hypothesis, explains why the top parts of the objects are illuminated. A third expert then decides that, once these two effects are accounted for, the remaining image looks like a face, these exchanges continue until every bit of the image has received a tentative interpretation. (Stanislas Dehaene).

If you read this book, keeping observer of observer in mind, you would see how the details fit perfectly with what is known scientifically. I hasten to add that this is not the only book, paper, or article I have read on consciousness or the brain. Dehaene does, however, have a great conclusion on free will in the last few pages, which I hold to. These ideas have been forthcoming for years now, and it is worth looking at this quote as well:

> Perception is a form of activity which has a very variable nature, for by one of its extreme limits it encloses conscious reasoning, composed of three verbal propositions, and at the other end it becomes identified with the most elementary and automatic acts, such as reflexes. (Alfred Binet)

We see a face and recognize it—perception, cognitive memory, in the right hemisphere and retrieve a name (cognitive memory) from the left hemisphere, our language hemisphere, which are both introduced somewhere in our brain for our observer to consider. This should not be confused with split-personalities.

The first observer(s) act quickly and accurately, while the second level observer(s) act slowly and consciously, attaining an actual thinking process. The thinking is observed by the third level observer(s), where it too, can interact, pass judgement, veto an action, accept an outcome, or ignore the process altogether—our normal state. Think shadows on the cave of Plato's Republic. We rise one more level in psyche. We have already established nervation as the movement of body. Now we have established psyche as the knowledge of our movement.

Additionally, we can establish psyche as the viewer of our actions and knowledge. Resistance is futile, you will be assimilated. Call it one-knowing or self-knowing. This seems to fit both the psychology and physiology of being, but something is still missing! Full blown sentient or conscious being? The following chapter deals with this.

Connectome

As you know, I started this chapter with cells watching cells. Cells have no eyes, you object. I concede! Or do they? The connectome is how these cell: cell 1, cell 2, cell 3, cell A123, and cell 1ABC come to have vision and combine into a collective.

Neurites, genetics: dendrites, axons, and synapses; specifically, do act as eyes. They act as all our senses. There are over one hundred chemicals that can potentially signal to the brain. We have both electrical—firing of synaptic gaps—activity and chemical activity to consider in forming neuron activity. A chemical cocktail of information to include in the discussion. It also includes what we call hormones.

It is widely accepted as true that the last brain feature to evolve was the neocortex. It is this neocortex that makes us humans...human. Other mammals have a neocortex, too. Monkeys have a neocortex. If you follow the evolutionary tree, we are removed considerably. There is a marked difference between other brains with a neocortex and the human neocortex. The human neocortex is bushier due to many more dendrites, axons, and synaptic connections.

The connectome is the "cool kid" term for synaptic connections within the brain, partly guided by nurture as well as nature. The term, connectome, was coined in 2005 by Olaf Sporns et al.

The connectome has selection ability of nurture over nature. One could, and should, interpret this as learning ability over instinctual ability. It is how individual personalities are shaped by a few factors: other individuals, likes, or taste—stimulus you "apply attention" to over other available stimuli, as well as interpretation of environment. Extensions of genome and phenome, connectome would be the inclusion of a connectotype, phenotype, genotype or extended phenotype. Memotype and memenome could also be added in an unexpected way. Meme, being, Richard Dawkins most famous work, if the internet is any indication.

If this is actually evidence of higher thinking, which I believe it is, then logical knowledge or the ability to analyze information must be the connectome driving factor. This does not rule out genetics and mutations, but enhances them.

Think of it in the same way that raising cattle, which allows humans to drink milk, supported a mutation that allowed adults to ingest milk and process it for food. Lactose intolerance would have been our normal state before the mutation happened.

In fact, for a large chunk of the world population (75%), lactose intolerance is our normal state. This is due to the fact that only certain populations used cattle for dairy consumption at the time the mutation occurred. Again, in Western countries, namely North America, 90% of adults drink milk because the larger population came from European populations where the mutation originated.

It is not scientifically accepted that a mutation happened, which caused an instinct to arise for starting herds of goats and cows, which led to adult milk consumption. The evidence suggests the mutation was present, but non-active, or not triggered, until milk started being consumed. Why would the connectome be any different?

With the few pages I have devoted to this subject, I must examine it without minute details. I will do most of the examination after we explore what is known as critical threshold.

Critical threshold is the point where a process builds, without purpose, nor necessary use, until the critical point is reached where it becomes purposeful or useful. When I say purposeful or useful, I am not being literal. If it had no use, it would not happen at all. I really mean that the use changes state, set for another purpose or use. Zero, nay, minus zero degrees is the critical threshold for water turning into ice. Ice keeps your drinks cold on a hot summer's day, which is a completely different use.

Examine the connectome for its pre-state use and see if it can happen. Humans are completely defenceless when we compare ourselves to other animals. We have no claws, fangs, or superior strength. We have brains for defence. Monkeys, at least, can take to the trees. Both species have a neocortex.

Humans were forced to use our neocortex more than any other animal species. We had to learn how animals, our predators, hunted us so we could avoid them. We had to learn how to hunt for prey without the natural tools so we could eat. This requires, by default, more connections of brain cells as the brain learned to tap into the knowledge within the brain cells containing that knowledge.

This would lead to knowledge of knowledge being manipulated within the brain. There would also be a slow natural selection for bushier neocortex brain cells. The extra connections would lead to more knowledge being available to analyze, leading to yet more connections being formed.

To form the current meaning of connectome, nurture must enter the picture. Besides having instincts, humans learn from watching other humans interact with the surrounding environment. It is called an interaction instinct.

We learn from watching our parents, friends, teachers, and society. Some things come naturally as they are directly acquired by instinct. However, instinct can be short-circuited and rewired. We learn articulate language from our parents and others, which just might short-circuit our acquiring cries and calls of our natural protolanguage. Articulate language might be instinct based, but nurture altered. Language has the most powerful logical discernment capabilities of any other instinct in man.

According to some studies I have read, women have the lion's share! She, too, would have spent more time rearing offspring, thus raising larger connectomes.

I know this is a poorly treated theorem without too many details, but a conclusion can now be drawn. If the connectome began small, but was well used, it would grow in potential, thus, at some point, it will reach this critical threshold. It might only take one more act of understanding before it is breached, or changed states, into higher thinking, what we call sentient beings—homo sapiens sapiens, wisest of the wise, or human. I submit for your scrutiny that the connectome was the last, and most important brain feature to be selected for, not the more common neocortex. At least, in humans!

I need defense here! This is based on fact and not idle speculation. Fact: humans do have bushier connections in the neocortex. Fact: natural selection works to preserve instincts and traits. Why would selecting naturally, for a connectome, be any different? Is it different from memes being selected naturally? The brains with the ability to grow the most connections would survive better and their genes would pass on to the next generation just like any other trait.

I could add many more properties of being human. I would not be brazen enough to write this theorem of the soul if I had not considered, perhaps, a hundred such properties and counters. I can find none that cause this thinking to fall apart. They only add strength to it. I can't cover them all. I will recount the two conclusions so far and add this other information to it, forming three conclusions. The last two additions came from the faithful phenotype.

First definition:

I, the observer, am paying attention to the stimuli, while allowing for my brain, my body, and my soul, becoming the properties of the highest observer. Any highest observer in the brain can say, I am observing my other observers, thus my thoughts.

Second definition:

I, the observer, am paying attention to the stimuli, while allowing for my brain, my body, my soul, and my choices, becoming the properties of the highest observer. Any highest observer in the brain can say, I am observing my other observers, thus my thoughts, with free will, apply over them.

Final definition:

I, the observer, am paying attention to the stimuli, in a sequentially structured order, with the power of prophetic wisdom, and memory, while allowing for my brain, my body, my soul, my choices, and my autobiography, becoming the properties of the highest observer. Any highest observer in the brain can say: I am observing time structured events, produced by my other observers; my memories, thus my thoughts, with free will to apply over them, in a faithful, logical manner.

That is my final current definition. We could add other factors and conclude another one. I have added enough information to draw a conclusion. I could add many more details and factual information to this process, like love, which also falls under the spell of "I get it" undertaken next.

Love would, perhaps, be better undertaken in another work. I don't have space, nor would I allow it, as the topic is quite extensive.

If this does not convince science that a soul and spirit exist as a naturally selected brain condition, rather than a lucky accident or unexplained phenomena, nothing will. If this does not convince the religious that both, a soul and spirit can evolve and there is no need for divine intervention, or impartment of a soul, nothing will. Does this information fit with our actual development? The answer, in my mind, is yes.

Chapter Seven

Impartment of a Soul

Until the Cognitive Revolution, the doings of all human species belonged to the realm of biology, or, if you prefer, prehistory (I tend to avoid the term 'prehistory', because it wrongly implies that even before Cognitive Revolution, humans were in a category of their own).

—*Sapiens*, Yuval Noah Harari

Revelation carries more than one meaning. Reveille, wake up to. Revealed, as in uncover how something is done. Reveal, as in showing someone else how something is done. Revolution carries that connotation. It carries the notion of erudite, which is having a greater knowledge. We need to examine this erudite cognitive revolution in biological terms and "eureka moments".

This forces us to undertake the terms cognition, cognition of cognition, and cognition of cognition of cognition. In short, "I get that I get it." What if I told you that you can get that you get, that you get, that you get, that you get, and it really means nothing. The only thing it means is that you got something. You are just adding meaningless levels of I got it. The main reason is in kind, it is the same in kind and we need different in kind, not more of the same in kind.

Try this and see if it improves anything. I get that I can get it. Once you get that you have the ability to get something, a new door opens. "Can get" is different in kind. You can now apply this knowledge to everything. If I can get this, then I can get anything. As Aristotle would say, "Neither this quality nor that quality, but some other quality."

Everyone has heard someone making the following statements:

If you can do that, you can do anything! (Belief reasoning.)

If you can figure that out, you can figure anything out. (Logic reasoning.)

Respectively one of the statements is faith and the other is reason. Both attributes have a common denominator—ability—as depicted by the word can. "Getting" that you "can" is only one more "I get it" but it is a game changer. The fruition of wisdom! See, *Tilogos: A Treatise on the Origins and Evolution of Language* for more information.

Archimedes sat in his bath trying to solve a problem. As he sank deeper into the bath, he "noticed" that the water level rose as he sank. The volume of irregular objects was thus solved and, reportedly, he ran down the street naked screaming "Eureka!" What was Archimedes trying to do? Solve a problem! It takes knowing you can solve a problem before you waste time thinking about solving a problem. This is a result of I can get it, not I get it. While he was in the "can get it" mode of thought, he noticed the water level rose as he sank and the famed "eureka" moment arrived.

When the brain is primed with "can get", then it becomes heightened for attention to details. Archimedes, primed with "can get" and his "problem to be solved" was heightened for a solution. He was set up for a related trigger to the problem. The rise in water level became that trigger. His body displaced his irregular shape in the water. He could now measure the water displacement in a regular shaped container.

Apply this trigger to a previous chapter's emotional intelligence trigger of shame. If I "can" get my shame, then I "can" get your shame. This becoming obvious to you might lead you to the conclusion that the other person "can" get it, too.

This becomes together-self-knowing, where both parties make an acknowledgement of it. What I wrote in the last chapter applies here as a consequence. Together-knowing becomes an awareness known as the theory of mind. The mind is the same as soul, spirit, and our psyche. Self-knowing is knowing how you are agency, emotionally, as well as cognitively. Together-knowing is knowing another shares the same self-knowing agency, emotionally, as well as cognitively.

If you know another person's mind works the same as your mind, then you can suppose it to think what you are thinking. You can also learn to communicate ideas better, develop articulate language through the manipulation of your calls, cries, grunts and other noises. You can start to question things and analyze concepts, in short, you can begin the search for knowledge.

The basis being, if you can together-know, then you can together-learn and together-teach your offspring. This is what we call consciousness. Your observer understands that others have the same observer in kind. If you can place agency of "I" on yourself, then you can place agency of "I" on someone else as separate from you, but same in kind.

Oddly enough, we carry this "I", and "my", over to our many possessions, offspring, mates, and friends. We understand we can teach this "can get" ability to our children as well. They can also form agency and agent, with questioning abilities. Us versus them is a compound of the collective "I". I, my friends, my family, and my social members are a collective. Them, they are foreign and become everyone, but the "I" collective. This applies to religion, first, then pro-life versus pro-choice later.

Animals have curiosity as much as humans. Curiosity is also linked to our "can get" discussed above. Albeit, I did not include it as a factor in this dissertation. When talking about sentient beings, we must include levels because animals can "get" some things but not other things. Curiosity, when the critical threshold is reached, will build into investigating, thus asking "how" something is done. How something is done is different than "why" something is done.

Under natural processes, we have been able to convincingly establish that soul can be created from the selection of observers. Also, the soul is not an extra entity, or rather, it does not need to be an extra entity. Agency, both as cause, and agent of cause—I—have been tagging along as well. Some readers might say that this Imparted Soul at conception is debunked. We need to examine biology again and see if it passes that test as well. We need to see how becoming conscious ourselves promotes conscious in children.

When an animal develops in the uterus or egg, they don't start by growing a full complete skeleton, then growing muscle onto the bone, then grow nerves into the muscle, complete with the brain stem and nervous system. Everything grows together. Of note, the brain and nervous system does start sooner. In fact, the brainstem, nervous system and backbone are among the first to appear.

When an egg is fertilized, the very first thing that happens is that DNA orders the cells to start dividing into nothing more than other cells. If the embryo does not start to develop properly, then a mass of lifeless cells accumulates and a spontaneous abortion occurs. I have discussed this in greater detail later in the book. In the case of placental animals, the first real thing to start development is the placental attachment, by the orders of the DNA. The placenta is needed to support growth in the uterus. We will not concern ourselves with that process.

Once the cells start to multiply, a basic form is taken, which is the same in all species of embryos. It is called the primitive streak because even primitive animals started to form this way. At this primitive streak stage, the layout of the organism is set. This is the point in which it can be said a real lifeform exists. Before this point, there is no guarantee anything will develop.

This is one of the arguments around when life starts, which is an argument we will return to later. Once this point of primitive streak is reached in embryo construction, the nervous system layout and position of the head is located under DNA control, along with where the limbs and organs are to be located and cells start to differentiate. That is the sweetened condensed version.

Cell differentiation spreads throughout the embryo system and they develop systematically as the differentiation occurs. This means that bones, muscles, and nerves all grow into the embryo at the same time and rate. Every muscle as it is developing also has control of nervation growing at the same time.

Nervous system learning can and does take place during development. This is why chickens hatch fully developed and start scratching for food right away. The phenotype is complete, which includes instincts. All that is left is for the phenotype to mature into adulthood.

This, of course, is all guided by the genotype, or DNA during development. For this reason alone, we can safely accept the learning of instincts and the proper neurological wiring of nerve cells observing other nerve cells as postulated. That does not need to change! The instincts just need to be developed, or fine-tuned, after birth, or hatching.

This means cell learning occurs in-uterus, or shell. We can still say muscle control, heart rates for different circumstances, limb movement and such, along with the "instinctual knowledge" of those movements is learned in-uterus. For example, the rooting instinct, where if you brush the cheek of a baby, she will automatically turn her head toward the touch and try to suckle—a level of inner observation—is present at birth. One thing that is missing is the out-of-shell world presentation, but that gets learned quickly as there are pre-set triggers. This is fine for a newborn as they are being cared for.

Humans are helpless at birth. The reason is believed to be that human babies are born premature by several months. This is believed to be due to the head size versus birth canal size problem. To have a human infant in the same advanced state a chimpanzee infant is born would make gestation between 14 and 18 months. It would never be birthed!

> An upright gait required narrower hips, constricting the birth canal—and this just when babies' heads were getting bigger and bigger. Death in childbirth became a major hazard for human females. Women who gave birth earlier, when the infant's brain and head were still relatively small and supple, fared better and lived to have more children. Natural selection consequently favored earlier births. And, indeed, compared to other animals, humans are born

prematurely, when many of their vital systems are still under-developed. (Yuval Noah Harari)

Infant chimps can move around on their own at birth. This happens with humans around 10 months to a full year of age. Most of the human development can happen in the uterus, where both movement control and instincts are developed before being born. Not all human development can occur though. We can see this by the faces babies make. Their nervous system is still learning facial expressions, which would be already completed with a normal gestation period.

Everything about being human must be learned inside or outside of the uterus. This makes certain properties of development advantageous. Calls and cries, our communication system, would normally develop during gestation. Being born premature allows us to short-circuit this development. We speak to our babies in articulate speech, thus articulate knowledge forms. This allows our self-together-knowing to be learned at an early age.

Both of my daughters, my granddaughter, and every other child I have observed, have made the exact same mistakes with expression. Most notably, "I am too big," or "I am too small," when comparing their size to another size. As mentioned, brain relativity would place a holistic concept of size differences within the brain. The triggered holistic concept would be I am too size different! We articulate—make into smaller chunks—that holistic concept into too big or too small—and these must become learned in context by our children. Sometimes, they get it right; other times, they get it backward. It also starts them off with a special feature—thinking with articulation from an early age.

Another observation must take place here. Every child practices their complete spectrum of sound until mastered before they attempt to speak. This is likened to the facial expression, which needed to be learned outside the uterus. If they gestated longer, then they might be fully capable of making these sounds at birth, or, at least, every call and cry from whence they originated. There is no evidence for this evolution of calls and cries into articulation, but there is no evidence against this either. There is evidence for learning language:

> As mirror neurons seem to code actions, there is increasing evidence that they also code the meaning of the actions with the sound related to the action, and that increased experience reinforces the association of the acoustic signal to the action. (Namhee Lee et al).

The neocortex is where most conscious thought takes place. There is evidence available in the literature from the studies on the neocortex. It is known that the neocortex only assumes operation around six-months of age in children, at least, according to Cairns-Smith.

> It seems indeed that a small baby does all that touching baby stuff—kicking, sucking, gurgling, mewling and puking—without seriously engaging her neo-cortex. (A. G. Cairns-Smith)

For the most part, babies do everything on automatic pilot and survive quite well. The six months before babies start to use the neocortex suggests that the neocortex is still developing post gestation. This means the highest observer is not yet active.

Both of my daughters, and my granddaughter, along with every child I have had the pleasure of observing, perform this same act. When they are around the age of six-months-old and recognize something or someone familiar, they get a funny smile on their face and place one hand on their head. The hand placement, as far as I can remember, was in the same place: the right-side, just above the ear, the place where the brain stores faces. The most likely cause of this is that they are starting to have their, now mature, highest observer kicking into place. In turn, they "see" what the brain sees and it feels funny to them. They smile oddly, and place their hand where they "see" the lower level brain functions revealing their content.

These are three examples I have given of post gestation growth for things that would have developed in the uterus gestation period for many other species.

Assuming the highest form of observer defines humanness, we can safely compare it to the chicken. Now the child is complete and only needs to learn the environment at about the same level as the chick in maturity. True, even at six-months-old, they still lag behind the chick. They can't talk or walk yet, but mental form is almost complete. By one-year-old, mental form is becoming quite complete, comparable to a newly born chimp, monkey, or deer. The state they should be naturally born in. It is only after puberty, when the final adult brain starts to become manifested and studies are still determining the age our brain stops growing. The latest studies show how our brain changes right up to death. We only need to examine development until we are fully self-functional souls. It does, however, beg questions about the degeneration of the soul.

Walking is another oddity. I noticed many times before, but the light never clicked on. My final observation was only a close guess. I was familiar enough with the house, that after-the-fact coloration was possible. When my six-month-old granddaughter was just learning to walk, with help, not on her own, she would move her legs funny. Sometimes, placing her left leg across her right leg and forward. Sometimes, placing her right leg across her left leg and forward. At other times, she was placing her leg straight in front of her. When we walk, the latter is natural. We place one leg in front of the other.

It occurred to me, upon reflection, she was offsetting for the Earth's rotation when crossing one leg in front of the other. From memory, I tried to recreate her movement in that house, with reference of what was facing north. When she faced either north or south, it caused the crossing of legs. When faced either east or west, she put her leg straight out. Close, anyway. The brain must learn balance of rotation. Most animals are born ready to walk and run, but they are mostly four-footed.

This begs a question! If children only start to have the highest in-brain observer at six-months of age, is that the age they become fully human souls? The definition of soul being an extra observer in the brain that can interact— watch and have control—with the brain. Natural selection dictates this moment is when children become observers of observers.

This marks a special context. We short-circuit normal learning and replace it with our more advanced learning from birth forward. Babies don't grow up and, at some critical moment, cross that threshold, and become aware, then learn to de-articulate information and re-articulate it into some constructive articulated language and knowledge. They do it as they grow into adulthood. De-articulate, here, means to create smaller concepts from larger ones. Recall my use of "the hot of the hot is its hot" earlier. Sub-concepts allow temperature and energy, thus: the temperature of the heat is its energy. When do we claim fully formed souls? The age of majority? Before six months of age? After six months of age?

Sudden infant death syndrome—SIDS, or crib death— is when an infant stops breathing and does not restart its breathing automatically again. This, by the way, is a normal human trait. The prospect of this happening has a higher occurrence before 6 months of age. 90% of all SIDS deaths occurring before 6 months. 75% of those deaths occur before 4 months. This, too, begs a question. Does this soul not get imparted before six months of age because the child might die before then? Why would God waste an otherwise perfectly good soul? Blasphemy?

It also begs another question. If natural development can account for an observer of the Cartesian theatre in the brain, then why would an impartment of a soul even be needed?

This leaves us with the words of Aristotle:

> We have now determined in what sense fetations and semen have soul and in what sense they have not. They have soul *potentially*, but not in *actuality*.

I will introduce some of the concerns published in books I have read on embryonic stem cell research. If a soul is imparted at conception, and the egg becomes identical twins, does this mean two separate souls were imparted? What of the development of twins that stops mid-way and reforms into a single fetus? What of the eggs, that start to develop, then abort? Did God forget to impart a soul in those special cases? What about twins born sharing a single brain or other organs? Did God mess up? Perhaps a few quotes directly from one source:

> Let us examine more closely the presumed correlation among individual identity, soul, and unique genome. Three phenomena occurring within nature are relevant to assessing this correlation. The first is fetal wastage. Estimates of the number of naturally fertilized eggs that are flushed from the mother's body before they can adhere to the uterine wall range from 50 to 80

percent. Consider how many unique genomes depart for the woman's system! What is not known is whether the woman's body expels the fertilized ova or if they depart on their own accord.

Second, there is the phenomenon of twinning. In the early embryo, each cell is totipotent—that is, each cell can make not only any tissue in the body, it can also make an entire person. In the first few days, the agglomeration of the cells can divide into twins, quadruplets, octuplets, or in principle even into 16 individual embryos. All of these have the same genetic codes, even if they become separate individuals.

The third phenomenon within nature that challenges the Vatican association of an individual human person with a unique genome is chimerism. A chimera is a single individual with two or more genomes. Within the mother's body, *in vivo*, frequently two or more eggs develop simultaneously, each with its own amniotic sac, two babies will be born at the same time... However, something else can take place during the first few days of embryonic development. This pair of zygotes can combine to form a single embryo. If brought to term, the resulting baby is a chimera, a single person with two genetic codes. (Ted Peters et al)

These three related quotes were taken from *Sacred Cells?* by Ted Peters et al. They show that things are not as easy as one egg equals one soul. If a chimera results, does the one individual have two souls?

Oddly, the scriptures are clear here:

Male and female He created them; and blessed them, and called their name Adam, in the day they were created. Adam lived an hundred and thirty years and begat a son in his own likeness, after his image and called his name Seth. (Genesis 5:2-3)

Adam is the Hebrew name "man" indicating species type and in this case plural, not singular as in Adam, the first man. From this point, humans generated humans in his (a male) own image and likeness. If it was speaking of a daughter being born unto them, it would be "and begat a daughter in her own likeness, after her image and called her" It is treated in the plural because it takes two to multiply. Biblical fact! It does not say that Adam and Eve begat children in the image and likeness of God.

Science has a really big problem here! Refusal to accept that soul, or mind as it is called, exists as a real thing! The literature is combustible with this argument. The common theme now is that, somehow, the brain has tricked itself into thinking there is an observer with control. Like the useless steam coming from a steam engine's exhaust after doing the work of pushing on a piston, mind is considered the same type of a by-product. [unknown].

We just walked through a formulated context where an essential, interactive observer can become selected for with all the necessary components of psyche, which is not an illusion. Psyche taken as the power of movement causes movement of body, by means of nervation, naturally occurring in some cells, known as physiology. Psyche taken as movement also allows for the inner working of the brain and the high level of conscious access and perception. Psyche taken as movement also addresses the movement of ideas within the brain or psychology.

This makes the assessment of when a person is a person a different problem than an imparted soul. Can a fertilized egg be a living soul at any stage? One might say that, as per my own writing, this is true. I did, after all, start out with single cells observing one another. I did so as a means to make our model of understanding the need of observation relevant.

In that first case, every cell was independent and became a collective. In the case of the heart, I did make the act of controlled beating contingent on an act of nervation causing controlled animation of an organ—over and above random beating.

Understanding the development process helps make this clearer. Before the primitive streak appears, then no soul nature can be claimed, because the embryo has not committed itself to development yet. It could just become a mass of unorganized cells. Once it commits, then it is only a potential soul until it is born into the living and takes its first breath. We see that only when Adam started breathing—the breath of life—did he become a living soul in the book of Genesis.

After all, an observer needs something to observe and there is nothing to observe before said certain features begin to develop. The formation of the primitive streak is the starting point of the development of features, which will become animated by nervous acts. It forms a full fourteen days after conception—bilateral symmetry. I might add here it is a full six months in uterus gestation before the cortex develops. The neocortex is where all the highest soulful activity takes place. Not restricted to one brain location only.

Everyone concerning themselves with consciousness, either hold it to be a happy accident—the majority, I suppose, or impossible without something added. We see headlines like the following. *Materialism alone cannot explain the riddle of consciousness,* as posted on aeon, by Adam Frank:

> Some consciousness researchers see the hard problem as real but inherently unsolvable; others posit a range of options for its account. Those solutions include possibilities that overly project mind into matter. Consciousness might, for example, be an example of the emergence of a new entity in the Universe not contained in the laws of particles. There is also the more radical possibility that some rudimentary form of consciousness must be added to the list of things, such as mass or electric charge, that the world is built of. Regardless of the direction 'more' might take, the unresolved democracy of quantum interpretations means that our current understanding of matter alone is unlikely to explain the nature of mind. It seems just as likely that the opposite will be the case.

I have just shown, with biology alone, it is possible to explain the rise of consciousness, complete with an observer, using strict materialism. Due to space requirements, I limited the information to a minimum, but I give enough information to draw a strong conclusion of possibility, if not probability. Peer-reviewed articles are commonly accepted with "happy accident" referred as the cause. Many books, too!

If you accept my limited theory as true—it has not been peer-reviewed, nor scientifically verified—then the end conclusion will naturally follow. If you think this is wrong, then you must admit some other such way is possible, as there is more than one way to be alive, many more ways to be dead. If you are bent on the religious view, then you must admit a soul can be part of natural development. All views depicted conclude a soul does exist in a real manner. A soul can be selected for. It does not need to be a happy accident of other factors, nor does it need to be imparted at any stage of development. If the question was posed: did a living soul evolve, then you could opine no. If the question was posed: could a living soul be evolved, then the answer is yes.

People are scared to accept the soul and body as one, because it plays foul with their afterlife. How can they enter the afterlife without a separate entity? If an afterlife exists, then it exists somewhere other than the physical universe. It must account for its own entry product and entry system, has no bearing on physics, therefore does not affect reality, only an after-reality, making it the problem of this after-reality.

As I have pointed out in several contexts, we have place here for a level playing field. Suspending God from the argument, or admitting Him into the argument, has no bearing. Admitting God as I have shown does not affect the universe in any way.

As soon as the universe is started, it becomes self-sufficient and self-sustaining. It admits no necessity of control. God does not need to adjust levers, rotate knobs, or sprinkle pixie dust. This applies to physics as well as biology and psychology. All we are left looking for is the truth about this lifecycle of the universe and everything in it.

That is as level a playing field as you can get.

Chapter Eight

Clash of the Titans

Those who avoid the sin of intellectual sloth could be called "engaged." They are more alert, more intellectually active, less willing to be satisfied with superficially attractive answers, more skeptical about their intuitions.

— Daniel Kahneman

For reasons I have already pointed out in previous chapters, both faith and reason are needed. Faith and reason are the two biggest titans of what it means to be human. Why should there be a clash? True, sometimes the clash happens within us as we lay witness to something that differs from what we believe, such as an ugly fact. This is what it means to seek knowledge about our beliefs. We reconcile these differences within our brain and form new beliefs. This is acceptable when it comes to ourselves, our own beliefs, and our own knowledge.

How are you going to recognize the enemy if you don't know what the enemy looks like? It's easy for the religious to blame the sciences for its woes. Likewise, it is easy for the scientific community to claim all their hindrance problems on the religious. The real enemy here is not science or religion! Science is not perfect, not anywhere close, and it does not have all the answers.

Religion is also quite far from perfect and does not have all the answers. I suggest the lack of answers is the real enemy! Personally, I believe in both a deity and the theory of natural selection. If that stuns you, I will reply, in my defense, that there are a million reasons God would use evolution, and not one reason I could come up with not to use it. The Holy Catholic Church conceded to evolution under the sheer mass of overwhelming evidence.

So, I find it easy to listen to what both sides have to say, of course, with a grain of salt. Since I am writing this book with the greater intention for Christians and to some extent a few Christians feel that they have attained perfection. I must point out some of our faults that society picks up on.

It is Saturday, March 3rd, 2012. I was spending time on the internet and spotted an article on the MSN web page. The article was on a famous celebrity breastfeeding her baby in a public restaurant. I thought it might be a "critical review" and decided to click on it. On this web page, there was another link to a page dealing with breastfeeding in public. It was a story that dealt with one specific case involving religion. A woman, breastfeeding her baby in church was asked to leave, allegedly with the comment that it was as "indecent as a pole dancer in a strip club." Really? I must ask that one more time. Really?

We look at a double negative in scripture and we see that, "thou shall not, not give suckle" means that you shall only breastfeed your children. It's not only in the nature of all mammals, but under divine ordinance as well! With comments like the one this minister allegedly made, I am almost embarrassed to be a Christian! Really? Pole dancer at a strip club? How are you going to recognize the enemy if you don't know what the enemy looks like? If what this minister allegedly said is true, he should repent in ashes and sackcloth.

This does not mean religion is the sole problem either. Several comments made in the literature lately have suggested that religion is completely useless. Really? Religion completely useless?

We may have our faults, but for the most part, religion does "good" in the world. I won't make a long list, because it is outside the scope of this book but it is important to make note of some examples of that good. We've had a bishop's walk for the cure and raised money for cancer research. I saw one church was raising funds to buy goats to give to a poor nation. I even witnessed the Anglican Church passing a motion to be mindful and in support of clean drinking water. Not to forget the PWRDF, Primate's World Relief and Disaster Fund.

I could list many more, but I'll stop with these. Religion completely useless? Maybe science should do their equivalent of repenting in ashes and sackcloth for that statement as well.

Science has filled the planet with enough toxic chemicals, pollutants, and potential radiation to completely destroy it. In many cases, unwittingly driving the war machine of religious conflict as well as political conflict. Robert Oppenheimer, quoting from Bhagavad-Gita, laments, "Now I am become death, the destroyer of worlds," upon seeing the first nuclear explosion.

On the other hand, the scientific community has also done good through curing many diseases and creating incredible ways to simplify life. Apparently, both sides do some hideous evils along with some life-saving goods.

Again, how are you going to recognize the enemy if you don't know what the enemy looks like? The enemy is the evil that *both sides* do. The good that both sides do should overcome that enemy.

Nicholas Copernicus died before his life's work was placed under arrest by the Catholic Church. Bruno was burned at the stake for heresy, and Galileo was imprisoned for life after being forced to renounce the mobility of the Earth. I'll be damned, the Earth really does move! These things were done with the church standing on Aristotle, as well as the Bible, I hasten to add. The church carried the bible in one hand and Aristotle in the other.

Since the Enlightenment, religion, and science have been at odds, and not rightly so in all matters. Taking the two extremes of religious fanatics and atheist fanatics, who have the loudest voices. It is true we need both of these voices to push for better answers for the questions of our place in the universe.

At some point, we need to open our eyes and realize we have much in common; we share this Earth, and we want a better level of life. The Greeks were known for their search for knowledge. Abraham was credited with faith, which spawned three religions. From a Spiritual point of view, don't you think it's strange that God sent the Apostle Paul to Greece?

Who has not heard the saying that opposites attract? It is used to describe relationships that should not take place, or should not have taken place, because the individuals are so different. Well, when it comes to faith versus religion, opposites don't attract and this needs a closer look. This analogy is taken from magnets. Two south poles repel and two north poles repel. The two opposites: north, and south, attract.

The analogy is a poor one in my thinking. Nature does not have this problem because magnets never attain this form of *delinquent* behavior. Throw a bunch of magnets on the ground and they self-align. This is in their nature! Define opposite! In one magnet, there are no opposites of north and south because they are at different ends of the same magnet and the field is free to traverse the magnet. In two magnets, the opposites are two north poles or two south poles because the magnetic flux runs counter or out of magnetic alignment.

One cannot imply that the root cause of faith and reason not getting along, is that they are opposites. They are not opposites at all; they are just going against their self-alignment nature. It's like trying to force two north poles together. Let's say the north poles is belief that becomes the south poles' knowledge. Like this magnet, from another chapter, we have already observed that we need to believe something before we can begin to question it for knowledge.

Placing two different beliefs together would repel one another, much like south to south or north to north would. Trying to deny faith or belief creates the problem of placing knowledge head to head with knowledge and they repel. Reason has tried to create a magnet with two north poles and they conflict with the faiths knowledge in natural form. The church, on the other hand, took their faith as knowledge and created a magnet with two north poles as well. It would not matter what was said, they would repel.

If you will remember from history, both faith and reason were staples of the church. The entire problem with this is that the reason always had to indicate the hand of God. However, church reasoning was slow, in the face of facts, to accepting new ideas. A wrong? I would agree somewhat, but not completely. There is ridiculously fast, whereby huge mistakes can happen, then there are times when a slower, well-thought, thorough pace would be best used. There is ridiculously slow, whereby one is left in the position of catch up. The latter resembles the state of the early church.

Nicholas Copernicus's fact-based ideas, took over one-hundred years to catch up to, with the Newtonian system being accepted quickly. Copernicus was only really apologized to in the twentieth century. Charles Darwin's theory on origins of species, took over one-hundred years to catch up with. The former Pope John Paul II, October 23, 1996, declared evolution true and suggested that his millions of followers do the same. Now, that is slow!

The thing I want to point out here is that, if you cut a magnet in half, you have two separate magnets, which still behave the same. If we say the north pole of the magnet is knowledge and the south pole of the magnet is faith it can help us discern much. It's only when the magnets are then forced against nature, to become combined again, but with the like poles face to face with each other, that they repel.

Both the church and the Enlightenment were after the truth all along, but when it comes to factual thinking within the church, especially in the early days of the Enlightenment, faith got in the way. Only it was not really faith that got in the way, the knowledge being used, got in the way.

Two like magnetic poles were forced together. Aristotle's knowledge, which the church embraced, clashed with the Enlightenments' new knowledge system for reasoning. Because it was the church and religion, faith got blamed for the bigger error. Had both parties continued in the same direction, then, even though there was a break in the magnet, the magnet would have held together. If both faith and reason had their like pole of reason facing the same direction, and their like pole of faith facing in the same direction, there would never have been a problem to begin with. In fact, if you place two magnets together they form one stronger magnet and can do more work.

Oddly enough, it was Rene Descartes, who plagued thinking as much as Galileo. Descartes was the first to take thinking to a whole new level. He postulated that a mind was watching the inner actions of the brain, and is famed for the phrase *I think, therefore I am*. We currently call the Descartes mode of thinking, the Cartesian theatre.

The Cartesian theatre made a separate soul, abiding in the pineal gland, as a viable possibility. Aristotle's soul, on the other hand, was one and the same as the body. The war still rages on today of whether we have a soul or a mind, or whether the brain tricks the brain into thinking it has a mind to control. I did my very best to convince you that both Aristotle's and Descartes' postulations were correct. Only, not in the normal manner of conceiving them.

I would like to believe the point was taken here, but I don't think it ever will be. When we place things together the way they work best, you get the best results. Because you have strong faith in God and refuse to give up on a deity—a good thing—does this mean you're still required to believe the world is flat? The world can't move if God really exists? I don't think God considers a moving planet any opposition at all! Most importantly, God has never been the problem anyway. If religion is truly the problem, then religions hold the keys, singularly, to that honor, not God.

Even though the separation was claimed to have started at the Copernican revolution, science was still religiously driven through the nineteenth century in works such as inheritance by Gregor Mendel. Mendel and Darwin were close to the same period. It was not until Darwin and Wallace, when evolution was discovered, that things really fell apart. Even circa 1929, Pierre Teilhard de Chardin, a Jesuit priest, worked on Peking Man conforming to evolution.

Since that time, the church has conceded to evolution, with a few exceptions but they have not conceded to other facts, such as the virgin birth... The fight wages today. Why? Not because religion and science are not compatible, but because atheists have advanced their religion—the religion of no god—into the mix.

Some would claim it was science that brought about this conflict and not religion. The world is on the verge of human-caused utter destruction. We can no longer afford multi-religious conflicts, faith, and reason conflicts, nor political scientific conflicts. We must learn to live in peace, each seeking the betterment, not only of mankind, but the ecology of this planet as well.

I do have to have some faith in my arguments and I feel I have shown well enough that our God, or any other god, would require us to obtain all the knowledge possible. I do see someone picking up on the above argument and saying this might be true of knowledge, but not of faith. Whether the reasoning-minded people of the world want to admit it or not, they most certainly have faith; even if it is not in a god. At minimum, they have faith in their ability to discover real facts and use these real facts for the advancement of humanity or themselves.

It is again, only when these two opposite poles are forced together that they repel one another. When you bring the two greatest powers together, faith and reason, in relationships, which are against their very self-evolved nature there is bound to be a clash. Faith and reason were never naturally intended to oppose each other, but work together. They were naturally selected, one Darwinian step at a time; both producing a survival advantage.

In defending my own belief, I call natural selection God's modus operandi, and then I leave controlled design out of the modus. I can state evolution is true and even a soul can evolve, which I believe I have proven. I can also state I believe in a deity. One can believe in both faith and reason, without inner conflict. Why are we creating outer conflict? The short-sighted vision of science, where God must adjust knobs, or religion, where God must hold everything together, is both limited and flawed.

For those who still hold onto creation as God's modus operandi, I suggest he would never have created both faith and reason if both were not needed. Unless you apply an attribute of a combatant God—omniwarring—and this was his main venue of guaranteeing constant conflict. You would have to defend the fact that the Bible calls us to live in peace, which I don't have to contend with. The bible does say, "Study to show yourselves approved unto God, a workman who cannot be put to shame." I can hear some irate now saying, God created faith, the devil introduced knowledge.

I think it is high time for humanity to overcome their delinquent behaviour, realign their moral poles, and end this clash. It has become an all-or-nothing nightmare, which the world would be better off without!

Worse yet, it has become the filthiest of possible words: political, prejudiced, profane, and perverted, the four horses the horsemen of the apocalypse ride in on. It seems no one will settle for anything less than all or nothing. Why not take the best from faith and the best from reason? The biggest self-fulfilling prophecy is to not do something because you lack the knowledge.

One all-or-nothing problem we see on the regular basis. Every time there is a meeting or event about stem cell research—embryonic or otherwise—going on, we see the pro-life advocates holding anti-abortion signs. What does the study of stem cells have to do with abortion? What do you mean by pro-life? I can feel your heart rate elevate already. First, we must take time to consider life and dignity.

Chapter Nine

Goodbye Cruel World!

*The general (as I believe) contempt at suicide
(even when no relatives left to lament) is owing to
the feeling that the instinct of self-preservation is
disobeyed.*

—Charles Darwin

Due to complications, later in this work, I must examine, closely, euthanasia or what is considered suicide. I cannot bring myself to be as open as I probably should be for several reasons.

One, others might be directly, or indirectly, involved and it is not for me to make public another person's life. Two, I think everyone would agree that some things are better left in one's own brain where they truly belong. Three, which is another strong consideration, is the effect it will have on loved ones reading this.

I think that, for me, opening up a little will impart a feeling unto the reader, which must be obtained, at least in part, for the consideration and justification of mercy killing. This will lend itself well when considering the abortion issue and the right to die.

Before entering darker areas, I must first make a distinct clarification. I am the sole reason for my own life's choices. Every "yes" decision that was made, was made by me alone. Every "no" decision that was made, was made by me alone. If I am in a mess, it is because of my own defective discernment prowess!

I was sitting in my psychologist's office, during a session of marriage counselling, when I told her about the previous night's incident. I was driving home, on a country road, when a deer ran out of the woods and brushed against my car fender. I did not even so much as skip a heartbeat, neither during nor after the incident. I felt no surprise or fear, whatsoever.

She, my psychologist, then asked me if I was willing to take the depression test. I must have aced the test, because she offered me a free night stay at a five-star hospital for observation, meals included. I declined!

I was diagnosed with severe depression. She advised me to see my doctor, get a referral to a psychiatrist, and go on medication. I knew I was depressed, but I did not know how bad it was.

The simple fact was that, at that moment, I was not ready to be official about it until that day of agreement. She saw me once a week for a long time and I underwent much pain. It would be almost three years before I finally got a physiatrist assigned to me due to the delay in medical systems in Canada.

Several medications were tried and failed. My marriage came to an end, at my insistence, right or wrong. Since that time, much has changed and I am still seeing my psychologist on regular intervals. I might be for life! I feel bad for her! After all, she must deal with me.

Digging a little deeper into my case will reveal some state that my mind is in, but I will exclude anything relating to how I got there. My depression started out with a somewhat normal brain state—I have been tested on other levels and I am not bipolar, attention deficit hyperactivity disorder (ADHD) or any other notable labels for mental health problems. My friends might argue with these diagnoses and state there is definitely something wrong up there! Hell, if two physiatrists say I am normal, but depressed, I am running with that! Sorry! My brain tends to wander in its dark musings! Back to the story.

As this does relate to mental states of brain and brain function, I must, at least, touch on them, even though there are few, if any, scientific articles I can refer you to read. At some point, I began to shut off emotional inputs. I give this the greater power over my loss of fear as noted in the deer incident above. Every time an emotion would arise within me, I would do my best to purposefully stop it from taking control. This was my doing, directly, no matter where or from whom the stimuli came.

There is no complete theory on wiring the brain by purposely ignoring stimuli. I am not a professional physiatrist or psychologist, by any means, but I was interested enough in these topics at the time to pay close attention to what my brain was doing inside of my skull. I can describe them in no other way!

On a conscious level, I was purposefully wiring my brain to ignore emotions, which I considered dangerous to my wellbeing at the time. Empathy being a huge danger here. If I put myself in another person's place and felt their hurt, I would change my mind, and back down on this issue! (The book: *The Brain That Changes Itself*, Norman Doidge, M.D. lends some support).

My thought pattern was: this issue is causing pain! My pain! I want this pain to stop! Block that empathy! After a couple of years, tears no longer worked on me! I used to have a feeling of butterflies in my stomach on my way home from work. Almost as if I was running into trouble, possibly anxiety.

There was not always trouble, mind you, but that did not matter. There were almost always butterflies! I had a hard time shutting these off, but I was successful in the end. This was probably helpful in discouraging my fear as well. Whether science backs this notion with data is not a major concern at this point. What is a major concern here is that, even today, I can't seem to actually feel emotions like I used to. Cognitive function has not been altered. I still know that tears mean hurt feelings!

I allowed pain to become my guiding light as pain was the only real emotion that seemed to be looking out for my wellbeing. The pain was telling me I would not survive until I made a change in my life. That is backed by science; *Listening to Depression* by Lara Honos-Webb. I did not even know what changes I needed to make to change my direction. I made the changes anyway! Some of these changes included controlling more emotions. I also found myself with the unrelenting need to be left alone to cope. At one point, I was ordering myself to go to the hospital before I killed myself. I could not stop crying! I could not stop the pain!

I am currently completely off any medications and rely solely on intellectual cognition without what could be termed as emotional cognition. This does not mean I don't know right from wrong! I also know moral from immoral. The difference is I must cognize without feeling them emotionally. I have resigned myself to being in this state for the rest of my life. I function without the joy of function. Who should tell me that I must continue living because I can, without the joy of life?

My outlook has become rather dark! I see happy shit on social media and must make my inner comments. I read something pertaining to choosing life through hard times, or even God knows and has planned a way out, and make the following inner comment, "Yeah, live through this pain so you can get even more pain later." Then I find it funny and laugh! Sometimes uncontrollable laughter!

It is not always outwardly noticeable that I am severely depressed! I am learning control! The old saying, never put off until tomorrow what you can do today has become one of my favorite lines; put it off until tomorrow—I might be dead by then and won't have to do it at all.

I might as well go deeper. These are the statistics for 2002. There were 873,000 reported suicides in 2002 worldwide. This number does not contain the attempted suicides. We should examine the attempts as well, even if there are no statistics available. We should also include suicidal thoughts that are not followed through with. The biggest deterrent to suicide might be pain! Think of worse things! No, not hell!

The worst thought, you ask? What if cutting your wrist, ended not with death, but the loss of your arm? Think about hanging yourself. What if you break your neck, end up paralyzed, but still live? What if while hanging yourself, suffocation leads to brain damage, but not death. You could be fully cognitive, forced to continue living, having well-meaning people visit you with nonstop idle chatter, which you could not even respond to, nor stop from happening.

There you'd be, paralyzed, unable to even speak, helpless against assault. Your friends, family, ministers, and specialists will gather together to tell you how lucky you are to be alive. Thank God for His mighty power as He has spared your life through grace and mercy. You could think, but not begin to communicate, that had God held mercy for you, he would have allowed you to die and be with Him in peace.

The main reason your gatherers would expound this is that they are looking at life through rose-colored glasses.

You are better to be alive in your pain, than dead and void of all feeling. You would see things through much darker glasses: I can't stand this pain any longer, please, someone, kill me! Unhook my life support! Should rose-colored glasses be judging yours or my right to die? Perhaps, the dead should bury their own dead.

Jesus said he came to bring life more abundantly, not less abundantly. Life is more than a beating heart and expanding lungs. If you have limits on joy, you are not living abundantly.

Since I am Christian, what about religious counselling? Great, have someone, whom you would otherwise respect, sit there telling you that God will not give us more than we can handle? If you have these problems, then God knows you can handle them! What about the people who do succeed in killing themselves? God did not know he was giving them too much pain to endure? Maybe, just maybe, God wanted them to be with Him and suicide was their time and way to go.

Maybe it was the devil's way of taking them to hell? They did, after all, take a life—their own. As a biblical fact, there is no mention of suicide ending in hell. Unless I missed it in four complete readings from cover to cover. How many attempted suicides in 2002 ended with the victim being made worse off? How many people suffer such thoughts, without attempting suicide?

I did say I was only sharing a small portion of my life. Good-times are not considered here, but other factors must be added. I will enter back into my depression toward the end of this chapter. Now, I must add other matters to this mess.

I previously wrote a book, and I was in the process of selling it. I sent it out for reviews and a contest, receiving some good reviews, and a Finalist Award. I was promoting it and it just started to sell some small amounts. My, then, "vanity" publisher was continuously contacting me with more promotions—more money spent. I decided to lose them and go full self-published. I did! Just in time to lose everything I gained.

I just published it under Idein Publishing and received that phone call. My stepmother had stage four cancer. I was the closest one to take care of her so I did. Some nights I would return from the hospital in time to get ready to go to work. My books, and writing was halted. Including other things I had in the works.

Her estate was in a poor condition when she passed away. I had to step up and care for the property until the executor of the estate was contacted, and worse, entered Canada from another country. My funds were strained until I was finally reimbursed almost a year later. The same year I received the bad news that my father-in-law had cancer. He passed away in the same calendar year as my stepmother, making it the third person close to me who succumbed to cancer. At least I was heavily medicated at the time.

I had just switched to a different medication and it was killing me physically. I had to take sleeping pills to offset some of my medication problems in general. I doubled the sleeping pills with this medication. The problem was that these medications made me tense. I woke up one night, my arms sore from squeezing my pillow too tightly. I'd held it like one would hold a fifty-pound sack of potatoes.

Another night I woke with a crack-sound, and found a piece of broken tooth in my mouth. My body could not relax at all. After spending hard earned money fixing that tooth, I cracked a piece off another one.

Add, to this, one more problem. I have a hard time when I hear people complain about being too short. I wish I were taller! Trust me when I say this. Be thankful you are not. I stand six-foot-four inches in height. My biggest curse in life! It might have been different if I had another occupation. When I am not writing, I am an automotive technician. Car hoists are built for people who are not over six feet tall. Imagine standing, sometimes for hours, under a ceiling that is six inches lower than your head.

The doctors have not come right out and said it, but my physiotherapist did. Not in this much detail. I must guess somewhat here. Being too tall for my work was stated. How I became an invalid overnight was not. Remember how I just wrote that I was unable to relax at all? Imagine this thought experiment.

You are bent out of shape all day while standing under a short ceiling—the floor of the car while you work on it. Normally, when one sleeps, one relaxes and your vertebrate disc decompress. When one cannot relax, this decompression does not take place and your vertebrate disc tend to remain bulged. Serotonin makes the brain happy, but it also gets used in muscle control. It smooths muscle movement and control. If you are always tense—activated nerves—then serotonin might allow higher activation of these nerve induced muscles. I was not decompressing, I suspect, and I started to suffer a shooting pain in my right arm.

Also, at that time, I started to cut my arms—work injuries—and not notice any pain. The outside of my right arm was numb. I used to walk 5km every day, but had to stop as my arm would have pins and needles up to my elbow.

Finally, one exhausting day, I hastened to throw out all my medications. Even my sleeping pills. I was to the point where I couldn't function. Mistakes happening at work included. It was several days with even worse sleep before I recovered the ability to sleep unaided. The tension persisted and I finally went to the hospital for help. I was referred to a neurologist for testing. He sent me for an MRI after determining I had carpel tunnel in both wrists, similar problems with my elbows and possible neck problems. I was sent for physiotherapy to correct for bulged discs in my neck.

While I was being treated for my neck, my right shoulder started to hurt; worsening with every visit. The therapist stopped treating me because I was getting worse. I was referred to another specialist for my right shoulder. I don't think he liked my answer when asked how I hurt my shoulder and I said it had started during my physiotherapy treatment. He insisted that I must have injured it.

The new specialist gave me two more shots of hormone in my shoulder and said I would not need surgery. It did nothing to fix the pain. I was referred for another MRI and a neurosurgeon. By January that year, I could not even lift my arm. The pain was keeping me awake! I went on sick leave. There were problems with that, too, but I will avoid the details.

Finally, I was called in to see the neurosurgeon. He started to pass it off as normal wear and tear until I told him I'd seen the results from the first MRI. He then said there was nothing they can do for me. "Science has not progressed to the point where we can replace your entire neck" or very close to that statement. He concluded by telling me traction would benefit me—in other words, physiotherapy again.

After a few more weeks, I received the MRI on my shoulder. Seven problems in total, but who is counting. I saw my doctor and was sent to a specialist in physiotherapy. She was the one who diagnosed me with frozen shoulder syndrome. She treated me for months and I am finally back to work now. She also treated my neck. Her words "It is like a brick wall." This is not her fault; of that I am sure. While she was treating me, my vertebrate began to hurt. Maybe, this was due to these damaged discs starting to move. Or maybe it is arthritis. I was never formally told. I continued to do the exercises and stretching, even in pain.

My neck, my whole back—vertebrate—still hurt even now. The pain might never depart. My shoulder has become a lot better. I wake up in pain most nights and must reposition myself carefully to relieve the back and neck pain. I had to stop doing most of the exercises as I was working again and spend most of my day with pain. At least I can feel my arm now, and the shooting pain is gone, unless I overwork myself. When I do, the shooting pain returns. This, too, might be my permanent condition. Not bad! Severe depression and always in physical pain.

One more kick should be enough to conclude. I was on sick leave and due to complications, the insurance did not pay for my medical treatment. Not only was I earning half my income, but I was spending $200.00 a week in physiotherapy so I could return to work. I had my entire savings budget wiped out and became quite broke. I am sure I lost a lot of possibilities for my planned future in writing. For instance, this book was supposed to be edited and published by 2014. It is now 2016, and I have just started editing it, now being pushed into 2017. I must start all over again from nothing and I must do it while depressed and in physical pain.

It was only a dark joke, but I think I meant it. One of my coworkers, and friend, made a comment about being careful so I don't end up dead. My reply was, "Why worry about being killed, think about it: no one bugging you; not having to get up in the mornings; a peaceful night's sleep; no more pain; no more working; it does not sound all that bad to me. Why is everyone so scared of death?" He made jest of it! I thought about it! What sounds so bad about death?

This brings me to what does sound bad about death. Your loved ones will suffer! What you are trying to tell me, then, is that your suffering is less important than that of your loved ones? True, I hate to make my loved ones suffer needlessly, but death will consume me one day.

How much suffering is wrong for me to live through, just to make it right for you? When do I have the right to say I have lived in pain long enough and want to die with dignity and peace? How much real joy can you get from interacting with another person, knowing that they are suffering being alive, just to make you happier? To what extent should you be responsible for someone else's happiness? Or misery?

Imagine you have just had your first baby. There are complications and a dire result. Your first born is now dying and in severe pain. So much pain that the doctors mercifully keep her drug induced. She has five days to live. You could sign papers allowing immediate termination of her life, thus ending her five-day pain-filled life. Besides crying your heart out, what would you do? She can't answer for herself, so what do you do? Do you have mercy on her or greedily cram in the most of her first and last five days? I hope you never have to answer these questions!

What about knowing you are pregnant and the fetus is not going to survive? Do you intervene and end the process? Some would say let nature takes its course. We have no right to interfere with natural processes?

The purpose of writing this painful chapter is not to elicit your sympathy for me—please send money! Thank you! The real purpose is to expose a higher reality. Paper money, not chump change! This desperately requires the examination of pain and empathy.

If I tied you up and cut off your foot with a saw, while you were fully conscious, would it hurt? If you tied me up and cut off my foot with a saw, would it hurt? Would your hurt be less painful than my hurt? Would your pain be different than my pain?

In almost every source on psychology I have read, there is a common theme, including the above-mentioned book, *Listening to Depression*. Only you can know your hurt and the pain you feel. No one else can understand what you are going through emotionally. Obliviously, this is wrong!

Is physical pain different than emotional pain? We both feel the same when having our feet cut off, but we don't feel the same having our hearts broken? Yes, yes we do! The only difference is that someone else broke your heart, not mine. Relate this to you having your foot cut off with a saw, while mine was cut off with another instrument for cutting.

The problem is not of kind, but of "Whom". We consider our uniqueness to never transpose (projection or transference) to anyone else. Except in the case of some personality disorders, where you transpose your thoughts to another person, making them the problem and not you. An example being, when someone says, you know how you are always talking about forgiveness. You say to yourself, I almost never talk about forgiveness, but let them continue talking. They are, in fact, transposing their need for continued forgiveness in their continued transgression, so they feel justified in transgressing. They make you think you are always talking about forgiveness, their need, so they seem innocent.

You can never understand how I feel is our inability to transpose our hurt onto another person's ability to hurt. It does exist and we should be able to force ourselves to transpose. This is what I am asking. If our abilities to transpose us onto someone else exists, then we can transpose someone else's unto us. Someone might say that empathy is what I mean to say, but empathy is slightly different. Empathy recognizes pain, where transposing extends it further and under different set circumstances. "What I feel to be good—is good. What I feel to be bad—is bad," Jean-Jacques Rousseau.

Jesus was not a Christian. He was of Jewish descent, anointed of God, for the purpose of forgiveness and healing. To be a Christian, one must share in the anointing. Christ, meaning oil—like Crisco oil—meant to be infused with. Christian denotes sharing in the infusion. How can the anointed share in an anointing if he is the source?

Commonly, the church realizes this fact and extends it to suffering—we must suffer as Christ did. This is advantageous! Occasionally, the church professes we must emulate the anointing of forgiveness and healing. It is not certain how far that emulation reaches in holistic terms.

Remember, from above, the Westboro Baptist Church, and the "God Hates Fagots" sign—forgetting God hates hatred! Where did the suffering come from? He took our nature upon himself so we would no longer be under that yoke. Seldom do we ever take another's suffering upon ourselves—transpose it, and offer them mercy, forgiveness, and healing.

Transposing is not, nor could it ever be a cure. One can only sample. Take your worst day into mind, extend it to a continuing nature, transpose that onto how someone else feels. They feel my worst daily, hourly, every second of the day. The emotionally depressed cannot transpose their best day unto themselves and create happy continuity.

One of the best things to happen in recent medical history is the right to death, known as assisted suicide. This is not legal in every country but has recently become legal in Canada.

First, attempted suicide is not always a cry for help. They could just be failed attempts. Secondly, making euthanasia easier prevents one from making their abominable suffering worse, in case of failure. Neither of these deals with the suicide inducement of internet bullies, the lowest feeding maggots on society.

Fine, if you are alone and dying anyway, or in the case of depression, already dead inside. What if you must decide this for someone else?

The propose of this chapter. What if you need to make this decision for the unborn? Unless you are looking through rose-colored glasses, tinted with the luck of never feeling pain, physically or mentally, then you can do this. If you can't transpose the pain, then try to cognize the pain. Please learn to transpose! This brings us to dignity and a quote:

> The major argument for doing embryo research is that it promises to reduce human suffering and promote well-being. The major argument against using embryos for research is that they have the moral status of persons and thus should not be destroyed, no matter how great the human benefit. (Erik Parens)

For the reader's information, whether it is true—de facto— or just an illusion of the truth, the two forms of souls have been argued since the times of Plato and Aristotle: both these writers argued the views of former philosophers. Plato's view was that the soul was separate and Aristotle's view was that the soul was the total product of man, inseparable.

To show the bantering throughout history, one only needs to read St. Augustus or other writings all the way down to Pope Benedict XVI (Joseph Ratzinger) to see the swaying back and forth. The swaying is whether the body-soul is dualism or one and the same. The implications are important—the most important—in considering whether any stage of life has a soul, in what form, and whether a soul means that the dead body left behind is sacred, and, therefore, has dignity.

My belief is every human, no matter what the stage of development has dignity. Dignity, on the other hand, has nothing to do with the stem cell issue, in my opinion, and is a smoke screen. My whole body has dignity, and by consequence so does the separate parts of it. If my kidney is too dignified to donate upon my death to save another's life, then it is too dignified to rot in the ground, becoming food for the worms. Smokescreen! Plain and simple! You think granting dignity onto any stage of life will prevent its decay? Call it royal dignity if it pleases you and see if it escapes decay. Smokescreen!

On the other hand, any stage of life does deserve respect and dignity, and to this end should never become experimented on whereby it suffers, or become transformed into other entities against its nature. To create stem cells for the purpose of saving lives does neither. To the extreme, mutating these cells to grow cancers—which are natural to man—to learn how they work, could not be considered experimented on unless they were grown upon a viable fetus. Once "anima" does not take place, they are simply cells lost of their potential to become life.

Where is the moral status of persons—human dignity— in suffering? To the contrary, it is morally indignant to allow human suffering to go on. True, to destroy a human embryo is wrong, but these are human embryos, which will not become living souls. This will be taken up in the following chapters.

I must make another observation here.

The religious seek to impart the will of God, implement the saving of your soul by giving yourself unto God, accept your pain as needed, and live a destitute life in the pleasure of knowing it serves God, kinships, and society.

The scientific seek to impart you with good feelings by filling you with hormones: serotonin, serotonin reuptake inhibitors, dopamine, convince you to interact with other humans to form dopamine producing habits, to make you feel good about living in pain, administer painkillers, and anti-inflammatory—at least you are alive—so you can remain a contributor to society and kinships and pay taxes. Neither of which produce a cure, and both I find... distasteful!

Not to belittle anyone. If spirituality and psychology help to improve a patient's mental health, then all is well. Sufferers need to see things can be worse. They also need to see that they have power over their suffering. They need to see that they can change things for the better, when possible. There is good, better, and best. Best would be to cure them without drug dependency, or spiritual crutches.

I had to take another route after getting off medications. I had to accept what I could not change! I had to reprogram my brain! I am in pain, so I accepted this as fact. No one is going to, nor can, do anything for me. I must accept this and become automated, as opposed to animated. Get up for work every day, because that is how people earn a living. Eat, because that is how people sustain themselves. Go out to movies, because you need to interact in society. Life, more abundantly?

Accept the fact I will never "feel" again, as described as "normal feeling" by the masses. Replace this with a new kind of feel. Cognitive recognition of feel, as opposed to chemical recognition of feel. In other words, I am more like a Vulcan, without the "Live long and prosper." Spock would be fascinated. Yes, I do find that funny.

I might not feel the *euphoria* of serotonin or dopamine flooding my brain, but I know I still love my children and granddaughter. I would still put my life on the line for them. I can't say without selfish intent, but the end result is the same. Their lives over my life. Thus, I manage my depression by retraining my brain and getting out of bed every day.

Chapter Ten

Pro-life

They arise from our human limitations, which we know we have, whether we hold with the Bible that we are all sinners, or with Mark Twain that we are all partially insane, or whether in a more enlightened way we call this shortcoming a neurosis. All these assumptions admit of one exception only: ourselves.

—Karen Horney

It is time to examine the moral issues.

If I have not been able to open anyone's eyes to the need and place for knowledge, then God has failed miserably. I have failed miserably in my vain attempt, and there is no hope. I cannot rule out some pending factors extending from closed-mindedness or the blinding arrogance, the refusal to replace one belief with another, a better belief system—that knowledge is not restricted from mortal mankind, or an unwillingness to improve upon oneself. One must sort out those messes on their own.

I have used the Bible in the common form of sixty-six books, but we must remember the excluded books of the bible. Most people do not possess them, so I must negate them as well. Arguments put forth by most people are strictly based on these sixty-six books in the standard King James version.

What we need is a starting point. A platform to jump from. Most pro-life advocates know all the arguments for pro-life. Regardless of what I have talked about in this book, at my very heart, I am pro-life. However, I am not in an all-or-nothing fashion. I don't need to cover any pro-life contentions in detail.

However, I do need to look at pro-choice in detail. If one cannot, due to having a closed mind, examine both sides of an argument, one cannot see past themselves through to reality. Throughout this chapter, you will see closed-mindedness, all-or-nothing thinking, and extremely poor education in critical thinking.

There is something to be questioned about pro-life. What does it mean to be pro-life? What do you mean by pro-life? Do you apply it equally to every person? Is it reserved for special people? Is it black and white in every case? Is there an age limit? Gender limit? Is it fine for someone to kill another person, but not fine to kill the killer? Perhaps it could even be asked if you are really an anti-abortionist and not pro-life at all?

There is a reason I can ask so many questions here, all of which are legitimate. It is because the term is too all-encompassing. Too all or nothing. Yet, when asked to assess different circumstances, the meaning of the words block one's powers of reason. One feels attacked! As with any attack, one blindly defends themselves, and rightly so. Only with intellect, the reasoning stops and belief defends. "To argue with a person, who has renounced the use of reason is like administering medicine to the dead," Thomas Paine

Carcinogenesis is a word that is used in science. Let's examine it carefully:

Car: something you drive
Cin: short for Cindy or Cynthia
Genesis: meaning newly created

This gives us: Cindy has a new car!

You're not laughing as hard as I am while writing this! I am sure.

If you don't understand what words mean, then how are you to judge what is right from wrong when you're using them? This preceding word, carcinogenesis, is quite harmlessly misunderstood, unless you are about to walk into a room filled with poisonous gas.

Spontaneous abortion falls under this spell of words that science uses, which present great misunderstandings. Let's examine what the mind sees with this word:

Spontaneous: not premeditated, without influence
Abortion: forfeit of life
This gives us: Murderous Bastards!

Funny, how when your brain sees abortion in any context, it produces an evil image or thought process. I am not laughing so hard this time! Any time the brain sees abortion, evil becomes the brain's residue. Why not continue with the use of the older, well-understood terminology of miscarriage?

Also, peculiar to the brain is the example of a complete shut down when one enters into moral issues that are firm in our belief. A wall is erected and no data enters.

In truth, both sides of the divide must be examined in full detail. Every individual must learn to see the details of the opposition's thinking. I don't want you to change your mind about anything! I want you to see another person's mind!

One must start someplace before any meaningful discussion can take place. The beginning is a good place to start.

For many centuries, women were considered the possession of men, that is to say, they were man's property. It has some of its origins in religion. There are good reasons for me admitting the bible as a factual document. Anyone can, for themselves, read these things firsthand in any bible. It was assumed that God created woman to be the possession of man. It does not say, in fact, that God did any such thing. Read it for yourself.

First, examine the curses of Genesis, chapter three. The serpent was represented as Satan. The curses after the "fall" started there. Paraphrased, "The Lord God said unto the serpent: *because you have done this*, you are cursed above all other animals and shall crawl and eat dust all the days of your life." One might think that this serpent, being Satan, would be treated a little harsher. It does not say "I will punish you" rather, it says, "You are cursed." You are cursed indicates self-cause as in; because you did something, a curse will follow.

Check the curse of Adam! Again, paraphrased, "Unto Adam, He said, Because you have listened to the voice of your wife, and ate from the tree, which I commanded you not to eat of, cursed is the ground for your sake." Again, it does not say that "I will curse you" but it is indicative of self-cause; because you did something, a curse will follow.

Curiously, when Eve, the woman, is cursed, it says: "I will greatly multiply your sorrow" and the rest of her curses. Seemingly, God had it out for woman! "I" being personal! God himself placed the direct curse! Either indicating that there was no fault from woman, you did not self-cause this curse, so I must cause the curse. Or the curse was recorded in man's curse "Because you have listened to the voice of your wife" indicating that Eve deceived him.

Look again at chapter two! "The Lord God commanded the man, saying, of every tree…" Oddly, the Lord God did not command the woman. Apparently, she was free to eat of anything. The exclusion was to "the man" and the man alone. Note, that Eve's eyes were not "opened" until Adam ate from the fruit. Did a righteous God intervene and place a curse where one was not warranted?

Maybe, just maybe, because man has written the bible from his perspective, fueled by guilt, he personalized Eve's curse. I wrote on guilt and sentience in the chapter about the soul. Human nature dictates no one wants to shoulder the blame for any wrongdoing, especially alone. It could as easily have been written as consciousness will cause man to place the blame on you and he will cause your "desire to be to your husband, and he shall rule over you." In short, it would have been written, "He said unto the woman; because you have done this, cursed is your life." That still does not answer: did what?

If creation is true in any form, why did God create woman? To become man's servant? Again, look to the scriptures. "I will make him a help meet [mate] for him" when loosely translated means someone suitable to help in being human. Define help! Adam's own words make it clear what he understood from having a helper mate: "The woman that you gave to be *with* me" makes clear that she was not his slave. Define *with*! If you mix flour with eggs, you get pancakes. Something of a different manner and form. You don't get flour controlling eggs. You get a mutually beneficial union of stability, where one part—the flour—benefits from the egg; and the other part—the egg—benefits from the flour. Don't criticize my cooking skills!

If Adam did not understand it to mean "with", the words of his understanding would be written there instead. We would have read something like "the woman you gave me to be my servant, she gave me of the tree and I did eat" making it her fault. She was a disservice-servant and not a service-servant!

From the evolutionary perspective, one could be tempted to say that evolution evolved woman to become man's servant. You could add to this and say that religion is not the problem. If this is the path you choose for defence, religion must have also evolved, and, in religion, man finds dominance of women. In every religion, the world over, dominance reigns.

Fault of the woman or not, men have ruled over women for thousands of years now. Wrongly, in my opinion, but who the hell am I? Since these are all curses, and Jesus paid the price for our sins, thus curses, why are women not seen as equal helpers in life? True, the last "curse to be destroyed" is death, but why do women suffer any longer after Jesus's sacrifice?

Hatred? Perhaps. One still hears many ministers giving biblical support for the notion of man mastering woman. Not to mention religious couples' counselling, where women are expected to be submissive unto the male—quoted from scripture—as head of the household. This curse is long overdue for lifting.

Jesus respected women. He performed his first recorded miracle at the request of a woman, Mary, his mother. He first appeared, after his resurrection, to the woman, Mary of Magdalene. His greatest miracle, raising Lazarus from the dead, was at the bequest of women. He forgave the same "whore" several times. His first time in revealing himself as the saviour was to a woman at a well.

The afore few pages may have offended a few readers, but I must point out what is written and not what is assumed by mediocre interpretations of the word of God, fueled by prejudice. It appears to be more of a man thing, than a God thing, that we reign over our women. My opinion, but is it also fact? Let's offend a few more of our standard thoughts.

If you are raped, then you must not have dressed properly to avoid rape. In some countries, women who report rape are sentenced to being whipped publicly for going out in public without a male chaperone. What about the rapist—he does not factor into fault because she was asking for it in the eyes of that society. Her first sin was leaving the house without a male chaperone...her second was for allowing the rape. I have since seen a meme stating this same conclusion. Should not the rapist, whose predisposition to rape, influence him to always go out with a chaperone to control him.

What about in the United States? I have read that some judge has granted rights as "father" to the rapist. Currently, there are only seven states that have laws preventing rapists from gaining parental rights. There are seven states that allow rapists full parental rights. The victims have to make their children available to visitation rights while the rapist is serving out his criminal sentence. He is the genetic paternity, after all. The remaining states allow paternal rights with restrictions.

So, if I rob a bank and serve out my sentence, then I am free to keep the money? Oddly, no! Check the laws. Money is truly more important than women! Why should a rape victim want to keep the child? Oh wait, I know, because it will remind her to dress properly and teach her female children to dress properly! My feelings are made clear here. If you are found guilty of rape, then you have no rights. Why would you have paternal rights? True, the victim's feelings don't matter! They're female, after all!

We cannot hold males solely responsible here! There are women who would insist that these victims were asking for it. They say things such as they obviously wanted it because of how they [the victim] dressed and they [the victim] were not brought up properly! Women who are saying these things would never appear in public wearing anything sexually suggestive! They were, also, never raped! There are many reasons why women say and think in these terms but some might have been brainwashed by males into thinking with male motivation.

An "internet source" imprinted this thought upon me. "If abortion is not murder, then why is it a double homicide when a pregnant woman is killed?" This must be examined closely.

If a woman is pregnant and the pregnancy is planned, then a life is expected from the woman's efforts. That makes it, by default, a double homicide if she is murdered. Abortion in an all-or-nothing manner might suggest that the same should apply for the life of the embryo because it is treated as a second life in the previous case. I will not comment on the whole—all-or-nothing, but will comment on its parts. If the woman is just ridding her body of a mistake, then one could imply killing, but not murder.

Is abortion really murder? No! Murder is biblically defined as an act of hatred! The worst thing you can do to another human is to rob them of meaningful life, yet, let them exist through and after the robbery of their meaningful life, where killing them would be a blessing.

> Whosoever hates his brother is a murderer: and we know that no murderer has eternal life abiding [living] in him. (I John 3:15)

Is abortion killing? That is closer to the truth. One can say yes, but not in every case. If the woman was raped, then this is a totally different venue. The rapist should be charged with murder! Rape is a hate crime, hate is murder, not killing, and a life has been taken due to the act of hatred—raping a woman. This includes drugging her to have sex, under the illusion of loving women. You lust after sex, therefore, lust after women, you do not love them. These victims mean nothing to you, except to fulfill your lust. You lack feminine respect. Disrespect of people carries hatred. I should finish with rape before moving on to others points of conflict.

First, while I am at it, I might define rape and sexual assault as never being the victim's fault. I don't care if you see a woman walking completely naked down the street, she is not yours to rape. If you drug her, it is rape. If she resists you without saying no, it is rape. If she says no, it is rape.

Recently, a news article stated that a judge made the decision that oral sex performed on a drunk girl was not rape. This too was rape! It is never the victim's fault, including in a marriage, or in a relationship! It is not a moral person who blames the victim, but the immoral person who does!

I know it is impossible for you to be raped, and that rape only happens to girls who are looking for it. You know I am being sarcastic toward that frame of thinking. That fits with "one exception only: ourselves" and is so wrong!

Suppose you were raped and conceived. It is easy to assert your pro-life stance when you must never make any self-decisions on the matter. I am a man and I find it hard to imagine what it would be like to be a rape victim impregnated by my assaulter. I can, however, imagine being a husband whose wife was impregnated by a rapist.

I love children! Would I accept this child as my own? Would I want my wife to go through life knowing this child was a product of her rape? Would I treat this child differently? Would I insist she abort? Would my pro-life stand in the way of it being aborted? I cannot answer these questions because I have not been faced with the problem! All I can say is that I would back whatever choice my wife made. I can't even say if backing her would destroy the marriage. I hope never to find out any of this!

If you were honest with yourself, you might say the same things as a woman. I don't know what I would do! Would you keep the child even knowing it would destroy your marriage? Even if it meant this child would be a constant reminder of your rape? It is easy to say yes, because I am pro-life, and that is what pro-life means, when you never face the problem. This is because never facing the problem makes one the "one exception only: ourselves" in the solution one poses on others—pro-life.

Wonder why the world is going to hell in a basket? It is the laws that give rights to offenders instead of to victims. Going back to the rapist gaining parental rights, what that can be translated to mean is that if I wanted to "be a family" with you, all I need to do is rape you. Then I have a child, complete with visitation rights in jail. I wonder if the judge granted child support to the rape victim at the same time? What do you mean, again, by pro-life?

Known donors of egg and sperm can become liable for child support using a loophole in Canadian law based on biology. It won't take long before every maggot finds a way of using people for their own benefit, without cost, and it comes with a financial benefit, too! There are also cases of genetic disease being passed on with donor sperm. Why donate eggs or sperm? Why save the life of the child, who is the product of rape? So people can take advantage of your kindness?

Sexual promiscuity is a completely different topic than the topic of rape! Sexual intimacy is a completely different topic, too! I will comment on the latter, but not the former.

Sex in a marriage is not for reproduction, but for intimate bonding. Not to be confused with bondage! Many species of animals have a wham, bam, thank-you-ma'am calling toward reproduction. It's in, it's out and no formal contact before or after. If human sex were for the propagation of species only, then we would not take anywhere from one hour with foreplay to five minutes for a quickie. Kissing would be out, as well as other forms of foreplay. In fact, we would never want sex until we had the instinct to reproduce.

Sex is for bonding, reproduction is for reproducing. Both partners must consent or it is rape! So, is it okay that a man can rape his wife and force her to conceive and bear a child? So what if he does "rape" her and forces her to carry his unwanted child to full-term? They are only women after all, and, maybe, they should shut up and only speak when spoken to.

What about cases where a man, sabotages a mutual relationship and damages a condom, with the intent of getting his partner pregnant without her explicit consent? There has been a case of this happening in the news recently. If she became pregnant, is she now to be forced to carry out her unwanted pregnancy? What is her recourse? We blame the woman for this; she took her chances by having sexual relations. We don't blame the victims of robbery for being robbed. The same would apply in this case. He, the perpetrator, would be guilty of the crime.

As I have read on internet postings; there is a new rule: you must have a vagina before you can make decisions about a vagina.

A full half of the world's population are female. They can form an opinion about such issues. There are enough different opinions out there about the issue that they could and should decide it for themselves. My guess is that it would be banned, except for special circumstances like rape and mortality, even without the male input. That is just a guess. Most every post on the internet about abortion is posted by females. Why not let them settle the issue? It could be because many men are afraid to lose control over them!

The point is that there are enough females of different thought processes to decide what is and what is not acceptable to be done with the pregnancies of rape victims. Is it her right to have an abortion? The choice should be made by women, for women! Not by men!

In some countries, these abortions are performed at the hospital. Question. Who would be the murderer? The raped victim or the rapist who forced the pregnancy? True justice would dictate that the rapist bore the guilt of murder. Just my opinion!

The bible is not silent on rape either. The most famous passages being in (Judges 19:21) to the end (20:48). It relives the moment when a woman was raped to death, cut into twelve pieces and sent throughout Israel for the coming together to punish such a despicable crime.

> Onto the damsel you shall do nothing: there is in the damsel no sin worthy of death: for as when a man rises against his neighbour, and slays him, even so is this matter: (Deuteronomy 22:26)

I admit that it is taking a lot of energy to force myself to view some topics in a neutral state of mind. On a scale of one to ten for an opinion scale, I cannot form some opinions. I am not female, so I could never fully understand what it would be like to become pregnant with an unwanted baby, let alone, raped and with child. I would have an opinion of zero! No! I should have an opinion of zero! This would be the main reason to have vaginas deciding on the issues of vaginas!

Even this line of thought has problems. If only women decide these matters, without the input of men, they would likely fail into a worse state. It is probable, that, most woman would feel they would never be placed in a position of being raped. Those who are raped are asking for it, after all.

Introduce men, and we can admit a different perspective. Most men would admit, that if they chose to, they could rape any woman. This does not state they would rape any woman, only that they could. If you were never raped, then you owe thanks to decent men. Add decent men into the mix and you will find men are needed to be *with* women on these important issues. What would your significant other think of you being raped? How would he feel about you, bringing to full term, the progeny of an indecent man?

Being a male, it is hard to discern whether you would have an abortion if you became pregnant. We must compare apples to apples, while giving you a hint at it. It would only be comparative to a woman who was never raped judging another woman who was, but it is the best I, or anyone, can do for comparison.

Being male, imagine you were raped by another man, or gang raped by many, and someone took a picture of it. The law says that you must, because you were defiled, carry this picture around with you everywhere you go. You must have a 11X14 picture hanging in your living room and an 8X10 in every room of your house. Furthermore, you must carry a picture of your rape with you at all times and show it to everyone you meet. Once a year, on the anniversary of your rape, you must throw a party and set a 16X20 picture of the rape at the head of the table and celebrate your violation with your friends. It is the law! [unknown]

If you could see yourself obeying this law, then I applaud you. This only sets you on equal ground with a non-raped woman and not a raped woman because you only have to imagine it and not live it. This picture in the above story represents the child the raped woman would be forced to bear—ever present.

If you could see yourself being ok with having this baby or rape picture to carry around constantly, then you are perfect, at least, in pro-life eyes. As for the rest of us who could not bear living with the constant reminder of the violation, we fall into the imperfect, greater multitude.

Being imperfect allows us to feel what other people of the same impure caliber are feeling. We find it in our hearts to forgive and encourage these women, who aborted for this reason. I, being a lot less than perfect, would actually say to them, this is in no way your fault and you should not feel guilty of the act you felt necessary to perform. The entire complete sin is on the head of the rapist.

It would be interesting to write a book, several hundred pages long, containing these arguments, but I must do this in one chapter and, for that reason, I must now change topics.

A random postulation.

You die and, in a flash, you enter the house of God. You consider yourself to be a born-again Christian. As such, you worked hard to do the will of God throughout your life. He asks you one question, and one question alone. Why did you destroy my good works? What would you reply? I would ask what good works did I destroy Lord? That is, after all, a fair question. You need to know what you did wrong before you can answer such a question.

Behold, He replies, and shows you a vision of you, holding a sign calling women murders outside an abortion clinic. You defend yourself saying it is murder, but He stops you. He says, it is technically killing, which is different than murder.

- 230 -

As you start to defend yourself again, He stops your reply and says it has nothing to do with the killing. Puzzled, you inquire about what He means. He points back to the vision and you see a young girl being stopped by you and your sign. That is where you turned my beloved child away! He explains. She was my last hope!

What? I don't understand what my doing the right thing has to do with destroying your good works. Being a vision, He points out what happened next. You told her she would suffer eternal damnation and that I, God, wanted her to not have an abortion. She turned away from that fateful moment, went home and committed suicide. You celebrated another victory and praised your conviction in my work. What was my work?

Before you can even answer, He explains why she wanted an abortion! She was continually raped and molested by her father and brother. Her baby was the result of incest—fathered by her father. She'd been a victim of evil for many years. Where were you when this evil was happening to her?

Again, He stops you from giving an answer, only to point out to another of your fallacies. Why were you not holding a sign that read, "God loves you! Your sins are forgiven you! Live in peace with your forgiveness!" Why indeed? Is this not My will, whereupon I suffered death? Why do you think will exists? Left stumped, and without an answer, He then explains what would have been her fate and purpose.

She would have become a driving force—unparalleled in the world, against child abuse, rape, genital mutilation, and discrimination against women. Mighty laws would become adapted the world-over, not only to protect My daughters, but also My sons who suffer sexual depravities.

How was I to know this? I was following your word, thus Your will, you reply. All you needed to do was to tell her the true will of God, included in the last will and testament; that He paid the price for every sin for all of time—go in peace! Especially, since the sin was not hers! End postulation.

Haters, might say: Stop, you are making me cry! Nice try, but anyone can make up some bullshit story to his own end. True, I could never claim to make any real statement about what a real God would say or do. It is just a so-so story to make a point! I might add that there are infinite stories I could tell, from both perspectives, but it only complicates the real issue and does nothing to solve it.

If I leave pretending to be this God, then I can ask my own questions, without any pretense. How do you know what God's will is on an individual basis? "This is the Father's will, which has sent me, that of all which He has given me I should lose nothing," (John 6:39) "…Neither shall any man pluck them out of my hand." (John 10:28) "…And no man is able to pluck them out of my father's hand." (John 10:29).

You can only answer this based on the collective, which is put forth in general terms. Thou shalt not commit murder, by the way, is the real commandment and not thou shalt not kill. Collectively, that is the will of God! Stopping Hitler required a lot of killing and we are forced to believe stopping Hitler was the will of God. How could it not be? Yet, how many innocent lives were lost?

I might also ask, how in hell do you know any person's reason for doing what they do? God told you, did He? Does one just assume everyone, except one's own self, of course, are condemned until God runs the ideal past them first? Once you see what He allows, then you feel free to allow it too. If you accept your own misjudgements, then God has already accepted them too, without anyone else being consulted?

Not all rape or molestation victims report their assaults. Some, being wrongfully ashamed, might choose to have a discreet abortion. Maybe, the offending parent is forcing the child to have an abortion. If the parent is non-offending, they still may be forcing their promiscuous daughter to have an abortion to save the family name. Is this the crime of the daughter or her parents?

You might also concede, and say this does hold true for rape and molestation victims only. Completely different story if you are a "whore" or a "slut" and require an abortion. Remember too, rape victims are often called whores or sluts, "women who can't keep their legs closed". (An Alberta judge recently asked a rape victim why she didn't just "lock her knees together.") How does one "lock" their knees together? Are knees like Lego building blocks?

I can neither confirm, nor deny this, as I am not a woman. Therefore, it is impossible for me to make or form an opinion. The male could never form a proper opinion about such issues because it would bring up the question of male expectations. These "whores" and "sluts" are the product of "decent" male fornications? How does this make men innocent? Why are unrestrained males not called sluts? See! Hundreds of pages worthy to be written. Thousands of internet memes to be debated and exposed.

As I am editing this, I am also trying to keep current. I just read a news report on US News, about a *New Sex Craze Called Stealthing*. Reporting in a 2017 paper, published in Columbia Journal of Gender and Law, where removal of condoms in the middle of consenting sex…is becoming a thing:

> If your partner is agreeing to use a condom, you have the expectation that you're being protected from an STI and intentional pregnancy" say's Dr. Barbra Levy "If the partner is removing that condom without your knowledge or consent, that is domestic abuse if you use the broadest sense of the word.

Rape abortions, or as they are called sexual assault abortions, are performed at the hospital. They are, to some extent, contested, but, thankfully, allowed under current laws in some countries. We can ask, are these exceptions that one deems permissible under this law, not a valid source of stem cells to advance important scientific research?

Abortion will always be a combustible issue. The main thinking, in the free-choice department, is that women own their bodies. Who are we to force them to become pregnant and produce babies? That is possibly the most legitimate question to ask. Who are we to order the lives of others?

Should we dictate to women what they ought to do with their bodies? Every woman ought to have ten babies in a lifetime. Great! I think you can agree that this is just what we need: 70 billion assholes in ten years time, instead of the current 7 billion assholes alive today—ourselves excluded, of course. Your right to dictate is more important than their right to decide for themselves?

Yes, but the bible says… I would stop you and remind you of what the bible says: "the woman, whom you gave to be WITH me"—not under me or under my control, but with me. For the male and female to be bonded *with* each other—this was the intent of God! No, Adam and Eve were not married in a formal ceremony and possibly had regular sex before the "fall." In fact, sexual consummation, without ceremony, was the first form of marriage.

Maybe, Paul Simon should have added "people reading without rendering" to the *Sound of Silence*. The bible is not silent on this either. Everyone challenged on reproduction lays claim to the bible for inspiration. Go forth and multiply comes into play—without rendering—as a God-given right, nay, responsibility. Conveniently, the whole verse is never quoted. "Go forth, multiply, and replenish the Earth." I would concede if replenish was not used. Plenish, means to fill the Earth, or people the Earth. Replenish means to replace others, or to strike a balance in the population.

Every man receives according to his own faith were the words of our Blessed Saviour. If you have ten children faith, then please have ten children. If you have zero children faith, then who am I to force you against your faith?

Interestingly, the Bible is not silent on birth control. In the first book of the Bible, before any commandments were made, birth control was used. There are no recorded laws against birth control, I might add. Examining (Genesis 38:9, 10):

> Onan knew that the seed should not be his; and it came to pass, when he went in unto [sexual intercourse] his brother's wife, that he [pulled out upon ejaculation] spilled it on the ground, lest that he should give seed to his brother. The thing which he did [withheld seed from his brother] displeased the Lord: wherefore he slew him also.

Quick comments. It should not be assumed that birth control was what displeased God, but the withholding of seed from a brother. Scientifically, they would each share the same dose of identical DNA. It is obvious that pulling out just before ejaculation was known as a means of birth control. Not a perfect form, mind you, but a deterrent.

Even declaring the bible to be nothing but myth will not make this go away. Other forms of birth control have been established during ancient times, long before latex condoms or birth control pills were invented. It became a real problem, only in modern times, with the invention of the birth control pill—which the Catholic Church protested profusely.

The morning after pill, for example, is held as a legal means of abortion and is highly contested. An egg might get fertilized after all. The Catholic Church has taken it upon themselves to define life as a fertilized egg, along with the impartment of a soul. If the egg in question does not start development, then there is no life form to kill. It is no different than taking birth control pills before sex, in this writer's opinion.

Some education in biology may help. Many people have misconceptions about conception and many believe that as soon as the male ejaculates sperm, the woman's egg is automatically fertilized. This is wrong as it takes time for the sperm to reach the egg. It is impossible for my thoughts to conclude that if the woman were to take the morning after pill after having sex, that the egg would ever get fertilized. Opinion!

If it did get fertilized, you are only stopping the egg from adhering to the uterus. Simplified, without the greater details. How is this murder? Someone, please explain this to me!

How is this different than taking a regular form of birth control? The regular form tricks your body into thinking it is pregnant and stops the release of an egg. The pill dose is stopped to allow for a period in every cycle. Ideally, you will not produce an egg to get fertilized. This is good! Child rearing should be planned for and you must have the ability to support your family.

In a real case from the United States, a couple were charged and convicted for the death of several children. They could not afford to raise any children, but kept having them, losing them and then having more, in hopes that one would survive. Pro-life anyone?

To take any form of birth control is to ensure that you are ready and able to have a family. Life is hard and one cannot always afford many children. Seeing that sex is for intimate bonding and it is expressed in the bible that one should not avoid sexual contact with one's spouse, for relationship purposes, what can you do? Saying that they did not have this problem in the past is quite literally a lie. Times have changed and infant mortality rates have declined.

In the past, if you wanted one child to survive, you had to have many.

This is enough about birth control, specifically the morning-after pill. I like to leave topics on a fun note, but most of these topics will never be fun. This one I leave on a fun note. "No matter which [children's] book I read to my screaming baby on an airplane, the moral of the story is always something about a vasectomy"—Ryan Reynolds.

As I was making my observations on a website the other day, I came across this meme. It showed a drawing of a dissected pregnant woman with arrows pointing to the woman and the baby. The arrow pointing to the woman's body had the caption, your body. The arrowed caption pointing to the baby read, not your body. It was a "pro-life" meme. Under the picture was another caption, "A baby is not a female body part. Stop saying, 'My body, my right, when it is not your body.'"

Flaws anyone? An egg is not a female body part? An egg is a separate individual? Then to not have them fertilized and populated is robbing every egg-separate-individual of its life. We should stop wasting these lives and force women to fertilize them as soon as they are produced (around the age of 13 and even younger in some cases) and as often as they are produced (every month, except when pregnant). They are not female body parts, after all! Thank God someone thought about this and settled the problem. Ladies, your eggs are not your body to control! Get pregnant, and I mean now, before these eggs die!

The same should, in concept anyway, apply if the egg is fertilized, but unwanted. The fertilized egg is part of the woman's body. It is also part of the male's body—the sperm. Should the sperm have the final right over the egg? Here is an idea! If the sperm demands that this egg becomes a child, then let the sperm donor do the gestation.

Why not allow for the nature of reproduction? It is the right of the egg to become a life. It is also the right of the sperm to become life. Reproduction is driven by this. Why not make the right of the sperm or the right of the egg more important than the right of the people carrying them? Pass a law that says you must reproduce for the rights of the sperm or egg outweigh the rights of their carriers. Is this the leg you are standing on, the rights of the unborn, outweigh the rights of the born?

Masturbation, under these potential conditions, can be considered the murdering of—at least in males—potential life. Yet we do not, nor should not, charge masturbators with even the lesser charge of manslaughter. Is that because we are talking about males? Females do not produce or release an egg upon orgasm.

I even read somewhere that masturbation would fall under this category for men, at least. If you waste sperm, it is killing potential life. What about the millions of sperm, which don't fertilize the egg and die naturally? If no one ever masturbated—without prejudgment—then what about the fact that millions of sperm die with each copulation, regardless of whether fertilization takes place or not? It can only be considered prevention of life if an actual fertilization takes place and it is stopped with the intention of stopping a known fertilization.

You could retort, what kind of asshole is he anyway? No one is saying this! Fertilized eggs are the topic. I might even reply to your retort. How do you think eggs get fertilized? Magic? Awareness? Surely, no one has sex without the awareness that it could produce offspring? Do we make awareness the governing rule? Awareness would include: you cannot afford a child right now; you are too young to take care of a child right now; you have too many children already; you are medically unfit right now, and so forth.

A proper definition of fertilization should be made, with intent added. A fertilized egg becomes realized, after mutual consent, with the pre-intention of forming a living, viable soul, or with the mutual acceptance, thus post-intention, if an accident occurs during regular intimacy in the normal function of a marriage—consensual union.

We cannot allow ourselves the destruction of pro-life without some defence. You are a free person with rights. You do have the right over your body and can refuse to become pregnant. If you do become pregnant, then your right to not carry to full term is more important than the right of the fertilized egg. You have the right to transfer that resource, in the form of an embryo, to serve as a source for research, or a supply of stem cells for medical purposes.

That is all true! Many advocates of free choice do not have any problem with embryonic stem cell research.

However, one must add to this: responsibility, action, tricked into conceiving, ignorance, et cetera. There is no one-hundred percent way of controlling pregnancy. Contraception can fail. Condoms can break, diaphragms can leak. Oral contraception can be missed, even once, and an egg can be released from the ovary. Even taking a medication for a cold can affect the effectiveness of contraception.

If you are sexually active, which is your right, then you must admit to the slim possibility of becoming pregnant. That is your responsibility and no one else's.

If you take action, then you must assume responsibility. The right of the fetus does not override your right. It was your action that caused the event. Pregnancy is not miraculous. Your action caused it. Your action of abortion kills it. Yes, you are killing a potential life, which you created. Making it legal and acceptable does not change this fact.

Pro-life asks if you have the right to create, then discard life, because you refuse to accept responsibility for your consensual actions. Rape and incest being different. As is age of majority.

Your right to have fun includes getting drunk, but does not include your right to drive under the influence. To kill yourself is one thing. To kill someone else is another. Killing someone else, while under the influence is considered manslaughter. Unless you die, you cannot claim it to be "only" your problem. If you survive, but are permanently hospitalized, then you are my tax problem. You have a choice—don't drink and drive. If you have zero control over your drinking, then don't drive! No judge is going to say, You're right! You were drunk at the time of the decision so you are not accountable. Edited to note that since I wrote this chapter and started edits, there has been such a case of a judge not holding a drunk driver accountable. If you are unaware, simply search the internet for the affluenza defense.

In a perfect world, reproduction would be under the control of consciousness. You could have your normal sexual encounters for bonding without worrying about pregnancy. A couple would discuss having a child, then, in agreement, produce a child. The female brain would tell her sexual reproductive organs to produce an egg. The male brain would tell the male sexual organs to release sperm. The couple would unite, her conscious releasing an egg into the vaginal shaft, where he would ejaculate directly onto the egg, fertilizing it. The fertilizing of the egg would instruct the egg to migrate upwards, into the uterus and implant itself, but we have no conscious control over biology and conception does not happen in this manner. Instead, if you get pregnant, you must shoulder the intellectual burden over your biology.

Sex affords no choice. Accidents do happen. If you accidentally become pregnant, a real, potential life is in your hands. My body does not make it different than driving drunk—all fun, no consequences. Define ownership? Your biology owns your body as much as "sentient" does! Biology cannot be reasoned with! Cognition does not confer sexcognition, or biocognition!

There is no real way of making your biology understand that you are not trying to get pregnant. You cannot order biology to not release an egg. You cannot order biology to not release sperm. If you insist your body is yours, remember you are placing sentient over biology. Biology does not cognate that it reproduces, it does so naturally. Sentient cognition must assume the responsibility of *nativus*—innate biology, born into, and such things. Ostensible?

If a woman becomes pregnant and chooses to abort, is it killing? Yes, to the fetus. However, the fetus is an intruder in her body, by means of the alien—to her—sperm causing the egg to develop, and the final right of the woman's bodily state falls to the woman alone. The fetus's rights do not extinguish the woman's rights. This does not consider the real problem with children raising children, unless your niche is appearing on reality television. These are the main arguments and the questioning of rights. This leaves the rights of the fetus hanging. This is where the pro-life activists get involved. That was just a quick summation, although we could go on in-depth with this topic.

I must mention, in passing, that you can have six thousand, five hundred and thirty-two abortions and be forgiven for every, single, one of them. If you think this is not true, you believe in man's forgiveness, not in God's forgiveness!

The summation weighs heavily on the embryonic stem cell issue. Some embryonic stem cells do come from elected abortions after all. We are now forced to examine these dead embryos and fetuses. If we can donate our organs after death, why can't a woman donate a dead extension of her body? We can even donate kidneys, and part of our liver, while we are still living. I should bring before you a few examples of these arguments before moving onto another topic.

Three, not two, individual rights come into question here. The egg's rights, the sperm's rights, and the combination-fertilized rights. We can illuminate, somewhat, two guilty parties, but not three. If a male has consensual sex and impregnates a female, unaware, and she has an abortion without his knowledge, is he guilty of murder? That one seems flimsy as an argument, but still has asking power. Males are a vital part of reproduction and should shoulder guilt as well. Most anti-abortionist only blame the woman. On the second point, from any perspective, does the fertilized have any guilt from either the egg or sperm? That can be answered in the absolute: no!

As another addition to this work, Arizona will pass, or just passed a law, where a woman needs permission from the father to terminate a pregnancy. That could be argued as borderline acceptable, if it did not include "even if the baby was conceived by rape". America, home of the Free Offenders Act?

Should the sins of the mother or the father be applied to the offspring? The bible says no! Does this exclude any and every means? Rape is not the fault of the embryo. Male and female "sluts" are not the fault of the embryo. How is it that these elected aborted embryos are dirty with guilty sins? I will take a reason in either the religious aspects, or under humanitarian aspects. None? There are a lot of guiltless embryos in question here.

What of the embryos that come from abortion clinics? Are they not already dead? Are these embryos evil because it is their fault that they were conceived? What about the girls who are forced to abort by parents or angry boyfriends? Who is at fault? What about incest? True, if incest were found to be the cause, then the abortion would be done at a hospital under a sexual assault clause. This would be true only if reported or discovered. Remember that psychological reasons are also medical reasons, especially in the case of rape and incest.

Looking at it in an all-or-nothing perspective, the answer would be not to use any of them. Bottom line is that if it offends too many people, then it should not be used. The thought of abortion still upsets the innate "gross factor" in most people. To make this statement clear. If anyone gets an abortion for non-assault reasons, or non-medical reasons, then don't use the embryos as a source for stem cells because it offends too many people. Due to no other fact, but having a negative connotation—associated with murder—in the minds of some people, then they should be left untouched.

This gives the opportunity to separate sexual assault causes from elected causes. We could free assault caused abortions for use in medical research and application. Any hospital sources are mainly considered life threats or sexual assault in nature, and should be considered a valid source. At least you can be less all-or-nothing about the source. We can, in good conscience, make clear distinctions. We need to learn how to reason.

Speaking of reason, we should also understand biology. Two Facebook posts I've seen, almost back-to-back. One was a pro-life post. It showed a drawing of an aborted embryo, cut into pieces. Paraphrased, it said that the embryo, when aborted, was cut into pieces for removal. Starting with each leg separately cut off, followed by two arms, then the body was separated from the head and both pieces removed. The post made it a point to say that because the head was the last thing to be removed, the embryo felt every excruciating cut and part removal.

In a non-pro-life, non-pro-choice post, I saw a real-life picture, not a drawing, of an embryo, which was miscarried, then removed. It just fit into the palm of the hand and did not extend to the fingers. Small! In the same post, the text read that the embryo was 12 weeks of age. I went back and checked the age with the pro-life post. Guess what? The fetus in that meme was claiming to be the same age.

Which one should we believe to be correct? Both the same age, but the drawn one needed to be sliced up for removal, while the pictured one was removed whole? Untrue, heart-wrenching stories are produced to elicit emotion from the ignorant—unaware—public.

I was supposed to be the product of stillbirth. My mother was told to carry me to full-term, but I would be stillborn. Yet, you can read on the internet about how women are made to suffer—please send money—carrying aborted fetuses, rotting in their wombs, producing so much stench, that they cannot go out in public, because they are refused or can't afford abortions. Abortions here, meaning the removal of the dead embryos. Ignorance of biology has robbed many of their hard-earned money. What these people are doing is just as wrong as abortion: taking advantage of other people's ignorance on the issue! I might add, here, that my case (born alive) was an oddity. Embryos can develop to full term without becoming living beings. There was a case in the news, that one woman decided to carry to full term and she donated the organs to patients in need. They don't rot with stench!

Not related to abortion, but to the news, and believed, we have this story too. A story in the main press not too long ago, showed what seemed like the miracle of the century. A picture was taken—actual real picture—of a fetus's hand holding the doctor's hand after an operation. The picture was used to inspire hope in us. The baby thanking the doctor.

If you believe the story behind the photo, you have to believe that wasn't much of a doctor. In fact, I would say he was cruel because he not only performed surgery on a mother without anesthesia but he did so on the fetus. Of course, all one must do is think critically to realize that this is not the case.

If you are asleep and someone touches your hand, you have the instinct to close your hand. According to the doctor, the hand popped out while he was getting ready to close, the hand gripped, the picture was taken. The operation was performed for a bad case of spina bifida and the child survived! This is blessed news in and of itself, but it was not a soul reaching out in hope for humankind. I am not writing these things to take the wind out of anyone's sails, but we need to stop urban mythology, and start learning biology!

Most of the sources from the hospital actually come from miscarriages anyway. The sexual process needs to be examined here, and badly. Again, in trying to cover so many important topics in one book, one cannot cover them in explicit detail. For those of you, to whom the details matter too much, I suggest you read up on embryology and anatomy. I cover some aspects of development in the following chapter.

We can also add some variables here for consideration. A real pro-life advocate would ask what life is. Is it suffering in fear for your life every day? Depression from your violent attack keeping you from living this life? Since when is life only eating, breathing and popping sleeping pills?

A real pro-life advocate would accept that sometimes an abortion is about saving a life! Or having a life worth saving! In this case, one could become less all-or-nothing about abortion and become in-some-cases about it. Not if you are a true pro-life advocate you say? No! Not if you're are an anti-abortionist!

You can cover much hatred by renaming it as a good. It took some witty individual to see this. You hate abortion (women in general) and calling yourself anti-abortion connotes a negative, the negative is hate. Call yourself a pro-life person and you seem to be seeking a good, while covering up an evil—your hatred.

To claim pro-life, one must value all life and that includes women and their choices. I am pro-life but I don't need to hide behind the soft spells words cast. I can be against abortion and still forgiving and respectful to any woman who has had an abortion, without judgement or prejudice. Like the old saying, "Perfection is achieved, not when there is nothing left to add, but when there is nothing left to take away."

Chapter Eleven

Life in The Balance

When we examine the opinions of men, we find that nothing is more uncommon, than common sense; or, in other words, they lack judgement to discover plain truths, or to reject absurdities, and palpable contradictions.

—Philosopher, Baron d'Holbach.

Let's count cells and potential. The germline cell has eight copies of chromosomes in both sexes: male and female. The male divides cells, which become smaller at each stage of division.

The cell divides once to get four copies of chromosomes giving two smaller cells. These again divide into two cells each, giving four cells with the proper number of copies of chromosomes and smaller cells.

Males produce some 340 billion sperm over a lifetime. One ejaculation containing roughly 200,000,000 sperm. It would be a better design if the male just ejaculated the four sperm already mentioned, and the egg received the sperm closer to the opening of the uterus. Survival of the fittest? The "one" fittest: fastest swimmer, best at navigation, best at endurance swimming, would be the victor. At least, this is the current thought process on reproduction. In proper terms, the healthiest sperm would fertilize the egg. The loss? 199,999,999 potential lives destroyed. However, studies have shown that the fastest swimmer isn't always the one to fertilize the egg. As you can see, even the view on reproduction is changing as new researched information becoming available.

The female has the same germline cells at the start and must dwindle them down, too. There is a slight difference from the male. She must maintain a large cell. The same type of process occurs—cell division—but with a different outcome. The first division creates one large cell and one small cell, which halves the number of copies of chromosomes. The cells divide again making four cells, one larger, three smaller, giving the large cell or egg, the proper number of chromosomes. The other three cells die.

That, more or less, gives a summation of sperm and eggs. Three potential lives destroyed in egg development, several million potential lives in sperm development.

Once the egg is mature and released from the ovary and fertilized, it must be implanted into the uterus. Let's follow this with a quote from Morris's Anatomy:

Normally the ovum when expelled from its follicle is received at once into the fallopian tube, and so makes its way to the uterus, in whose cavity it undergoes its development. Occasionally, however, this normal course may be interfered with, the ovum coming to rest in the tube and there undergoing its development and producing a tubal pregnancy; or, again, the ovum may not find its way into the fallopian tube, but may fall from the follicle into the abdominal cavity, where, if it has been fertilized, it will undergo development, producing an abdominal pregnancy; and, finally, and still more rarely, the ovum may not be expelled when the Graafian follicle ruptures and yet may be fertilized and undergo its development within the follicle, bringing about what is termed an ovarian pregnancy. All of these varieties of *extra-uterine pregnancy* are, of course, exceedingly serious, since in none of them is the fetus viable.

Once a "normal" pregnancy is underway, there is still a chance that the pregnancy will not go full term or be lost. Sometimes the ovum does not adhere to the uterus or there are placental problems. Sometimes the development is such, that, a spontaneous-abortion occurs, better known as a miscarriage. Other problems include the sack, which contains the embryo during development, not expanding all over. In these cases, it can lead to an amputation of a limb, deformity or the death of the fetus.

Before ultrasound and modern medicine, a portion of stillborn births were caused by the umbilical cord tangling around the fetus's neck and strangling it to death. In some cases, the tube formed in the primitive streak stage does not close on the end and heads and brains are poorly developed. If you inherit two Y chromosomes and no X chromosome, the embryo will not develop since it needs the information on the X chromosome. However, having three X chromosomes does not produce death. There are other combinations as well: XYY, XXYY.

There are many defects in animals, and man is no exception. There should be some lists made so you can see the magnitude of the problems. There is no point, I think, in creating a list in technical names and adding a paragraph to explain the terms.

The list is quite extensive and I can't list them all in this book for expediencies sake. However, problems we can see in a fetus are hair lip, web fingers, web toes, six fingers, six toes, clubfoot, short fingers, short limbs, missing growth plates, missing teeth, missing ears, hairy— in excess, two different colored eyes, no eye lens, the most common defect is poor eyesight, no skin pigment, missing limbs, conjoined twins, missing tongue, and spina bifida. Indeterminate sex, poorly, or not, formed genitals (neither sex), born with both fully formed genitals (both sexes), at one in every two-thousands births in the USA. I could go on but you can see my point. There are many disorders that can affect the viability of a fetus.

True, many of these defects don't cause miscarriage, and they can be managed very well with modern science, but there are a lot of problems which do! I, personally, know three women, who had several miscarriages. One woman, specifically, had three miscarriages before she carried her first child to term.

We find ourselves avoiding desensitisation like the plague. The more often evil deeds are done, ignored, and accepted, the less evil they become. While I understand the importance of combating desensitisation, it is important to point out that desensitisation has some good qualities as well. It overcomes hatred and prejudice.

If prejudice is never spoken of as thought, it is too sensitive in nature, then prejudice will continue unabated. The same applies to ignorance. If ignorance is never shamed, then ignorance will continue as normal, welcomed, human behaviour.

The biggest task is to desensitise the use of fertilized eggs in special cases. This will never happen if we don't use dialogue about the issues to clear up the ignorance surrounding the topic. We need wisdom to prevail.

There exist conditions in embryonic development where the end of the neural tube does not close:

Anencephaly, Encephalocele, Hydranencephaly, Schizencephaly.

When this lack of closure occurs, the brain does not develop, or it leads to other deformities occurring. These conditions often end in stillbirths, or death within a few hours after birth. Spinal Bifida is a problem where the development of the spine prevents the muscle, skin, et cetera from fully closing around the spinal cord, but this condition does not always end in death. Neural tube defects are the most common defects worldwide with 300,000 cases a year. They occur during the gastrulation period of gestation.

Many other developmental problems occur in gestation, some of which are not life-threatening, but produce malformations or results in retarded developments. Any developmental or abnormal conditions occurring during gestation are called congenital, such as congenital heart disease. Congenital herpes simplex is not a developmental problem, but one inflicted upon offspring by being exposed to the disease in the birth canal at time of delivery. It is different in nature from developmental problems. We cannot count inflicted diseases in any numbers we might hope to attain.

Being Canadian, I should use the data afforded by my country; however, numbers in first world countries are comparable to Canada's.

These are stats taken from Statistics Canada for the year 2011. There were 380,454 births in Canada during 2011. In those births, there was a reported 2,818 stillbirths where the fetus was over twenty weeks in gestational age. Canada does not list the stillbirth rate under twenty weeks of gestation, where possibly, the majority of deaths occur through spontaneous abortion. It also does not include the number of infants born destined to die within hours, days or during the first two weeks of delivery.

- 251 -

Low birth weights of over 500 grams, but under 2500 grams are at 22,682 and should be remembered that, even 100 years ago, they would have been stillbirths or died within the first few hours.

None of these record the number of times a sexually active female becomes pregnant without even knowing she is pregnant. Although difficult to come up with numbers, it is theorized that two out of three sexually active women will become pregnant three times in their lives and spontaneously abort without having any knowledge of being pregnant. At least, according to *Stem Cell Now*, Christopher Thomas Scott, the actual number of unplanned deaths due to miscarriage is around fifty percent, factoring in deaths immediately after birth in any given year, universally. None of which have that intended outcome— planned abortion. If you cannot phantom that number due to the lack of universal numbers I use, then maybe we can agree that at least fifty percent of conceptions end in a combination of deaths or severe birth deficiencies.

These percentages mean nothing without looking at some actual numbers. The statistics for 2016 are as follows. The worldwide birth rate was 18.6 per every thousand of total population (2016). This tabulates to 4.3 births every second or 256 births every minute. If we use a fifty-percent miscarriage rate, then every minute 256 miscarriages happen worldwide. These numbers do not affect the total birth rate, so total pregnancy rate would be 256 plus 256 for a total of 516 fertilized eggs every minute in 2016.

If that number still seems very high to you, then remember that the only stories you hear about are the tragic ones reported in the media. The books I have read on embryology and stem cell research all conclude high numbers of mortality. They do average around fifty percent universally, which include underdeveloped countries with higher mortality rates than in first world countries, such as

Canada, or the United States. These numbers are what I must deal with while writing this book. We need to examine other data to determine why these rates are so high.

Miscarriages, or spontaneously aborted fetuses, are difficult for the parents when they are known, but many of these parents would happily donate those fetuses for the greater cause. To see that their loss means a gain for others and for humanity often helps to alleviate the pain of that loss.

There are a few estimates in the literature. One, which we will call it a high estimate, is that there is enough DNA in one human cell to stretch one-third of a football field. A shorter one, is that there is about six-feet of DNA strung together end-to-end from one human cell. The longest estimate I have seen or heard was that there is enough DNA in the entire human body to go from the Sun to Pluto several times. This estimate is composed of 30 trillion cells within the human body—an unsure estimate—which produces about 34 billion miles of strung DNA. The shorter estimate was from the Earth to the Sun several times—about ten. These numbers, as unsure as they are, are not off the mark enough to be mistrusted.

> For you knit me together in my mother's womb. I praise you because I am fearfully and wonderfully made (Psalm 139:13-14 NIV)

Why knitting? First, we need to clarify that the King James Version of the Bible does not use the word knit. Converted to modern English, it says, "For you have possessed my reins: you have covered me in my mother's womb" and no mention of knitting. Twice, I heard knit was a better interruption of the Hebrew word and in newer versions, it has become knit. Due to the properties of physics, which I won't get into, knitting produces a helix, which looks like the famous double helix of DNA. If you ever watched anyone knit, they must constantly be straightening out the knitted piece.

The pictured cover of this book has been taken from this analogy. The knitting is also wrapped around in the shape of the symbol for the cure, in this case pink, for breast cancer, which knowledge will someday produce. The white cross is meant to represent enlightenment, the direction which we should be heading toward, shining our light upon darkness. Thus, the reason for the black background. The title is self-explanatory as the difference between faith and reason are in constant conflict over morals. They are often indignant about one toward the other. My own indignation already mentioned: I must choose? The subtitle relays the message that stem cells are just as important to Christians as the rest of the world and we should resolve it.

Back to the main theme, we see that knitting and the famous double helix of DNA look the same and fit the prophet's analogy quite nicely.

Adam lived a hundred and thirty years, and begat a son *in his own likeness, after his image*; and called his name Seth. (Gen 5:3)

We also see that humans produce humans in their own image and likeness. For this to happen, then humans must pass on some form of knitting—having the flesh reproduced with DNA instructions, but also, we can derive some hint that it also forms the soul at the same time. In prophetic terms, God is knitting us together and there is no mention of inserting a soul in the process. The scripture could easily have said, "God knit a soul within us."

We must restrict ourselves to as many facts as we can, while those of us who have faith keep it. One can keep their faith unwavering and still give a space for the facts.

DNA does exist! DNA does mutate! Almost all diseases are caused by *defects* in the structure of DNA right down to poor immune systems! God does not cause these defects!

From this, it is only a small step to ask questions. Isn't it easy, with millions of kilometres of knitting, to drop stitches? Is God that careless to make so many mistakes? Could God not make a better replication device than DNA? Has sin entering the world corrupted our DNA? Feel free to ask your own questions with mine. A truth, which no one would deny, is that mistakes do happen!

I am surprised that the atheists haven't taken to accusing our God of murder. After all, according to the belief of many, God is the one who causes the miscarriages to take place. Is He careless with his knitting? Does He cause this imperfection? Or is He imperfect, or just mean to some people? Maybe his modus operandi is other than perfect creation as I have already suggested. Barring divine intervention, someone needs to do something to correct these travesties.

This brings us to the point of why checking statistics is important. On any given year, there is an average of a fifty-percent death rate due to miscarriages, including industrialized nations. Pro-life? I don't see anyone outside of hospitals holding a sign that read, "End Miscarriages and Birth Defects."

I also don't see pro-life advocates holding signs at stem cell research conferences that read, "We support the right to life and research into finding cures, including embryonic stem cells from clean sources." What I see are anti-abortion wolves wearing pro-life sheep's clothing.

Whether you claim Jesus as the son of God, a prophet, or just a man of his times, he is credited with pointing out an important aspect of life. "I am come that they might have life, and that they might have it more abundantly" (John 10:10) "He came to give life more abundantly."

This, by definition, suggests that life is more than a beating heart. It suggests that a higher comfort level should accompany life. Oddly, you almost never hear this preached from the pulpit. In Jesus's usual style throughout the scriptures, He does not place a minimum or maximum on this abundance. What is clear, though, is that life should not be lived in complete misery. Having a beating heart does not count as having a full, abundant life. Religious or not, any pro-life advocate should take into account a certain level of comfort afforded the living.

Woman and eggs are one and the same entity until the eggs are fertilized. Even then, that egg is nurtured inside of the female body for nine, long, months. It is connected to her through a placenta and umbilical cord. Literally, they are one flesh until she gives birth. Then, and only then, are they separated.

This unique oneness gets carried over into childhood and into early adulthood, which is the main reason why mothers have so much trouble letting go of their children when it is time for those children to leave home. Fathers never experience empty nest in quite the same way as a woman. A mother's love runs deep! A mother's love starts when she learns she has conceived. Her heart starts planning a future that includes her beloved child. At any stage of pregnancy, it would be devastating to learn that there was no future.

Sometimes you only have bad choices, but you still need to make a choice. There have been cases of criticism from pro-life advocates upon some woman having late-stage abortions for life-threatening complications. There is pro-life, then, there is an asshole. There is pro-choice, then, there is an asshole.

These women are devastated by their loss! Pro-life looks upon them with their rose-colored glasses and profess them evil? How dare you? Oh yeah, I forgot, some consider themselves the exception of evil! We will always have haters living amongst us.

Maybe, some of this hatred comes from living in misery themselves. No one to share that misery with or to give meaning to life. Maybe I should not be so harsh! If your hatred stems from pain, then please forgive me. If your hatred stems from ignorance, then all bets are off. It is a choice to remain ignorant! Perhaps this meme says it best!

> I don't understand evolution, and I have to protect
> my kids from understanding it. We will not give
> into the thinkers—I Fucking Love Science
> (quoted source)

There has been a case in the news, recently, where a woman died because she was refused an abortion. Her government refused to pay for the necessary abortion under medical insurance. Some medical abortions have to occur. If they do not, it puts the mother at risk. In rare cases, a fetus can cause death to the mother. You're pro-life and must make a choice here. Assume this fetus is still living, but killed the mother; we will cover the details later. If the mother dies, then the baby dies too. What do you do?

If you said do nothing because abortion is murder, then you are not pro-life. You are an anti-abortionist and a hater riding the coattails of pro-life advocates. A pro-life advocate would ask one question. Can we get life from this? Yes, abort the fetus. Doing math quickly—one death, plus one death equals two deaths—would supply the pro-life answer. One life it is! Spare the mother! Unless the mother is the one dying. Yes, keep her alive on life support until the baby is delivered. These abortions, too, are done at the local hospital. Are these not valid sources of stem cells? With consent of the mother, of course.

Why is it that every time a stem cell event arises, anti-abortionists are there waving their signs? For that matter, if they were, in fact, pro-life, then why not use their sign money to feed the dying? The simple fact is that they are sowing the seeds of hate instead of knowledge.

Chapter Twelve

Promises, Promises

Heal the sick, cleanse the lepers, raise the dead, cast out devils: freely you have received, freely give.

—Matthew 10:8

I cannot cover as many articles and sources as I would like. If I did, I would be unable to retain a brief chapter. As you may be aware of, there are thousands of papers, articles, and books to cover these subjects. I will need to limit the length of the citations I do use for the sake of expediency and not bogging down the book with too many outside conclusions and sources.

First, we should look at some hard facts. Men are no longer needed in the grand scheme of creation. Women can combine the DNA of their egg, with that of another woman's DNA and produce a female—only—offspring. This procedure can be repeated indefinitely as long as a female remains, who holds the information and technique. It has not been tried on humans yet! Although the technique was first reported in the journal Nature, 2004, by Tomohiro Kono of Tokyo University of Agriculture.

Males could become extinct from war and females could continue, unabated, long after. This is known to be true as laboratories have been successfully doing this with mice for a long time now.

This brings us, nicely, to a recent news report about a science article I read.

Three-person reproduction is finally a thing. Medical science has taken the egg from one woman, removed the nuclear DNA from it, replaced it with the nuclear DNA from another woman, and then fertilized it with her husband's sperm. She gave birth (2017) to the first three-parent human ever conceived. The procedure was done by Dr. John Zhang, New Hope Fertility Clinic in New York.

That might offend some people. Until you see the reason why. Mitochondrial DNA is only passed on in the female genome: the eggs. This specific woman had a defect in her mitochondrial, or mtDNA, known as Leigh Syndrome. If she became pregnant, she would pass on this developmental defect to her offspring and it would end in the death of the fetus.

Look at the medical ramifications closely. Now, this new human, if, and only if, she was born female, ended the defect. Her daughter could get pregnant naturally, without passing her mother's defective mtDNA along. The new unaffected mtDNA of the donor will get passed into her eggs. Long-term cure. As all of us have the same mtDNA, then it is the nuclear DNA that constitutes descendant heritage. The problem could have been effectively removed.

The effects of this procedure still remain to be seen, but the possibility is there! This procedure was made possible, solely by learning about DNA, development, and manipulation of genes.

For whosoever shall do the will of my Father which is in heaven, the same is my brother, and sister, and mother. (Matthew 12:50)

Even so it is not the will of your Father which is in heaven, that one of these little ones should perish. (Matthew 18:14)

John answered and said, Master, we saw one casting out devils in your name; and we forbad him, because he followed not with us. And Jesus said unto him, Forbid him not: for he that is not against us is for us. (Luke 9:49-50.)

I won't continue to quote scriptures throughout this chapter; however, they do ring true for those of us who believe. Unwittingly, perhaps, medical science seems to be doing where religion is failing. True, not all medical scientists, or any type of scientists for that matter, are atheists.

The great charge given by Jesus to go onto all nations in his name to make disciples, cast out demons, and heal the sick, is one that many can't do. I, personally, can't do it! I can't walk on water, cast out demons, nor heal the sick. I must admit I have not even tried to heal anyone.

In fact, I can't even stop from getting sick myself and I rely on medications just like everyone else. I don't even know, personally, any ministers of the Lord, who can perform miraculous healings, either. Maybe it should be an embarrassment to me that I can't heal, but I don't feel as if it is my "calling" to heal, either spiritually or physically. On the other hand, I don't feel any special calling per se and I only write this book because I believe in the cause. I also have enough questioning ability to keep my mind open.

Noted above in the scriptures is that Jesus did not care if others were healing in his name. You think he would care if healing took place for faith reasons alone? I.e. I know I can do this! What about the true religion of love? Healing because you love your fellow human.

The same as the rest of the world, in general, doctors were devout believers and did what they could, leaving the rest to God. Today, we still find some doctors who believe in a personal deity along with some scientists. I read somewhere that the ratio is the same in the population sampling of scientist as common people. Medicine has always been on the side of the Lord in our past even if, today, it has fallen in numbers. This does not stop doctors from trying to heal people, regardless of their beliefs.

When it comes to healing, doctors seem to be having more luck with that task, only I think it's not luck, but knowledge. I wonder which one of these revelations Jesus was referring to when he spoke of the healing miracles he was performing, saying, "I tell you the truth, greater things than this will you do."

His ministers laying hands on the sick or finding, through knowledge, cures for all manners of disease. If the former is being referred to, then the world has fallen short of God's expectations for a few millennia now. I also remember this scripture by Paul, "Death will be the last ENEMY to be destroyed."

That was the last scripture I will use! Promise! It was needed! Without giving up on God, faith, or belief, is it possible to support both efforts: science and religion? Shouldn't both be seeking to eradicate every disease on the planet? Unfortunately, not all diseases are caused by germs.

Most certainly, it is God's will to have his people healed. Science has this one main fact going for them. Not a single scientist will give up learning, testing, hypothesizing, searching, starting over from scratch and doing it all over again to cure even one disease. In addition, they do have morals and a moral standard, and no one can blame them for getting defensive when pushed by religion.

I have reasonably shown that medical science is doing a better job of healing. I have reasonably shown that we should be supporting medical science for their efforts in taking an active part in God's will, even if some, or all, are non-believers. It is still the will of God that the sick become healed.

According to a flyer I have collected from the Catholic Church titled *Stem Cells: Astonishing promises...but at what cost?* we are on dangerous ground:

> Most of the safety concerns are related to embryonic stem cells. Ironically, their danger lies in their greatest strengths: their capacity to develop into any cell type, and the ease with which they continue to multiply. Scientists have not yet found a sure way to control the development of these cells, so once they are in place in the human body, they could specialize into the wrong kinds of cells and divide uncontrollably into cancerous tumors.

One thing is guaranteed! If we don't try, then victory will never become tenable! Restrictions must be put in place, however. The pamphlet also made comments about future development of pluripotent stem cells, which will not harm human life. I think this has already happened, but it is not the same as stem cells.

Even if we could produce stem cells from a skin cell, or tease a pluripotent cell into becoming one, someone, somewhere, would challenge this, too! One of my biggest fears, which should also be any reasonable person's fear is that when a skin cell becomes reverse-engineered into an embryonic stem cell, it will be considered a human life because it has the power to become a life.

To be clear here, and not attempt to be misleading to the reader, I will explain in somewhat loose terms. Once an egg is fertilized, it is, for all intent and purpose, an embryonic stem cell that produces a living being.

Reverse-engineering is slightly different as there is no nuclear transfer. The genes are coaxed into becoming a stem cell, or, more specifically, embryonic stem cells, by reversion. Once they become embryonic stem cells, they can and do have the power to become a complete human being, albeit a duplicate of the source of skin cell—or clone. If they could become implanted into the uterus of a woman and produce life, all hell would break loose. I can hear them now. We can't create life with the intent of destroying that life no matter what good is derived from it.

Examination time here. John Smith has a failed heart and is placed on life support. Then a technician takes John's skin cell sample and heads to the lab. He reverse engineers an embryonic stem cell from this skin cell, then grows several in a culture for use in making a new heart. Some good-to-do, without a thought, barges into the lab with a court order stopping the process. "Can these cells produce a complete human embryo?" he asks.

"Yes, technically speaking," the technician replies. Then the man serves a court order to halt the murder of these lives in the culture dish.

Meanwhile, John Smith's wife finds out and she must lawyer up. "These are my husband's skin cells you are refusing to let us use and they are his property, the property of his very own body and they were taken to grow him a new heart with his own DNA match."

"Yes," the do-gooder replies, "but they are now a life form and to use them would be murder of an unborn life."

You might think this is a ridiculous scenario and could never happen because it is not reality yet. Wait until it does become reality!

If a skin cell has the triggered potential to become an embryonic stem cell, equivalent to a fertilized egg, then cutting your hair, or fingernails, will be destroying potential life. Where and when will the madness stop? Does it follow, that we should avoid creating stem cells for medical use?

In this next case, I will start with the objection first. The Catholic Church is against in vitro fertilization, also known as IVF. Producing offspring the old-fashioned way promotes bonding, as already mentioned. In vitro fertilization voids sexual intimacy and the church follows a saying of, "Begotten, not made."

We should look at a simple fact, having sex in this situation does not seem to be a problem for bonding, or just enjoying sex for fun. Why would you stop having sex just because you can't get pregnant? If anything, one would think spontaneous sex without worry would happen more often in a marriage where IVF is used. This would strengthen the bonding effect of sex, which is the Catholic Church's objection of artificial insemination or in vitro fertilization.

In vitro fertilization was developed by a physiologist named Robert G. Edwards; he was awarded the 2010 Nobel Prize for it. It was developed in 1978. If you remember the year, you may recall it was called "test tube baby" by the press. During the process, there were leftover cells, which were discarded, until James Alexander Thomson discovered they formed stem cells in 1998. Then, the moral issues ensued.

These leftover cells were, in fact, leftover eggs from in vitro fertilization, which will not be used in child production, will never be used. As I pointed out, it is not wrong to aid in becoming pregnant. It is not wrong either to not want your eggs donated to another woman, who you don't even know. It is not as though you are withholding seed from your brother or sister.

Does it sit better with you that these cells be destroyed and rot in the ground than to save a life with them? Not to mention that some eggs are of such poor quality, they would not be used for implanting anyway, but work for producing stem cells. At least, one can see these eggs are a clean source as they can produce stem cells but not life.

Stem cells, embryonic or otherwise, were not known until in vitro fertilization was invented. Stem cell discovery is a "happy accident" of artificial insemination. We now know they exist, and we must master them. Cloning was soon to follow with the world-wide publication on Dolly the Sheep. Dolly was to become a ticking time bomb as this brought forth several moral issues with cloning. There was a picture of an ear growing on the back of a mouse to replace an ear missing on a man. It was on the cover of Time Magazine the same year as Dolly. Through the heated debates, some good progress has been made, including discoveries, such as the immunity conference.

It is now possible to confer your immune system onto another person. This was just hopeful thinking not too long ago but it is, now, a reality and was derived from stem cell research. A recipient patient can have his immune system killed off, incompletely, of course. He needs to retain some of his own immunity or he would reject his own body. This is done by killing off the producers of white blood cells in the spinal fluid found in the vertebrae and bone marrow.

Once this process is done, a donor can give his spinal fluid for transplant into the recipient, where both immune systems grow together producing two different white blood cells in compatibility. Thus, the patient can accept a kidney without tissue rejection. That is the hope, anyway.

Recently, a patient with AIDS, received a spinal fluid donation from a person who was immune to AIDS, technically, he was immune to the HIV that causes AIDS. The patient also became immune to HIV and was cured of the disease.

Deletion of HIV genes in cells has been accomplished, but the treatment is still suspect. The virus might still be "hiding" somewhere in the genome that hasn't been spotted by researchers. Temple University School of Medicine published these finding, but they were done on cells, and are not ready for human trial. This poses problems for haters, who insist that HIV was a godsend to punish homosexuality.

Haters should consider it offers hope to the many who contract the disease by other means. I would not deny the healing to anyone, as we all drink of death—chose your poison. Deletion of genes will allow for insertion of repaired genes.

Some ministers have, and would, say these people, who lose a child through miscarriage, are being punished for a sin by God. Really? God punishes the child for the mother's or father's sin? Well, I am glad, for one, that these ministers enlightened me on the matter! I didn't realize all these "spontaneous abortions" were the punishment God placed upon the heads of the child for the sake of the parents' sins.

This sounds as bad as when the people were told if a child died without being baptized, it went to hell. I, for one, would not bend a knee to any god of their imagination. I am a little more astute than that; show me where it is written in the bible. "Neither has this man sinned, nor his parents." (John 9:3).

Confusingly, visit the sins of the fathers to the third and fourth generation of those who hate me does not cut it. If the father is drunk all the time, then the alcohol intake affects his sperm as well. If a woman uses crack during pregnancy, then she has a crack-baby born unto her. If defects are caused in any child, due to drugs, beating women, malnutrition or any other reason, then the parents can be said to have passed on their sins, not God!

Once defects have been introduced into the lineage, it can take a few generations to pass, if at all, unless fatal. You pass on your mother and father's DNA to your child, not your direct DNA. There is a germline generation gap involved in inheritance. If they did wrong while they conceived, they could pass it to their grandchild and have it miss their child. Both, you and your parents have some influence on the third and fourth generations.

The process of editing genes, called Gene-Editing Therapy, is becoming a real thing. European researchers reported in the Journal of Science Translation Medicine that editing of DNA had saved the life of two babies recently. White blood cells were genetically programmed to destroy cancer cells. They had acute lymphocytic leukemia. They programmed white blood cells from a donor to do the job. One child had to have a bone marrow transplant to fix a subsequent problem, but is doing fine as of the articles date. The second child appears fine.

With some success, viruses have been used to insert "repaired chunks" of DNA into living cells. In some reported cases, patient improvements have been forthcoming. How can we say it is not worth the risk? Not worth knowing? The same applies to Nanobots.

> These legions of nanorobotic agents were actually composed of more than 100 million flagellated bacteria—and therefore self propelled—and loaded with drugs that moved by taking the most direct path between the drugs injection point and the area of the body to cure. (Sylvain Martel)

Basically, bacteria are infused with iron so they are guided magnetically to the source where they are used as a cure. This same process can include repair for DNA into isolated cells, not endangering any other body part. No human trials have occurred as of yet.

Further, doctors have begun the process of not attaching the tips of amputated fingers back onto young children. The main reason for this is that the tip grows back on its own. Young children still have active embryonic stem cells at work in their bodies. The critical age of when this stops has not been conclusively determined. Knowing how stem cells work can become beneficial in creating this effect later, and longer, in life. Think how nice it would be if you could grow back an arm lost in an accident. Repair arthritis damage to your bones. Regrow the nervous connections back into the brain, past the brain-blood barrier, when paralyses occur. Currently, this is not possible. However, injection of stem cells into the neck does help with nerve damage prevention.

We not only know that this happens with starfish and some amphibians, but we know, at least on a small scale, that small children have this limited ability. Darwin, in Origins of Species, noted that fingernails sometimes grow back onto amputated stubs where fingers used to be. The potential is there. Some cancers are the result of "growing a jaw, complete with teeth," into someone's leg muscle: known as teratoma. Not only could we prevent teratomas from occurring, we could cause them to grow into replacement parts, hands complete with the original fingerprints.

Embryonic stem cells are the first cell types to appear in development. They have the ability to become any cell type in the human body. Adult stem cells are slightly different. Adult stem cells remain in the body and are utilized by the body when repairing organs and tissue. However, they are not as valuable as they have limits to cell type production, as do pluripotent cells.

This would be the main reason for studying embryonic stem cells as no one yet knows what triggers the differentiation of one cell type into another cell type. This information can only come from the study of embryonic stem cells.

For example, how does repair cells become activated for healing broken bones? How is this distinguished from differentiated cells forming new structures, such as growing a bone in the first place? These can be examined, at least, in part.

Did you know that molting, the act of shedding the exoskeleton in Arthropods, like lobsters growing new shells, is physiologically triggered? The entire system has been explored, recorded, and tested. We are even aware of which genes do the work.

To explain this in the sweetened condensed version, arthropods have their skeleton on the outside of their bodies and their outer shell is segmented. When the body grows large enough to touch the shell within certain limits, a nerve firing takes place.

This complex action of nervation controls turning the DNA on. Once on, the DNA begins the sequence of building a larger outer skeletal structure. We know how this process works because it has been studied! The exact process is too complicated in detail to go over in this book, especially since we are not looking at arthropods but stem cells. We only need to understand the basis of physiologically triggered enactment upon the DNA.

Properly, we need to be able to ask the following questions. Nerve firing can't be responsible for prompting a change in the other nerve structures or cell structures? In other words, does the contact of the flesh with the shell, in the case of lobster, cause a nervous act to trigger the alteration of the genes by activating/deactivating them? This would be helpful information to grow new limbs, or organs. How about nerves and actual neurons? What about growing more dendrites, or longer axons? Chemically activated neurons such as the ones that are affected by dopamine or serotonin, which promote concentration and stability. How would this knowledge affect sufferers of Parkinson?

It is well known that a hierarchy exists within the DNA structure. Some genes only purpose is to switch other genes off or on at the appropriate time. We have progressed through our understanding of DNA from where we thought a genome was made of mostly junk DNA to accepting that all genes have a purpose.

We've come to understand this purpose, but we need to observe cell transformation into different cell types, the starting and stopping of structural formations, and what triggers what to happen. There is only so much information to be obtained from the study of other animals. We need to know how human, embryonic stem cells work to perform cell differentializing.

The human genome project catalogued the entire gene sequence of the human body. This does not mean every gene function is known. Far from it. We still have no hierarchical structure in which genes switch which genes. We also don't know how many genes are involved in any single biological function. There are often several genes involved in one function. To rebuild an arm, we must hit the right gene, or several genes if applicable, and in the proper order of switching.

You can't have too many examples to draw upon for conclusions, can you? Teeth are well known to change color when the nerve is damaged or destroyed. They commonly turn grey or brownish in color. The tooth does not die and fall out within seconds or even days like when you lose a part of a finger. Disconnecting the nerve from the tooth cells does not kill the cells as they can still get nutrition from the body. Sew the finger back on and you lose feeling in it, but it heals and lives on. The end of your finger does not turn grey or brown. With that knowledge, we have to ask, what is the difference? The logical question to ask is, does the nerve order the tooth to be white? Does the lack of nerve connection, thus communication, stop informing these tooth cells on how to work? Does it allow the cells to switch on or off their DNA? No one knows.

One more sweetened condensed example and I shall move on to another topic. Bone cells are not made out of the hard materials or chemicals you look at when looking at bone. They are soft cells like the rest of your bodily cells. These cells mingle their "dendrites" or "tentacles" into one another in a mesh-like fashion. Then they collect the harder chemicals needed to build a hard bone: i.e. calcium. These chemicals are stored around the cells mesh-like structure and create a hard bone formation.

Once the bone is initially constructed, it only needs normal maintenance. When you break your arm or leg, it is not the calcium or other chemical solids that heal you. First, contact is crucial between the broken ends of the bone. The soft bone cells then touch each other and communicate that there is a break in structure. The cells grow new meshing and fill them in with chemicals. Does the initial disconnection of the bone cells trigger these cells to search for a new connection? How do the bone cells know there is a disconnection and not the stop-growing signal of the genes?

Let's try some answers. First, these tentacles touch each other. Could this be the communication signal for these cells to build material around themselves? The exterior of the bone is not a problem with this thinking. Once the cells reach full size and are "turned off", the outer cells are still in partial contact with the next level down. They, too, would surround themselves with materials to build hard bone.

As soon as a break occurs, the cell is no longer surrounded with material. Cell contact is also lost. This leaves the cells with a question and the answer is to grow new cell connections and fill in that gap with material. Remember these cells were damaged, but were not told to stop growing. To regrow an entire arm, one needs to understand the difference between lost connection: repair; and outer limit: stop growing. We need to be able to trigger the bone cells to re-establish continued growth and not just a repair. No one knows how this would be accomplished. Stem cells need to be studied.

This information is needed to grow replacement parts and repair heart tissue damage. The heart scars, as opposed to repairing itself, reducing the heart function. The heart is non-regenerative and when heart attacks happen, they leave scar tissue, which is not good for the constant flexing of the heart muscle, making it less effective. Injecting new heart stem cells into the damaged area may allow new heart cells to grow and eliminate the scaring.

Conjoined twins pose another problem entirely. If twins share one heart, who gets the right of the heart upon separation. Are they destined to live as one soul even though they have separate brains? It might be nice to have the ability to grow an entirely new heart so both can become separate, self-efficient, living souls.

An article I recently read suggested that the purest liver cells ever seen have been coaxed from pluripotent cells. How long before liver cancer no longer exists?

Brain and blood do not mix, blood actually destroys the white matter, or myelin system in the brain and spine, not in the body though. The blood-brain barrier. It is actually the oxygen in the blood, or exposure to outside air, which differs from body nerves to brain nerves and neurons. When someone breaks their neck, some damage occurs on the spot, of course, but until bleeding stops and the myelin stops degenerating, the damage is unknown.

First, it has been proven that injecting stem cells into the damaged area helps prevent additional damage from occurring, which helps the healing take effect. Second, new nervous tissue will not cross this blood-brain barrier, which causes permanent damage. Stem cells, however, may regrow new wiring in the nervous system past this blood-brain barrier the same way it developed in the embryo in the first place, thus curing paralyzed victims. Sure, it might take nine months, the same as gestation of a fetus, but it is better than a lifetime in a wheelchair or worse.

I want to point out even some scientists caution against making promises. I believe all cancers will be defeated, birth defects will become non-existent, damaged organs repaired, paralysis cured, or restored nervous system from damage would be a better statement. Amputees grow new limbs, blindness erased, the deaf will hear, and people will live their lives until they are full of years.

It is even conceivable that, one day, these spontaneous abortions will become fixable. Either directly in the uterus, or replanted after the repairs are made. One day, we might not even need to use embryonic stem cells for research because we will be able to coax them from skin cells.

The thing is once you have the knowledge of how the cells work, how DNA works, and how to control the switching, more and more things become possible.

Hype? Maybe! Maybe science will never get all the bugs worked out. Maybe lots of mistakes will happen and new methods will be needed. One thing I can promise every single person on the planet for the next thousand generations is that if we don't try, these advancements will never happen. I promise! That promise you can take to your grave, knowing it is true.

Walk into a palliative care unit and take a good look at someone dying of cancer—skin upon bone, covered in tumors, which are the last appearance of flesh under the skin. Imagine telling them we should not care about their natural plight when we can take an already dead embryo, with living cells, and use them to find the cure.

When a person dies of unknown causes, the first thing the police do is to order an autopsy to find the cause of death. Are you not curious as to why these fetuses spontaneously abort? Or do we, as a people, resolve to just not care? An autopsy, in this case, would not be checking the heart as there is none, but would check why the heart did not form, for example. The tools used would be the only ones available: DNA, you guessed it—embryonic stem cell research. Only one example of it!

As a friend of mine pointed out. Every time there is a miscarriage, an autopsy should be performed to see what the actual cause of death was. This would promote inspecting stem cell development, DNA for defects, detect the actual cause and learn from them.

If the cells are never grown or cultured for stem cell research, the extra knowledge would be of little help. Nothing to compare to. Making them a clean source would be considered as a source of stem cells, anyway.

Chapter Thirteen

Learn to Compromise

We can't solve problems by using the same kind of thinking we used when we created them

—Albert Einstein

This has already been a long tedious argument, I know. I have taken the long path, guiding you through as many facts as I could. Some of those facts, I could only touch upon while others, I delved into the minutiae. I encourage every reader of this book to continue reading on these topics, like I have. Based on my non-aggressive arguments, we see the need to stop thinking in an "all or nothing" fashion.

We can learn to compromise, and start the process of settling on minimums. We can allow for natural sources of stem cells to be used to advance medical science. We can allow for a minimal cloning to produce organs, cells, and genetic material. We can allow for a minimal amount of genetic engineering to take place for defective genes.

Through this, we can disallow genetically engineered super-humans to replace the nature of man. We can disallow cloning a whole person for vanity sake. We can outlaw, completely, creating human life for organ farming.

With all the science fiction illustrated on screen, books and pop culture, it is not hard to see where the fear started and where it comes from in regards to these subjects and the surrounding moral issues.

Here are a few of the many moral issues: a person willfully producing child B, only to abort and supply parts for child A, or, worse, letting it go full term only for parts. Hand picking special attributes to raise super humans: blonde hair and blue eyes, desired heights, sex, build and the like. Becoming pregnant just to abort and sell the aborted fetus to research as a source of income.

We should include cloning as a matter of record, and cloning whole armies, which might turn on us and destroy us. For vanity; cloning oneself to live longer; this one is not, and never will be, possible. Cloning only makes a look-a-like; you are the totality of what you've lived, and experienced. Your genome can be duplicated, but not your connectome.

Add a thousand more moral issues, if it pleases you, but then ask the same question of it. Why can't we illegalize these immoral acts as they arise? Is it not possible to separate true, medical, life-saving research from the immoral? Can we not allow the one without the other?

Never should any life be created with the intent to use that life for spare parts. This is true no matter the need. Who gives us the right to create a human for human consumption?

There should never be, in any form, genetic engineering to produce any life form, which could not be selected for naturally. We don't need 20 billion blue-eyed blondes with a 300 IQ running around. If we, as a species using natural selection, end up with these things, then it is natural and permitted. However, to accomplish that feat of natural selection, we would require permitting only smart, blue-eyed blondes to reproduce, and a general genocide of the rest of humanity. If you don't forbid the mixing of people with whom they choose, this is a non-issue.

We should consider two types of cloning. Type one: to produce a complete organism from the original. Type two: to produce cloned cells or complete replacement organs.

Type one cloning should not be allowed in regards to human cloning. Type one cloning could be allowed for a few special circumstances. Like producing viable clones to help endangered species. Human cloning could be completely banned worldwide but we could still use type two cloning to advance stem cell research. This would advance the cure for many ailments. We can lawfully condemn cloning on the whole for vanity, while separating cloning for the origins of cells needed to cure illness. As this quote will testify, cloning is needed:

> Melton had no interest in making cloned babies. In fact, he remains opposed to using nuclear transfer solely to produce a clone of a living being. He instead was obsessed with the idea of exploiting the cloning process for its ability to yield stem cells from patients, because it would provide an unprecedented way to watch the cells as they grew, from stem cell to endoderm to pancreatic cell and eventually to an insulin-producing beta cell. It would also be the only potential way to chronicle why that cell loses its ability to produce insulin or respond to glucose. (Alice Park)

We know there is only a fifty percent chance of life occurring in any one egg/sperm fertilized combination.

The remaining fifty percent are miscarried embryos, which can't produce life. Why not make them clean sources for research? Nobody murdered them! There is no sin attached to their deaths! They belong to the mother as a part of her body until delivered! She is free after her death to donate organs to save lives, then why not donate an organ before her death if it saves lives? This should not even be contested in my opinion. If the woman can't do it, then fine. Should you judge her harshly if she can do it?

In no case would I consider a human soul imparted until the human form has taken place. The human form starts at the primitive streak, where asymmetry takes place, but this does not mean soul as my psyche explanation showed. Most religions accept the primitive streak as the starting point for life. It is accepted in the Islamic tradition. Some of the Jewish traditions only consider the death of an embryo after forty days to be an offence to the embryo. Before forty days, the offence is to the mother, not the child.

> The rabbinical text treats pregnancy as a continuous process, with the moral status of the embryo, fetus, and newborn gradually increasing along the way. pregnancy—along with a significant moral imprint—isn't officially recognized until after 40 days. "the old texts describe the developmental period before 40 days "like water," Zoloth says. "It makes practical sense if you think about it. If a pregnancy ended before 40 days, you wouldn't be able to detect a recognizable human form with the naked eye."
> (Christopher Thomas Scott)

To have a start date at the primitive streak should be acceptable to everyone. However, the primitive streak does not guarantee a live birth.

Politics is possibly the worst of sins. If we want a field of indignation, this is one of the greatest. You can't be liberal and adhere to a conservative policy? It matters not whether you use the term liberal or conservative, democrat or republican, or any other term. If the liberals say pro-life, the conservative must say pro-choice. If the conservatives say pro-life, then the liberals must say pro-choice. It is impossible to have both say pro-life, but allow for extenuating circumstances, such as rape and/or medical welfare. It is impossible for both to say pro-choice.

How would you get elected if both your platforms were the same? You are responsible for representing the public which contains both views, so you have to pick the opposite side of the competition.

Perhaps it is time to examine a comment I made earlier. It could be considered Christian in origins, but the world can learn something from it. I wrote about Paul saying, "I can do all things, but all things are not expedient." Adding, further, if you did not know what that meant, you were not alone.

All things are lawful for me, but all things are not expedient: all things are lawful for me, but all things do not edify. (I Corinthians 10:23)

First, if all things are lawful, then doing all things is lawful. This is where I get the term, "I can do all things," which I will use for an easier explanation. It should be examined under the laws of grammar. The word "can" represents the ability—lawfulness. The word "all" represents everything, without exception. The word "all" does not have any exceptions placed upon it because it is under ownership—lawful.

There is ownership between "can" and "all" without exception. Can—lawful, includes the ability to do all

- 281 -

goods, and all evils, without exception. This is meant to be covered under the blanket of complete forgiveness. Paul understood he could murder someone, and forgiveness was extended to him. That part of the sentence is firm and without exception. I have the ability to do every good or evil thing under the blanket of my sins having been forgiven.

He does not stop there. He adds an exclusion using the word "but".

But does mean to exclude something or make exception. He then chooses the word expedient. From the Greek "ex" meaning freed and "ped" from the Greek word "poda" meaning feet, or foot. This gives us freed-feet, or free from consequences.

It is made into the negative by adding "not" to the mix. When properly combined, this gives us "but all things are not freed of consequences." If Paul was to murder someone, he would still be punished for his crime, even though he was forgiven. So, what is the lesson? Just because we are on the verge of making everything possible, does not absolve us of any dire consequences.

To use the proper term of lawful complicates things, but my substituted word "do" makes for an easier explanation. Further, if we examine the word "do" in context, we can stipulate that one must do something. I can "do" all things, leaves out doing nothing—unlawful. Doing right requires no forgiveness. Doing wrong can be forgiven, but the consequences live on. To do nothing is also forgivable, but filled with consequences.

This can easily be converted directly from faith into scientific reason. To make a mistake is forgivable, but we must suffer the consequences. To do a good, benefits all. To do nothing, does not.

True, there will always be that special someone, who will find and exploit some loophole. Maybe, we need to coin a crime before it happens. *Exploitation of a loophole* might be a good idea. If you challenge a law, due to poor grammar of the law, or vagueness of the law, and exploit an evil, then you can be charged with exploitation of a loophole. Because money is involved, I am surprised this is not already a law. The government making concessions for exploiting tax loopholes, for example.

Maybe, it is time to divide the all-or-nothing conflict into solvable separate problems. We can solve the loopholes as they arise. The huge, all-or-nothing issue will never go away, but we can solve the smaller, moral dilemmas and conceptual issues to make progress into a brighter future. We can lawfully create clean sources of stem cells: the embryos of rape victims and medical welfare victims, where life is threatened, for one example; spontaneous abortion sources, for another. There are many other things we can do if we extinguish the demand of all-or-nothing!

The Gilgamesh Project aims to make men a-mortal. A-mortal meaning we won't die from natural causes, but can be killed by accident—or war. Gilgamesh sought to find the cure for death after seeing worms crawl out of his friend's body upon decay. Imagine, in the distant future, standing shoulder to shoulder, with your brothers and sisters, without room to turn around. For this not to happen, one would need to stop the propagation of the species, not limiting a couple to have one child, but no children. Unless a replacement is needed due to an accident. Then who is the one elected to propagate the replacement? Do we hold a lottery?

If scientists were asked why the research projects such as the Gilgamesh Project, the majority would undoubtedly answer, because we want to cure disease and save lives. As Harari writes in the last few pages of Sapiens, the question that science is asking is, "What is it forbidden to do?" I suggest we should set boundaries before they become problems. We should define forbidden before ethical issues arise.

Of important note here, it was a scientist who first flagged moral complications. It is best to take another quote:

> There was a very real possibility that man-made genetic horrors could harm not only the human species but the environment as well. So in 1975, Berg took the unusual step of convening a group of genetic experts at Asilomar, in California's Pacific Grove, to address the safety concerns the new science presented. After several days of discussion, the brain trust, which included James Watson, the discoverer of the structure of DNA, as well as past and present Nobel laureates, decided on a voluntary moratorium on certain types of recombinant studies.
>
> Known at the Asilomar Conference, that gathering remains a highlight of scientific policy-making. It was an example of effective self-policing, and the recommendations of the attendees later formed the basis of guidelines established by the National Institutes of health on the appropriate use of recombinant genetic techniques in research. (Alice Park)

Are we afraid we are not wise enough to step into the arena of morals around what it means to be alive? What it means to be dead? True, murder is illegal, but it still happens. Making some things illegal might open doors for crimes against humanity. Not opening doors are keeping crimes against humanity flourishing.

These crimes are allowing diseases, like cancer, which are flourishing, to go unchecked. I read a report that "two-thirds of cancers are unavoidable, even if you live a healthy life" The Telegraph March 2017.

Cancers triggered by copying errors could occur "no matter how perfect the environment", according to co-author Dr Bert Vogelstein, also from the Johns Hopkins Kimmel Cancer Center.

Maybe we have need of a moral, universally-acceptable definition for life? We need one that satisfies all religions, ethics, and the scientific community, one that includes: Spirit, Soul, Entity, Cognition, including Potential—in realizable terminology. Not so much one that states as soon as an egg is fertilized, it is a life. If the fertilized egg fails to copy the DNA properly, it will never become a viable fetus.

There are other reasons I understand, which could cause spontaneous abortion, like the mother's body rejecting the fetus; not her fault of course. It doesn't matter how many reasons there are, because, at the end of the day, it does happen. Fact! No one to blame! No one to blame? If we had a means to stop it, and did nothing…onto him, it is sin!

The "elected willful abortion issue" will never be resolved! Fact!

Can we, as a people, separate the two "abortions" in our minds? Is it easier to call it all murder, blaming God for the one murder and man for the other? Is there no middle ground? Can we, in good, Godly conscience, give our full support to the research on one, without giving in to the other; morally, if not financially?

As far as this Christian is concerned, it should become a leading Christian cause and be supported as such. Maybe,

Christians for Embryonic Stem Cell Research: supporting clean sources and the right to living life more abundantly.

Once a thing has been done, the fool sees it—Homer

Further Reading and References

Before I started writing this book, I spent many years reading excellent books on every topic I have undertaken to include in this work. The list of books read is large, however, I found that it is better to focus my recommended reading on the books I feel are important for people to read. I included these here, with comments, for your information and reference.

There are many books I have read on the stem cell issue, seven books are explicitly on the topic, four of those are quoted in this book. These are:

Holland, Susanne et all: *The Human Embryonic Stem Cell Debate* (2001)

Park, Alice: *The Stem Cell Hope* (2011)

Peters, Ted, et al: *Sacred Cells* (2008)

Scott, Christopher Thomas: *Stem Cell Now* (2006)

I also cited a pamphlet from Catholic Organization for Life and Family, Life Matters. On stem cells. © copyright 2007

Binet, Alfred, *The Psychic Life of Micro-Organisms* (1910)

Binet, Alfred, *The Psychology of Reasoning: Based on Experimental Researches in Hypnotism* (1899)

Bopp, Franz: *A Comparative Grammar* (1843)

Cairns-Smith, A.G.: *Evolving the Mind* (1996)

Cox, Brian et al: *The Quantum Universe* (2011)

Chown, Marcus: *Quantum Theory Cannot Hurt You* (2007)

Darwin, Charles: *Metaphysics, Materialism, and the Evolution of Mind* (1974)

Dawkins, Richard: *The Extended Phenotype* (1982)

Dawkins, Richard: *The God Delusion* (2006)

Dehaene, Stanislas: *Consciousness and the Brain* (2014)

Harari, Yuval Noah: *Sapiens* (2014)

Honos-Webb, Lara: *Listening to Depression* (2006)

Jammer, Max: *Concepts of Space* (1957) Einstein, Albert: quote from forward.

Kahneman, Daniel: *Thinking, Fast and Slow* (2011)

Krauss, Lawrence M.: *A Universe From Nothing* (2012)

Lee, Namhee et al: *The Interaction Instinct* (2009)

McTaggart, Lynne: *The Field* (2001)

Moffat, John W.: *Reinventing Gravity* (2008)

Mukherjee, Siddhartha: *The Gene* (2017)

Ovason, David: *The Secrets of Nostradamus* (1997)

Paabo, Svante: *Neanderthal Man* (2014)

Primack, Joel R. et al: *The View from the Centre of the Universe* (2006)

Randall, Lisa: Knocking on Heaven's Door (2011)

Segre, Gino: *Faust in Copenhagen* (2007)

Sheldrake, Rupert: *Morphic Resonance* (1981)

Walter, Chip: *Last Ape Standing* (2013)

The first book I would add to anyone's reading list would be: *Biomimicry*, by Janine M. Benyus. In its pages, Benyus does an excellent job of explaining some of nature's naturally occurring phenomena. More importantly, it gives us a feel for how we imitate nature through learning about nature. This, in and of itself, supports how humans evolved the capacity to become sentient beings.

Finding Darwin's God, Kenneth R. Miller, is a wonderful work. It has, possibly, the best explanation on how the sun generates atoms of different elemental structures. It argues clearly and concisely on how evolution works within the current framework of our knowledge.

The Elegant Universe, Brian Greene deals with string theory. More importantly, he does a nice job of covering the first few seconds during the creation of the universe according to string theory.

Warped Passages, Lisa Randall also does an excellent job covering string theory, including "branes" and "no braners", two terms commonly used in physics but specifically used in string theory.

The God Particle, Leon Lederman, does a detailed job of the historical search for the atom in a humorous, concise manner.

In regards to physics, the list can be inexhaustible when you consider both books and papers. Throughout this book, I have quoted from many of both, which I have read. It would be difficult to list all of the sources from years of research.

What I can say is there is not any one book that gives a full explanation from start to finish of how the universe came into being. However, after reading several books, which cover many of the separate topics from antimatter to black holes, one can, at the very least, get a good idea how the universe works. I leave physics on this note:

Concepts of Force and *Concepts of Space*, both written by Max Jammer are worth reading for a well-defined history of man's search for the nature of causation.

A Brief History of Mathematical Thought, Luke Heaton could be added here as it too follows learning through the ages.

We cannot ignore how matter learned to interact organically with the environment. *What a Plant Knows*, by Daniel Chamovitz, does wonders to explain the natural triggers of organic matter in relation to growth, ripening of fruit, and which way is "up" to a simple seed.

The Scent of Desire by Rachel Herz covers, in concise detail, some of the factors leading to our evolved sense of smell. It touches on some aspects of what goes on in the brain.

This is a good place to recommend some reading on the brain. *The Mind and The Brain*, Jeffrey M. Schwartz, has an excellent explanation on how neurons fire; in addition to mental control of brain wiring, and free will, or rather "freewon't".

The Other Brain, R. Douglas Fields covers the topic of glia—the white covering or coating of nerves and neurons. It gives explicit detail on the brain blood barrier, which is so important to overcome in order to cure paralysis.

There is no single book that fully explains consciousness, and *Consciousness Explained* by Daniel C. Dennett is no exception. However, the book does explain some very important aspects of consciousness, including new ideas not found in any other works.

Consciousness And The Brain, by Stanislas Dehaene, which I did quote, does one of the better jobs of explaining the goings on of the brain. It is worth the read. He also wrote another book: *Reading In The Brain*, which is quite detailed.

Another work of marvel on the workings of the brain, which no library would be complete without, is *Descartes' Error*, Antonio Damasio

The Brain That Changes Itself, Norman Doidge, M.D. will give the reader insight into how the brain can become rewired with conscious effort.

One could never understand the divide between woman and men without understanding the differences in brain function. *The Female Brain*, Louann Brizendine, M.D. does an outstanding job of using the proper terminology of brain and not mind, which makes it refreshing to read.

However, I award the top spot for gender differences to *Delusions of Gender*, Cordelia Fine. She makes the absolute best argument, that there is no difference, or very little difference between male and female brains. Little or no difference between the male and female brain is something, which I believed true long before now.

There is a book, which most scientists have read, that no one takes seriously. To the credit of the author, at least he made an attempt, using nothing but biology and history, to explain how consciousness came into being. *The Origins of Consciousness in the Breakdown of the Bicameral Mind*, Julian Jaynes.

In a work that stands alone, *The Emperor of All Maladies*, Siddhartha Mukherjee, is another must read. It covers the history of cancer and every conceivable attempt at a cure. It was so enjoyable to read, that I bought his new book: *The Gene*.

Which brings me to the very book. *The Gene*, Siddhartha Mukherjee covers the history of the search for heredity, genes, and gene mutations. Ideal for anyone who wants the details of genetics or cancer in one read.

This book is a more difficult to read, as it is written in medical terms instead of layman's, but it is worth taking the time. *Pathological Anatomy of the Female Sexual Organs*: Julius M. Klob. As the word pathological suggests, it is on the devastating conditions which woman suffer in their reproductive organs. Including many causes of miscarriage.

While we have covered science topics, I feel it is important to also include works that throw a shadow upon science. *Darwin's Black Box*, Michael J. Behe, attempts to discredit evolution by admitting Intelligent Design into the biochemical challenge of evolution. He does cover some problems with our current knowledge, but I must point out that, because we currently lack the information, does not mean that we will never discover the information.

The same can be said of the book: *Darwin's Doubt,* Stephen C Meyer. He takes the Cambrian record into account as a lack of evidence and tries to convince us there is not enough time in the Earth's history—from its beginning—to evolve as many species that currently, or have at one time, exist. This is based on how long it takes for mutations to happen. Thus, pointing to an intelligent designer. I might point out here that, in reality, only one mutation per cell type needs to happen. Once more than one cell type happens, then forms can evolve using the cell types differently while new cell types continue to evolve.

Going from a plant cell to a bone cell, for example, would allow for a separate evolution to take place as bone can evolve into different structures, analogous to snowflakes. This one objection alone, cuts the mutation rate from millions down to a few hundred to create viable selectable species.

At any rate, neither of these books hold up to arguments considering the newest theory on the beginnings of life on Earth. Nick Lane, wrote a book, *The Vital Question,* which answers to all challenges of intelligent design. I took a look at this above, where using nothing but natural processes of electromotive forces sets the standard of evolution to be broken.

A reading of *The Math Instinct,* Keith Devlin, will enlighten you on how the understanding of mathematical concepts allows for survival. This lead me to use the term, "mathematical relativity," when I explained time structured thought.

The Extended Phenotype, Richard Dawkins is undoubtedly the best work he has undertaken. It is refreshing to read something explicitly about evolution acting upon its environment causing change. It naturally follows, that the changes influence selection.

Finally, any of Charles Darwin's works are jammed full of examples of natural selection in action. He was very adept at details and it showed in his writing.

So detail oriented, was he, that one could tear out half the pages of any one of his works and still have a valid theory. It is my personal belief that one should never reject an idea until it is fully understood. If you have never read any of his works, first hand, then do so before passing judgement.

Unbelievably, there are vastly more Christians that have never read the bible than there are Christians that have read the bible. Until you have read it, and understand it, then the same advice should hold before passing judgement.